SHARED CROP

Life of a Black Tenant Farmer during Jim Crow

RANDOLPH T. HESTER

Stories Illustrated by Outsider Artists

Person County Museum of History
Roxboro, North Carolina

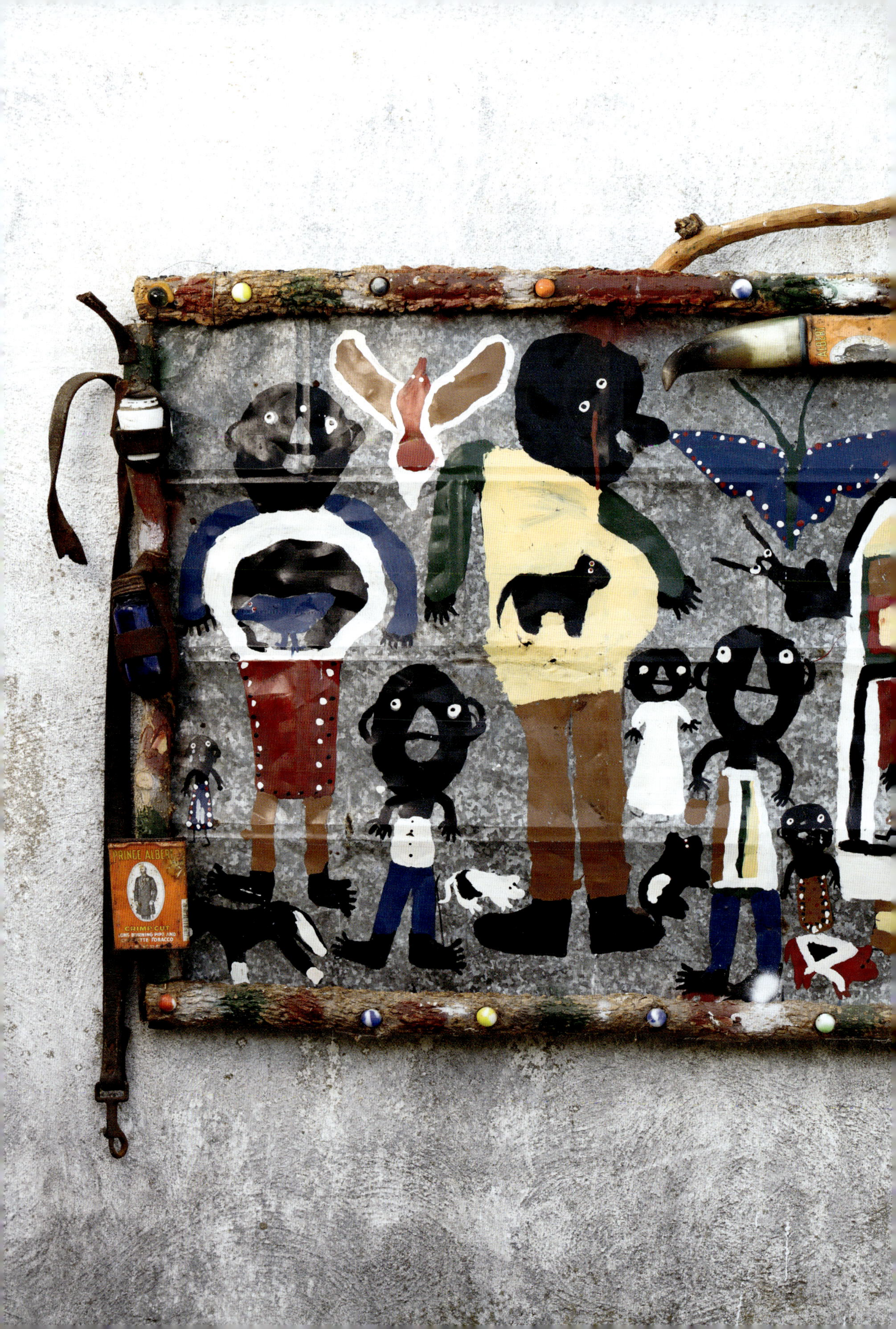
PRINCE ALBERT
CRIMP CUT

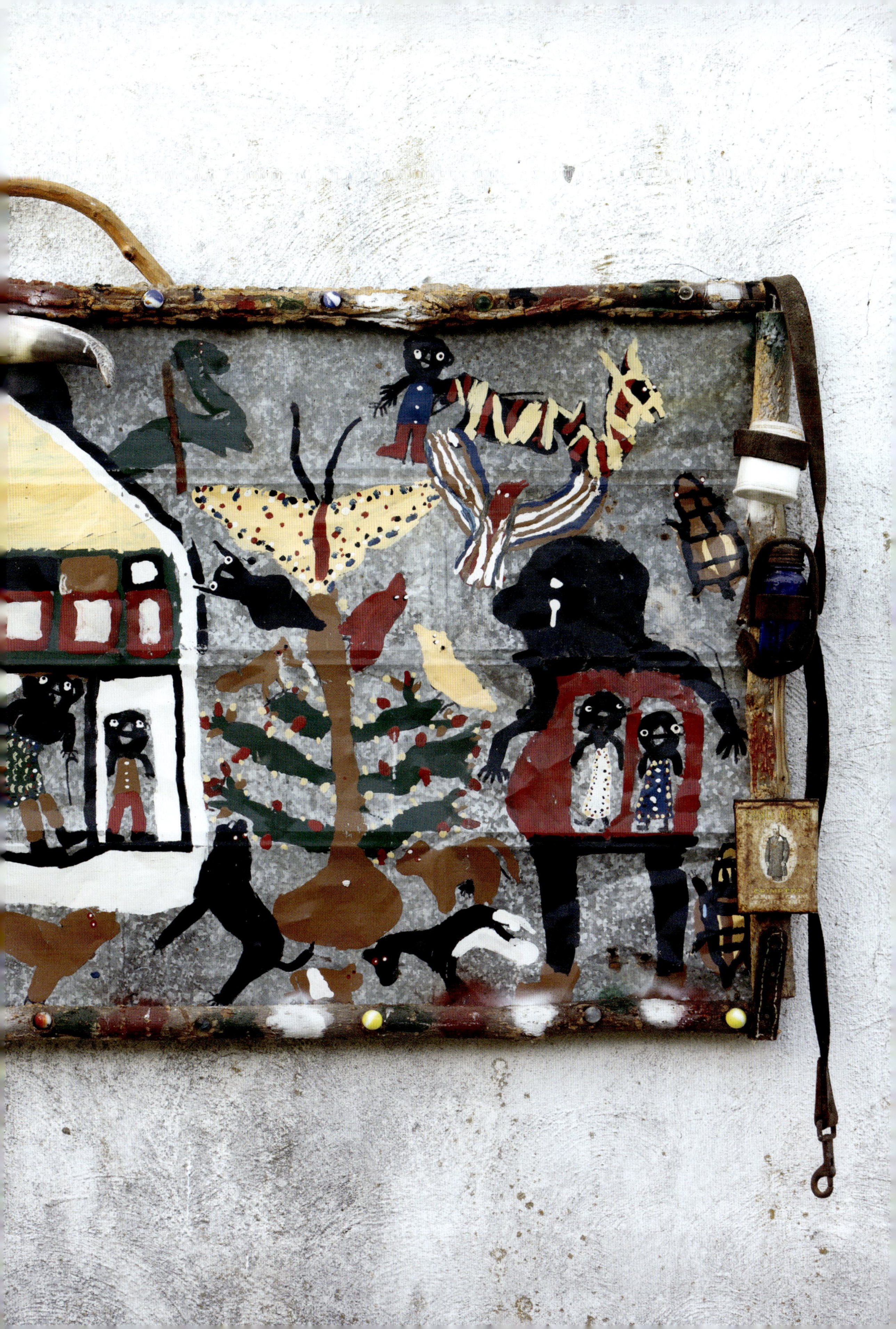

Contents

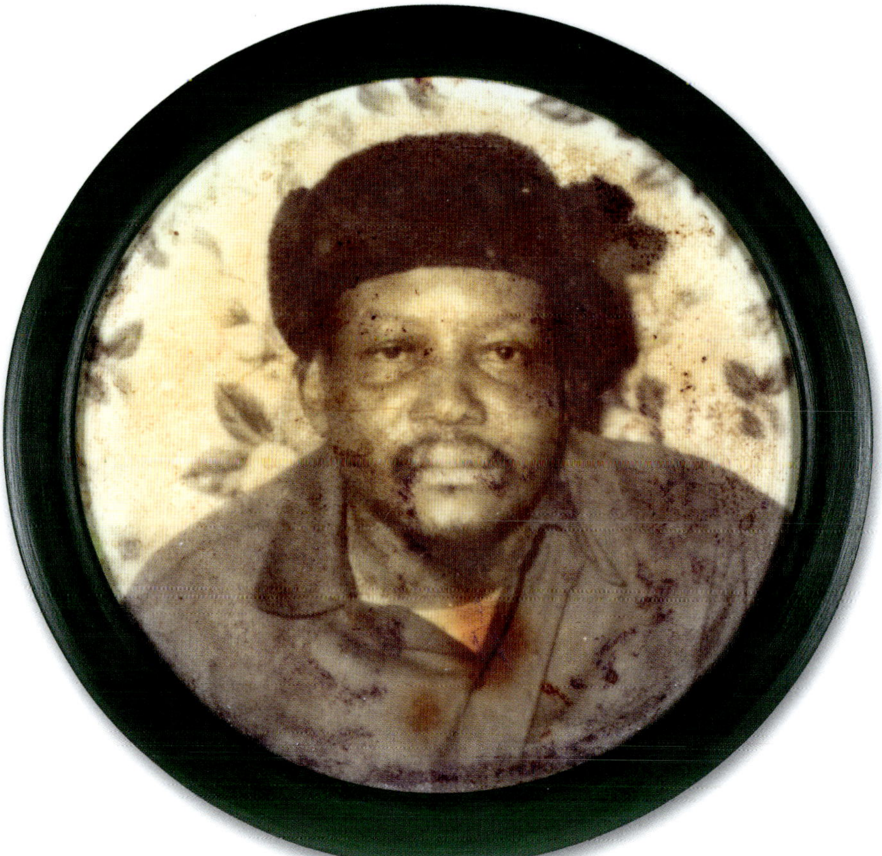

Introduction

This book is a tribute to a tenant farmer, Cornell "Shorty" Lawson, and the character he embodied. It honors him, his wife Annie, their children and grandchildren, his brother Sam and his wife Brenda, his half-brother Larry Dixon and his wife Stella and their boys, the Furges family who lived across the road, and the two million Black tenant farmers and sharecroppers like them who stayed put in the South during the Great Migration, deepened their roots and resolve during Jim Crow, and whose children helped shape a New South.

Stories and Pictures

The book depicts the Lawsons' daily life as tobacco farmers, their pain, pleasures, and wisdom, conveying it through stories Shorty's family tell about how they lived and the values that guided their lives. Each aspect of their oral histories is illustrated by African American outsider artists, other Southern artists, Larry's own art, and artifacts found in their house and around the farm they called home. Their home is now the Shorty Lawson Museum of the Black Tenant Farmer, located on Tom Bowes Road in Person County, North Carolina; the stories and art featured in this book are part of the museum's collection.

Cornell "Shorty" Lawson, the Man

Shorty Lawson was born in Caswell County, North Carolina, March 5, 1938. He farmed all his life, living as an adult in the house that is now a museum, working on halves with Randolph Hester, the farm owner.

Shorty's is a story seldom told. In the formal history he was simply a strong laborer who fueled the economy in the transitional era from Jim Crow to Civil Rights, but his life was far more than that. Yes, race and class constrained him, but his character was larger than social definitions. He was known throughout the community for his work ethic, strength, endurance, straight-ahead honesty, and how he and Annie raised their

(facing) Shorty Lawson, photograph made at North Carolina State Fair. Restoration and frame by Roy Lee Duvall. Gift of Carolyn Lawson.

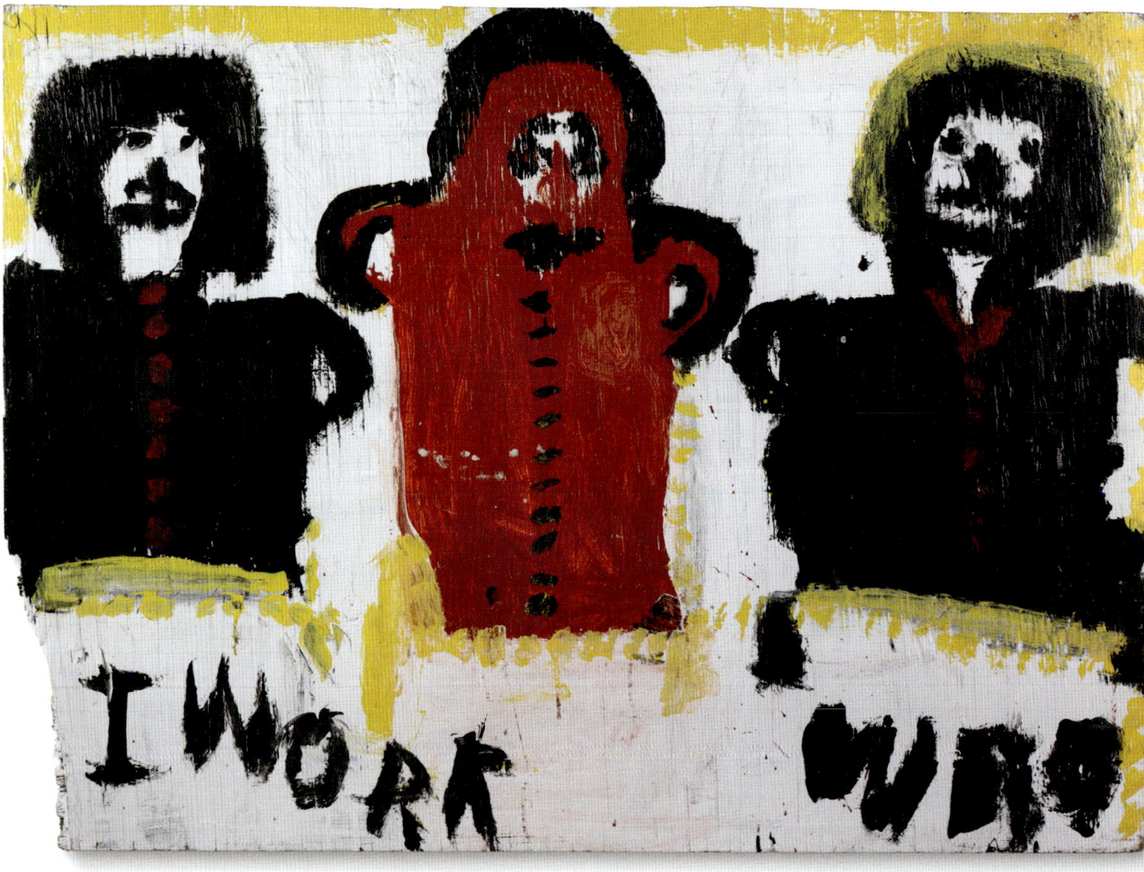

Plate 1. Mary T. Smith, *I Work*. Paint on plywood. 35¾ × 48 inches. Shorty Lawson Museum Collection.

children. He dispelled every myth of White superiority, not by a calculated strategy, rather simply by how he lived. And, in doing so, he lived a life of integrity that challenged his children, those who worked with him, everyone in the community, and all who knew of him, Black and White, landed and tenants. To each he left a legacy of a shared crop of steadfast lessons that continue to guide us. The gifts he gave us might serve others who seek to live by principles of hard work, integrity, ingenuity, and being true to oneself, firmly fixed in place.

Hard Work Is Its Own Reward

By unspoken example Shorty Lawson taught us to work hard, to not only endure hard work but to get great pleasure from it. That was his North Star. Some said, "He had to work hard, simply had to." (Brenda Lawson) Others saw it as inspiration. "He expected us to work as hard as he did, do it right, and if we made a mistake, correct it." (Carolyn Lawson) Maybe he inherited a driver mentality from enslaved ancestors. He was the first at a task and last to take leave. When harvesting tobacco, he pulled two rows while others worked one. "Then he met me, helping me finish my single row." (Randy Hester) Maybe he knew his children would need to be tough to survive. "He taught me to work from sunup to sundown and beyond, sweat running all down my eyes." (Larry Dixon) "We sure had good role models." (Carolyn Lawson) But his work ethic meant more for Shorty. He loved hard work. It was its own reward. (Plate 1) He thrived on work, knew it distinguished him. He got pleasure from outdoing all others.

True to His Word and Himself

Shorty Lawson did everything with integrity. He was forever true to his word. You could count on what he said to be the truth. A man of few words, he still called it like he saw it, not mincing his few words. And he was true to himself, unwavering in his sense of self. Arbon Lane describes perfectly how Shorty was under no White man's thumb when most tenant farmers were, "i am a man in the shadow of another man, and that is how i will always be, for i am a man in the shadow of another man, and that other man is me." (Arbon Lane) By standards of what mattered most in his community, work and integrity, Shorty proved his superiority every day, respected as the most principled man inside and out. Any child growing up under Shorty's care, Black or White, learned from his example. "He taught Larry to be a good man." (Stella Dixon) "Shorty taught me more about farming, hard work, and how to live than anyone I knew." (Randy Hester) But that is only a part of the story about his character.

Firmly Fixed in Place

Even though he was short in stature, Shorty had a presence that could be intimidating. Everyone had witnessed or heard of him deadlifting 200-pound bags of fertilizer in his teeth. Steadfast, he was firmly fixed in place, commanded his ground, his territory. His boys learned early that they better not fool around when their Daddy was harnessing the mules or plowing. And when they were old enough to plow, there was no horse-play or breaks allowed. (Plate 2) Folks in the community knew they had to honor his personal space, his home, and the land he worked.

Lived by His Own Hand

Shorty Lawson lived simply, did not want much nor did he want for much. He wanted to improve the lot of his family and did so, but he sought little material status for himself. He lived by his own hand, could make or repair most anything he needed. In an era when Jim Crow sucked away the dignity of thousands of souls, Shorty seldom bowed and was never broken. He never whined. Self-pity was beneath him. That does not mean that he did not know the score. He knew the deal and was prepared for the worst. His half-brother remembers that he himself feared the Klan but Shorty did not. "Shorty had artillery for the Klan." (Larry Dixon)

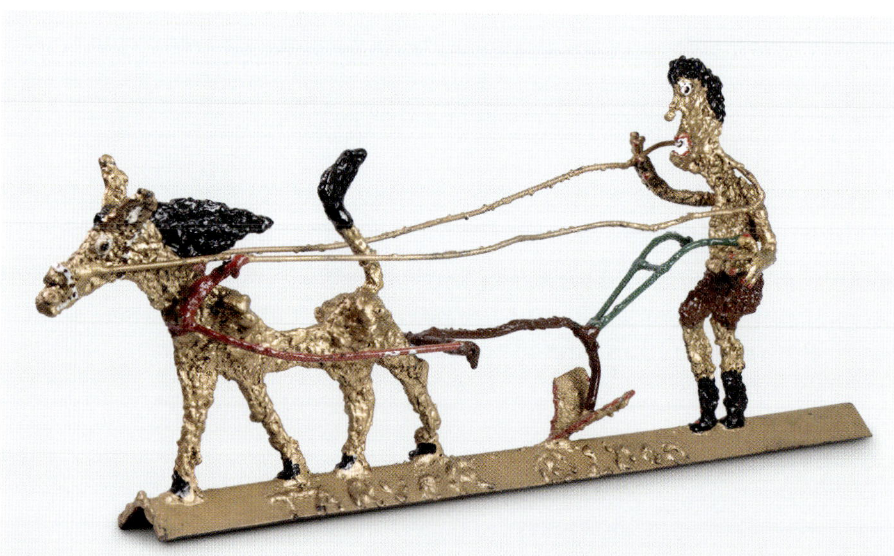

Plate 2. Willie Tarver, *Plowing.* Painted metal, welded with texture. 11 × 25 × 4 inches.

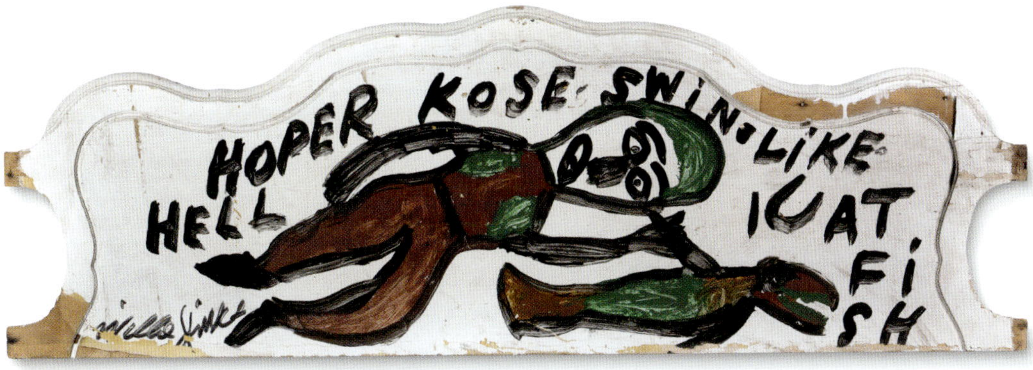

Plate 3. Willie Jinks, *Hell Hoper Kose Swim Like I Catfish.* Paint on headboard. 17 × 51½ × 1 inch.

Farm Seasoned with Pleasures

In spite of it all the Lawsons endured and thrived. They grew plenty to eat, were largely self-sufficient, and Shorty got so much pleasure from the farm and nature that he infected all the children with his enthusiasm. He knew nature's warnings, from threatening purple storm clouds to copperhead snakes and water moccasins, and he taught the children to escape those dangers. With a few cautions the farm landscape was a wonderland of free recreation. While most Black people he knew were deathly afraid of water, Shorty was a famous swimmer and taught all the children. (Plate 3) But he had one rule. When swimming one of the children had to sit on the bank and spot all the others. "He would sneak down to the pond, hide in the bushes to be sure we followed the rule." (Carolyn Lawson)

They all fished, and the boys hunted. Shorty himself got pleasure from nearby Saturday-night juke joints, cheap liquor, and an occasional trip to the state fair, the young ones left at home. The children learned the joys of nature firsthand. They knew rain was coming if they heard a rain crow call. They knew to answer an owl's hoot to avoid trouble. They knew the best spots on Crooked Creek to catch knotty heads. They made games of chores like getting water from the big house, feeding chickens and pigs. Games were everywhere waiting to be discovered as long as the imagination was engaged. "We learned things that kids today never do because they just stay inside and watch television." (Carolyn Lawson) All these, from work ethic, integrity, joys in a simple life of family sufficiency, sense of self-worth, and steadfastness, Shorty passed on to his children and anyone who worked with him. The children grew up to follow what he taught them, and he only taught by example. The children made something of themselves, contributing to a new world order.

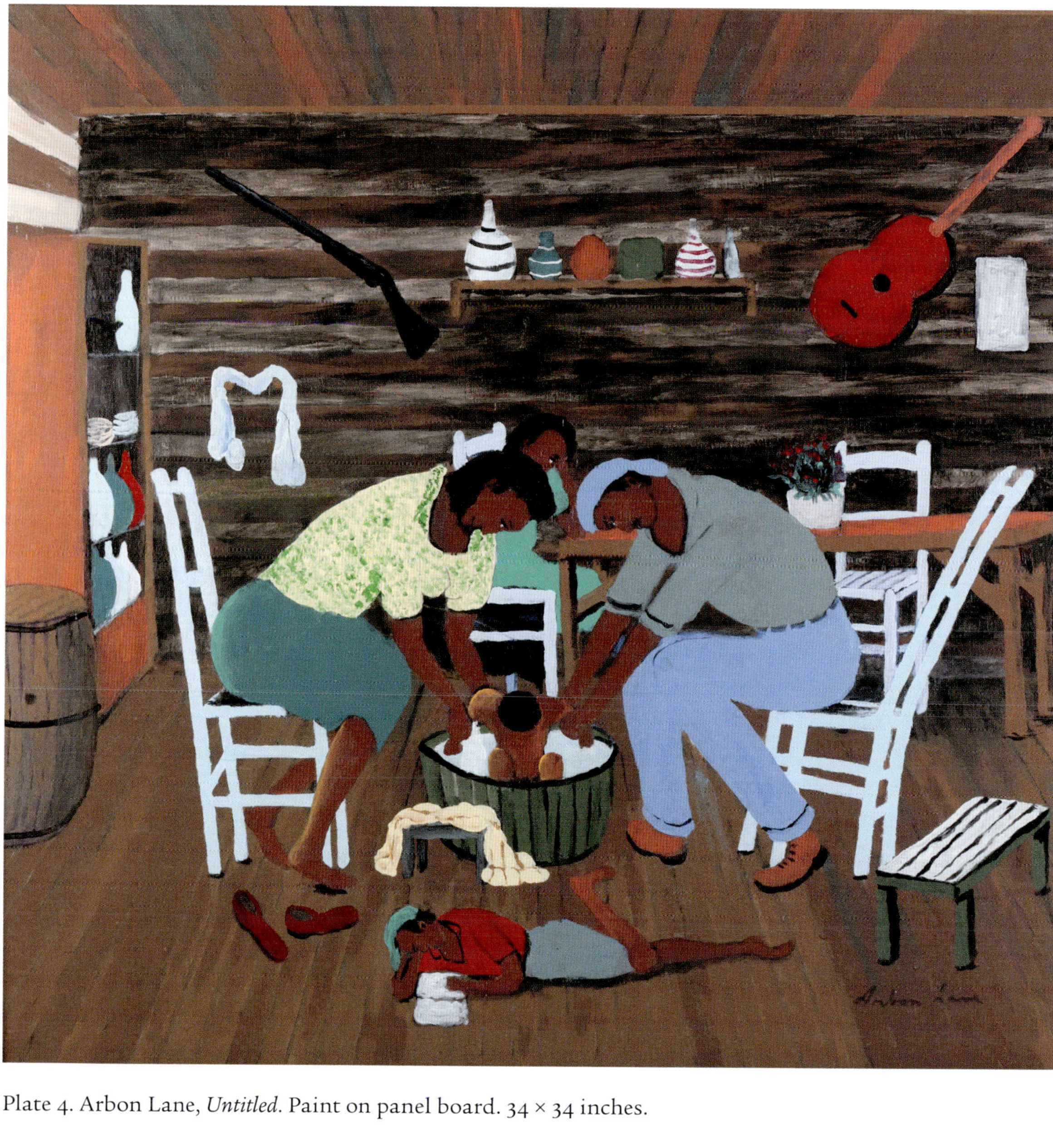

Plate 4. Arbon Lane, *Untitled*. Paint on panel board. 34 × 34 inches.

A Tenant Homeplace

The Lawsons considered the Bowes Farm their homeplace but never owned it. Annie grew up in the Church of the City of God in the Wilderness founded by Preach Wiley Bradsher, who witnessed for Black land ownership, but Shorty seldom went to church. Like three-quarters of the African Americans who remained in the South during the Great Migration, Shorty never owned land, but some of his siblings and in-laws, his half-brother, and the next generation did.

To the original four-room house on the Bowes Farm where his family lived Shorty added two rooms, created shelves and clothes racks. He recycled scrap into dignified things long before sustainability was a buzzword. He made things that performed beautifully. "When I decide the way I want it, I can make it. You can do things in your head. You can do things out your head. You ain't got to have a book for everything." (Creola Bennett Pettway) His family enjoyed electricity but never had a well, running water, or indoor plumbing. (Plate 4) Shorty and Annie had an adequate house, a solid roof over their heads. More, they created a good home, safe, loving.

Most of the family's domestic life, however, was spent outside. The outhouse and rain barrels served necessities without plumbing. Across the road mules were stabled in the feed barn. Beyond were fields, ponds, and woods, each providing essential resources. Shorty stewarded all these as his own.

Cornell "Shorty" Lawson died in 1974. Parts of his family continued to live in their homeplace for another twenty years.

Why We Made This Book

We want to convey an important story of the life of a man and his family whom history might not otherwise consider. We hope you will get a sense of the daily life, the hardships and pleasures, of the Lawson family during the last half of the century from about 1950 to 2000, a difficult time in America's own story. We consider how Shorty Lawson's character gained him respect, guided him through a period of danger and dramatic upheaval, helped him disprove racist stereotypes and challenge those who knew him. "America needs the Negro for ballast; his tropical warmth and spontaneous emotionalism form a counterpart to the cold and calculating Anglo-Saxon." (Anna Julia Cooper) It might serve us to consider the way he taught his children by example, let them learn from him and nature. His values may inspire us to think about our own strengths, biases, and

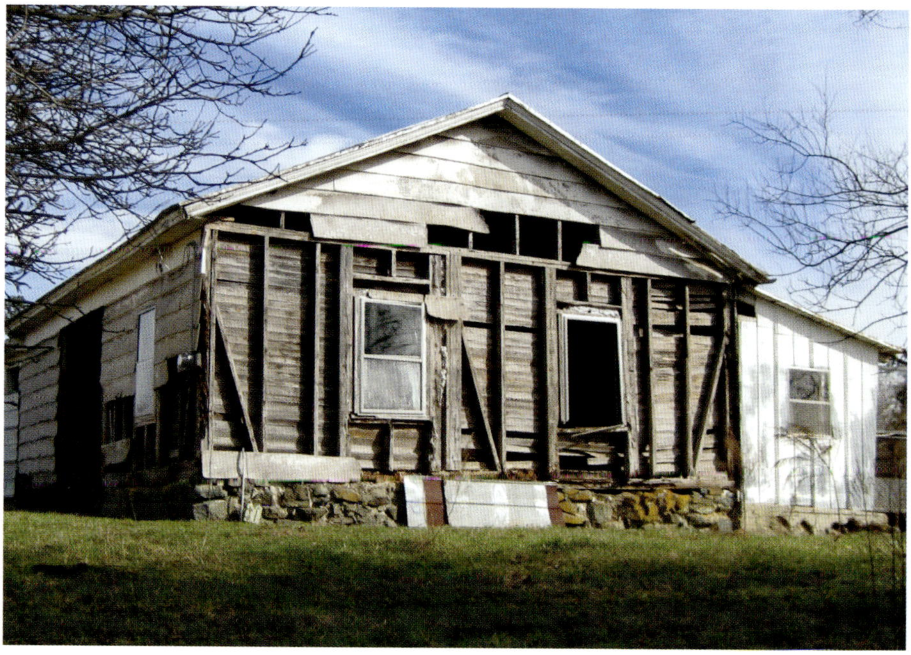

The Lawson house in disrepair in 2016.

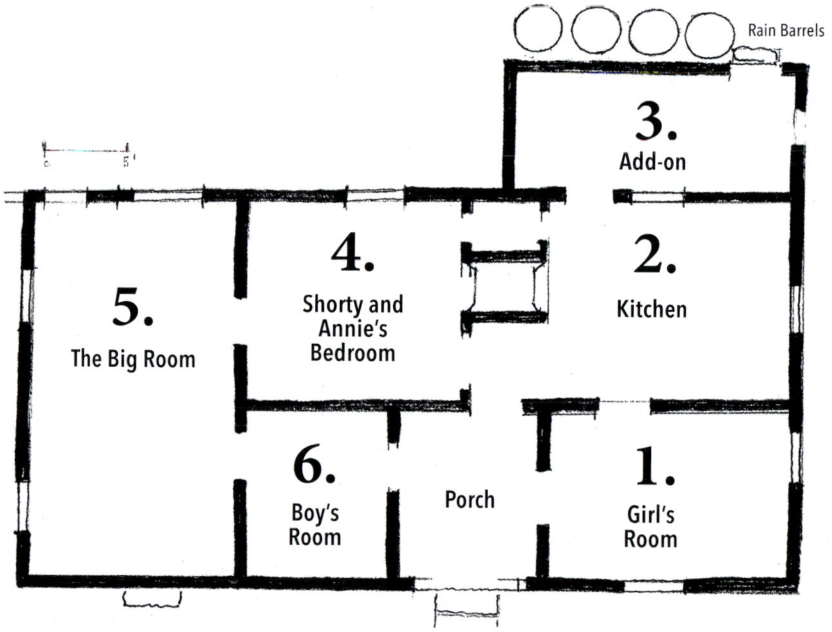

Plan of the Shorty Lawson Museum showing the rooms of the Lawson home.

love for homeplace and other people, the things we make well or perform beautifully, or aspire to. His life suggests that the dominant culture might not just tolerate but also learn from the little people. "If we want to change the world, we got to look at the little man. All these little folks out there—Black peoples, poor White peoples—got big minds." (Thornton Dial) Maybe we will internalize lessons that Cornell Lawson offers us.

How the Book Is Organized

This book is organized around the six rooms of the Lawsons' house like *Chambers for a Memory Palace.* (Donlyn Lyndon and Charles Moore) Two concluding chapters assess the larger meaning of the Lawson family stories and describe the creation of the museum. Some folks want to forget. "I hadn't so much forgot as I couldn't bring myself to remember." (Maya Angelou) The Lawsons remembered and continued a tradition of a vibrant oral history. Each of the six rooms depicts aspects of Shorty Lawson's life, his values, and the day-to-day events of the Lawson family:

Girls' Room: Life by the Seasons

Kitchen: Cooking, Eating, and Bathing

Room Off the Kitchen: Processing, Washing, and Fixing

Shorty and Annie's Bedroom: A Shared Crop of Values

Big Room: Work and Prejudice

Boys' Room: Failings, Fear, and God

Each room is made up of recorded memories, the oral histories of the Lawsons. Each story is illustrated with art, making visual the spoken words in much the way a graphic novel combines text and image. When part of a story is quoted directly, the person being quoted is acknowledged after the passage. In some cases, African American artists and authors who knew these stories themselves are quoted and acknowledged in the same way. This gives multiple views. "I can see the farmer man with a heart full of hope, I can see the old pa, pa, fishing in the brook, I can see the mothers hand as she readys her self to cook, yes all this I can see and mutch, mutch more, while satting up heigh, and looking way down low." (Arbon Lane)

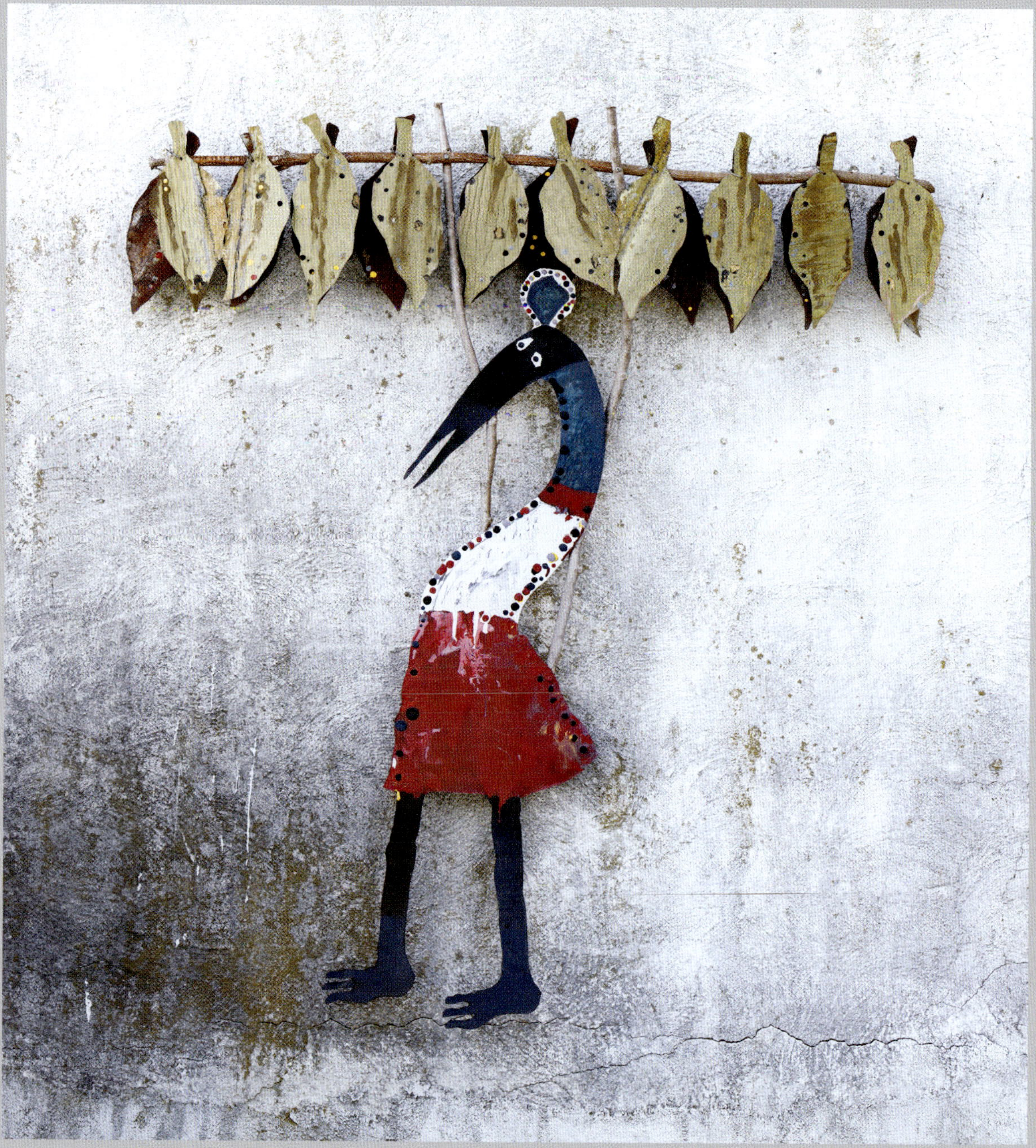

GIRLS' ROOM

Life by the Seasons

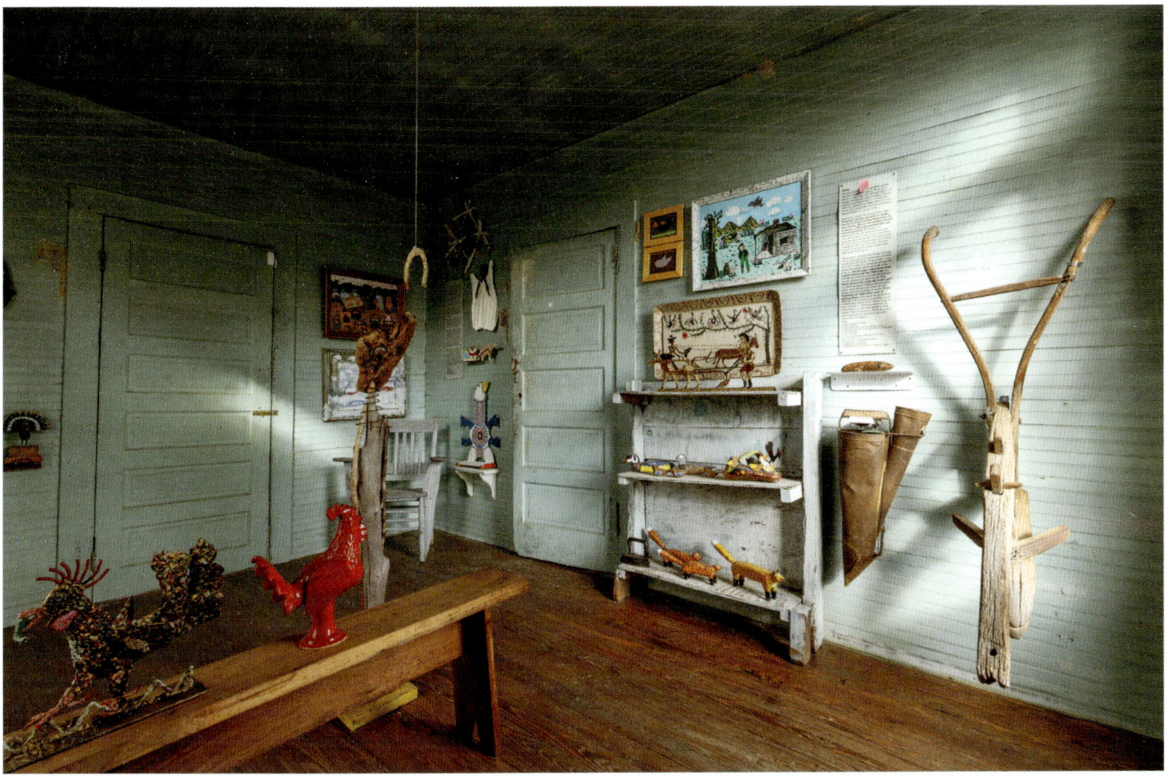

Plate 5 (facing). Randy Hester, *Taking Out Cured Tobacco.* Enamel paint on roofing tin, cutouts from metal siding, sticks. 43 × 39 × 3 inches.

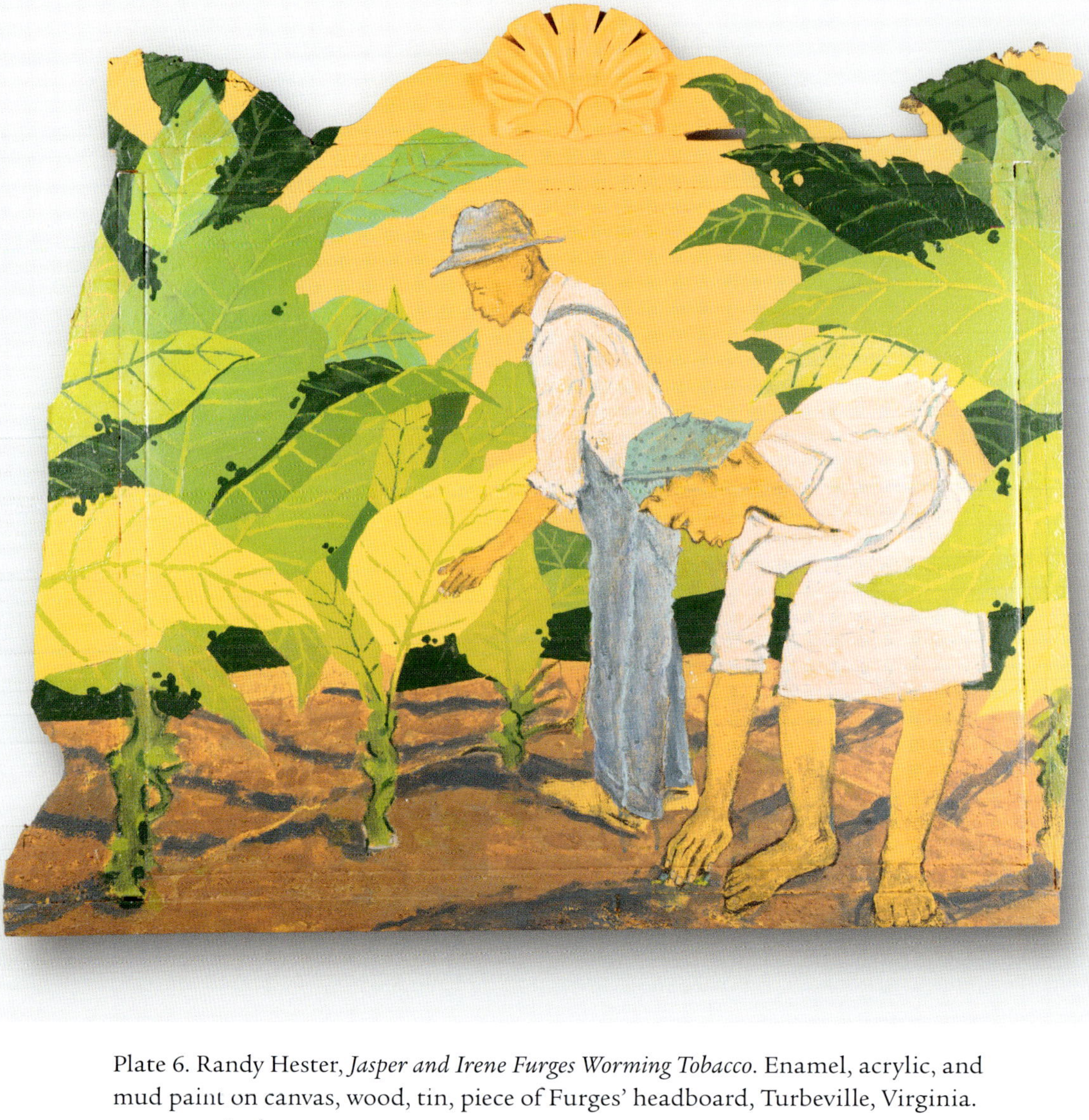

Plate 6. Randy Hester, *Jasper and Irene Furges Worming Tobacco*. Enamel, acrylic, and mud paint on canvas, wood, tin, piece of Furges' headboard, Turbeville, Virginia. 30 × 35 × 4 inches.

Summer

The Lawsons lived by seasons. Summer was tobacco season. There were other food crops, but the only money crop was tobacco. Before his boys were old enough to help out Shorty did all the plowing himself. He plowed with a single mule. They didn't have a tractor in the early days. That was in the 1950s. After late spring plowing of the allowed tobacco acreage, the fields were ready for planting.

Shorty and the farm owner's son, Randy, planted the tobacco one plant at a time. Any baby plants that didn't thrive they replanted in the following weeks. They had to go over all 15 acres to be sure there was a good stand. Next tobacco had to be weeded, hoed, plowed, and laid by.

If there was a slow week of tobacco work, Shorty plowed more fields for corn, beans, and the watermelon patch. When that was done, usually the tobacco needed to be topped, suckered, and wormed. Men, women, and children helped worm. (Plate 6) "Now that was a nasty job. You killed the worms by smushing them between your thumb and fingers. Everybody hated that job, but it was necessary. Otherwise, the worms would ruin the crop." (Carolyn Lawson)

When Shorty started farming, all tobacco work was done by hand or mule. Later untested chemicals like MH30 did the suckering; tractors did most plowing. You pulled tobacco from the ground up, in 90-degree heat and 90 percent humidity. Pulling bottom leaves required guts and stamina. If anybody whined about it, the old folks or Shorty himself always responded that it built character. Truth is they were right.

Usually, men and boys pulled tobacco, and women strung. At the end of the day, everyone helped put the tobacco in the barn. Then you built a fire to cure the tobacco. If done masterfully, curing turned the green leaves to the golden yellow that was most prized at market, brought the best price. As a boy Shorty cured with wood, sleeping at the barn to keep the fire going. You had to be careful not to let the fire go out; that could ruin a barn of tobacco. By the 1960s they upgraded to oil heat; it was easier to control the temperature inside the barn. And you didn't have to sleep at the barn to keep the fire going and the temperature inside the barn regular.

As a young tenant farmer Shorty Lawson sharecropped the 15 acres of tobacco on halves with the owner, who covered expenses up front and provided his son as labor. Later, they traded tobacco allotment from another farm and tended as much as 30 acres.

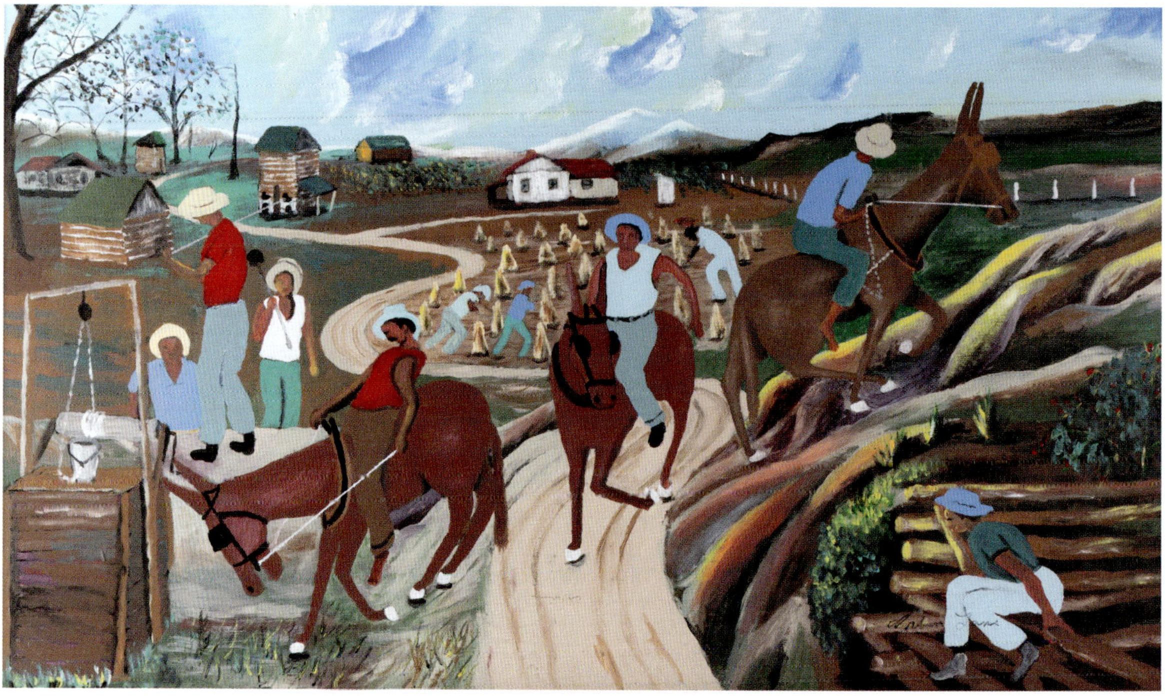

Plate 7. Arbon Lane, *Untitled*. Paint on wood. 26½ × 42½ inches.

Jasper and Irene Furges, another Black family, lived in the big house across the road from the Lawsons; that was the house Tom Bowes had built. Jasper had managed a farm himself so he was a master at curing tobacco. Their grandchildren grew up with the Lawsons, and "our two families farmed together. We kids went back and forth from one house to the other." (Debra Davies)

When Shorty and Annie's children got old enough to do men's and women's work, the family doubled the acres of tobacco they grew, always on halves. His family and the Furges family netted about 3,000–4,000 dollars, maybe even 5,000 dollars in an exceptional year, after all the crop and living expenses for that year were paid. That was 'long about the 1960s.

As soon as the children were knee high, they all did fieldwork. Annie and the girls did the stringing at the barn. No one was spared the hard work. "My brother Shorty was hard working, and he taught me to work. We all had a patch of tobacco that we got the profit from." (Larry Dixon)

Shorty and his family worked tobacco five and a half days a week, knocking off at noon on Saturday or when all the tobacco was housed.

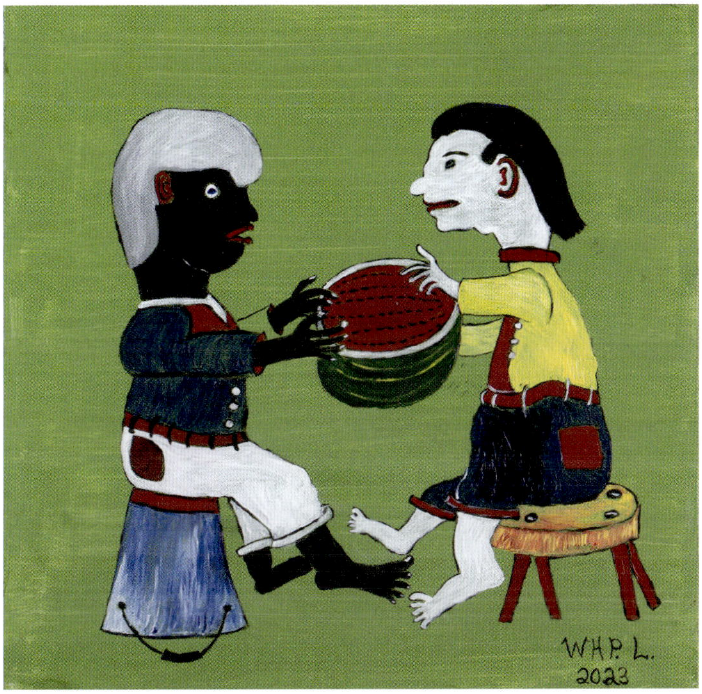

Plate 8. Wade Ledbetter, *Untitled*. Paint on board. 14 × 14 inches.

(Plate 7) Then they worked the garden. They always had a big garden that fed the family through the summer. Annie and the girls washed clothes, and hung them out to dry. Work overalls dried draped over the barbed-wire fence. The girls cleaned house. The boys' room often went unattended. Chores done, everybody found a place to cool off from the heat. On Saturday nights Shorty often went off drinking with friends. "He didn't bother anybody, just sleep it off, back to work on Monday." (Brenda Lawson)

Saturday afternoon most of the children went fishing at the old pond. Often, they fished and went swimming after church on Sunday, too. "We bank fished, never in a boat. I liked a cane pole best. We caught bream, bass, crappie, and catfish, enough for several meals. We kids fished the creek. And we always had a big watermelon patch, more than enough to go around. We shared with neighbors. Any time we were hungry for watermelon, we could go to the patch. Just get you one, bust it open, but you couldn't waste it." (Carolyn Lawson) Sometimes at the end of a day of pulling tobacco, Shorty would get several on the way in from the field, finish tying tobacco. Then they would sit around, have a feast. (Plate 8)

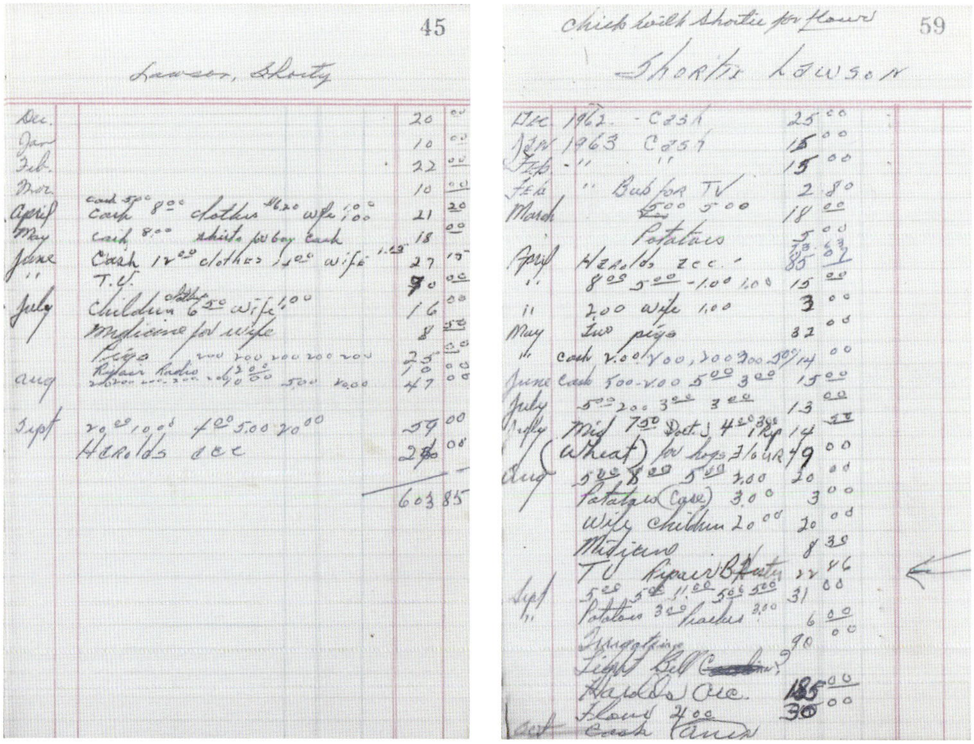

Records of purchase of television in 1962, television repair in 1963, and other expenses.

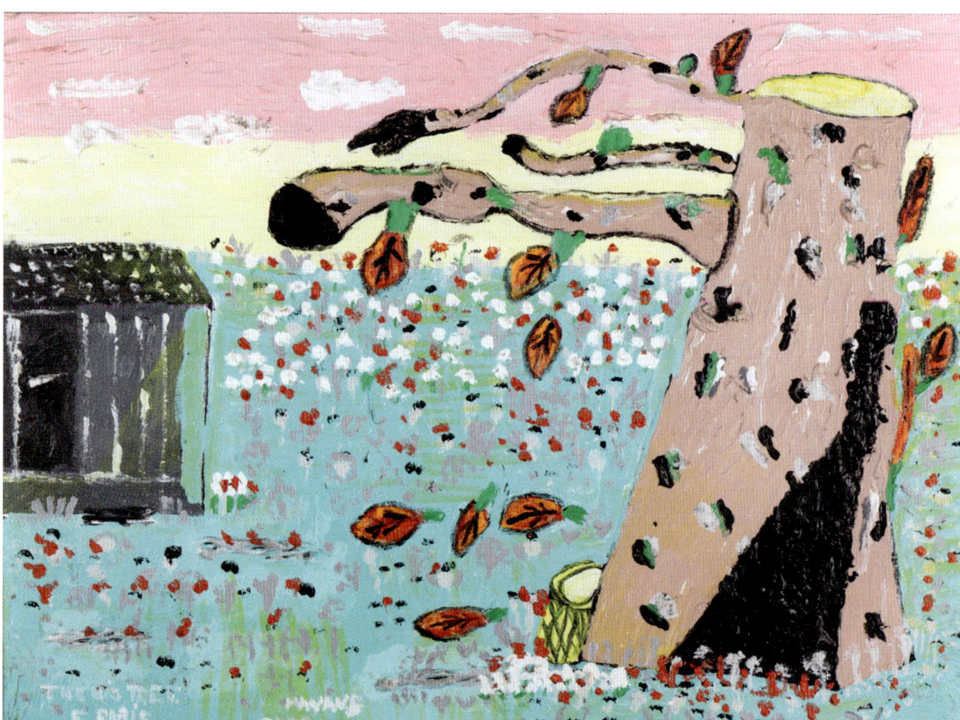

Plate 9. Eula Parris, *The Big Tree*. Paint on canvas board. 18 × 24 inches.

Fall

"It's like summer wear the world out, and by October everyone is just ready for a nap." (Ta-Nehisi Coates) Fall most folks slow down.

Not Shorty. This was a season to finish up tobacco and get ready for school, for hunting, and to buy something special. Fall was the only time of year that the Lawson family had extra money to spend. The rest of the time they lived on credit at the store and weekly advances from Randolph.

After tobacco was sold, Shorty and Annie would figure out what purchase would most improve their lot. Of course, winter shoes had to be bought for the whole family and some school clothes for the children, but each good year there was money left for something major like an electric kitchen stove, deep-freeze, television, or living room furniture.

Their first television was purchased for $70.00 in 1962, a bulb bought for $2.80, and the TV repaired for $22.86 in 1963. Older children got the profits from their own allotments of tobacco. "One year all us boys bought bikes and go-carts with our money, raced up and down the road. It was just a dirt road then." (Larry Dixon)

With a killing frost the world turned red, yellow, and orange. The big silver maple tree at Jasper and Irene's dropped its leaves, exposing old limbs, twisted from years of struggle as the only living thing in the swept yard. (Plate 9)

But Shorty was attending to other trees. He needed to make wood, enough to heat the house and feed the cookstove for the whole winter. In the 1950s Shorty made all the wood himself. When the boys got big enough to cut wood, he gladly shared the work. They found trees downed from a storm or cut some good-sized oaks, cut them into lengths, and wagoned them to the yard where they split the wood with a maul into stove-sized pieces.

In later years they rigged up a splitter to the tractor. That made the work easier but terribly dangerous. "Once the saw hit a log knot, bucked a piece of wood right at my head, missed by inches. If I hadn't ducked, I wouldn't be here today." (Larry Dixon)

Although the pace slowed, there was one most important job to finish. Everyone pitched in to bundle and basket the last primings of the tobacco crop before the market closed. After a barn of tobacco was cured, it was too dry to handle. So the Lawsons stored it in a basement with enough moisture to "bring it in order." After it came in order, was pliable enough to handle, you handed each stick of tobacco upstairs to the pack barn, where you stripped the tobacco off the sticks and put together a dozen or

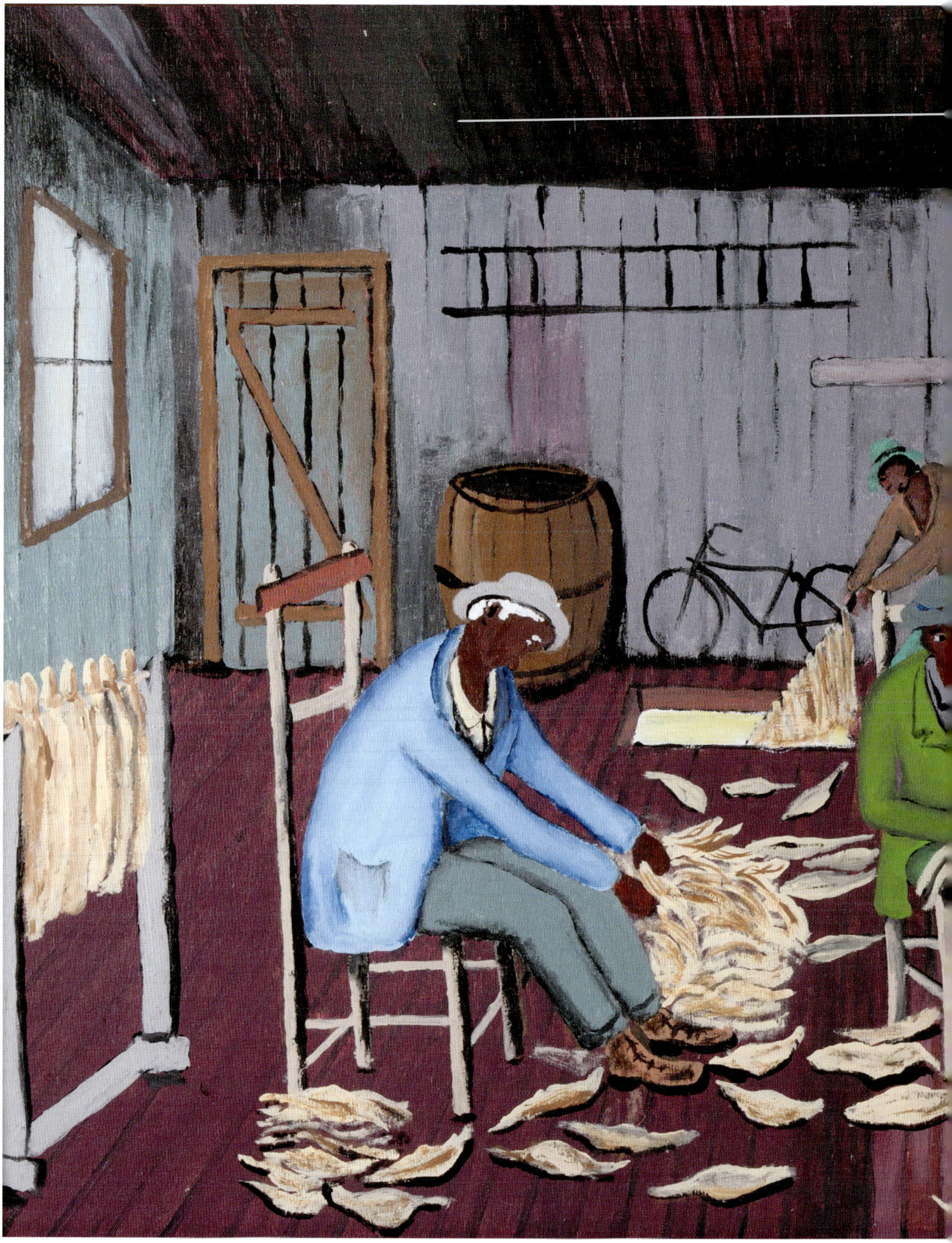

Plate 10. Arbon Lane, *Untitled*. Paint on plywood. 27 × 42 inches.

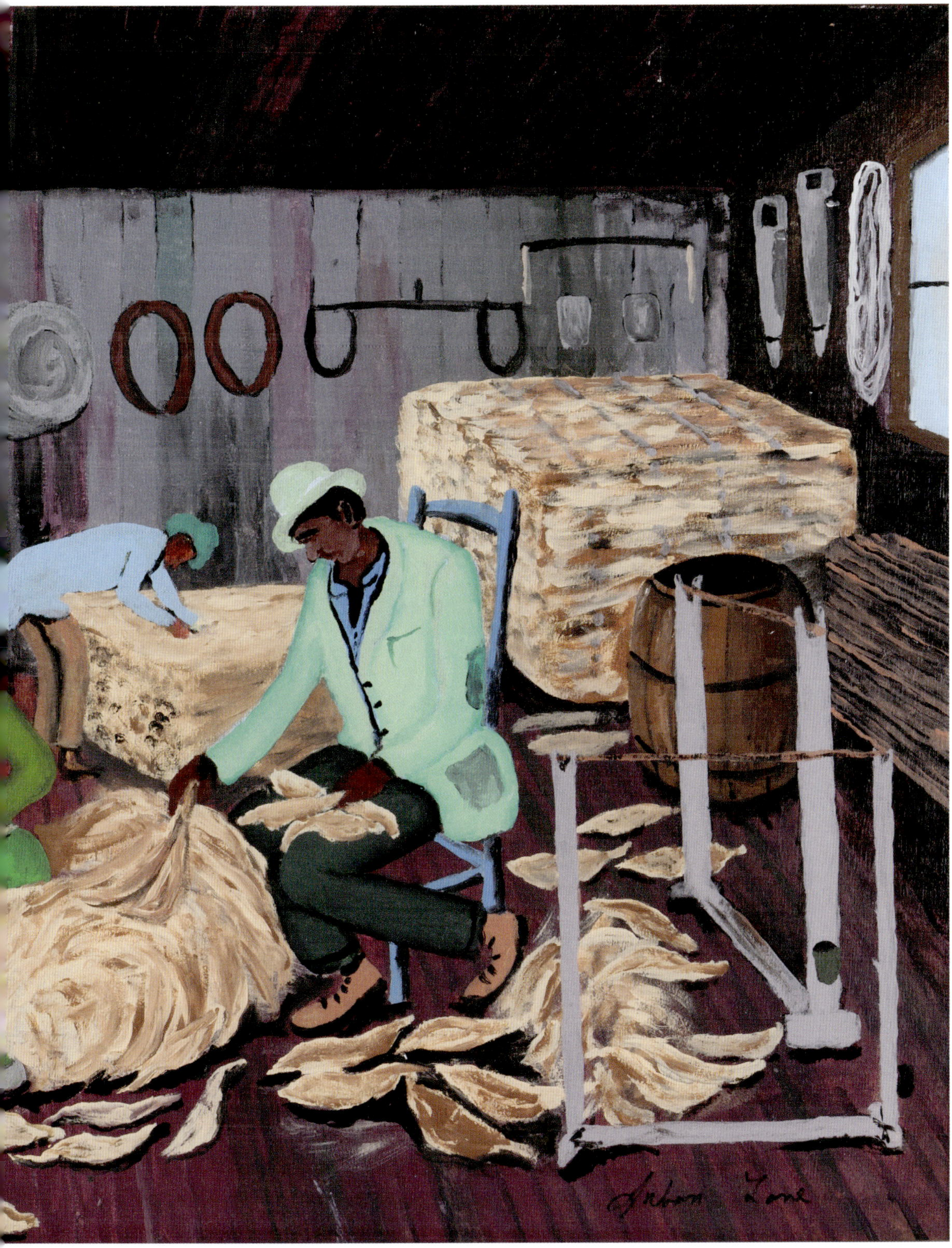

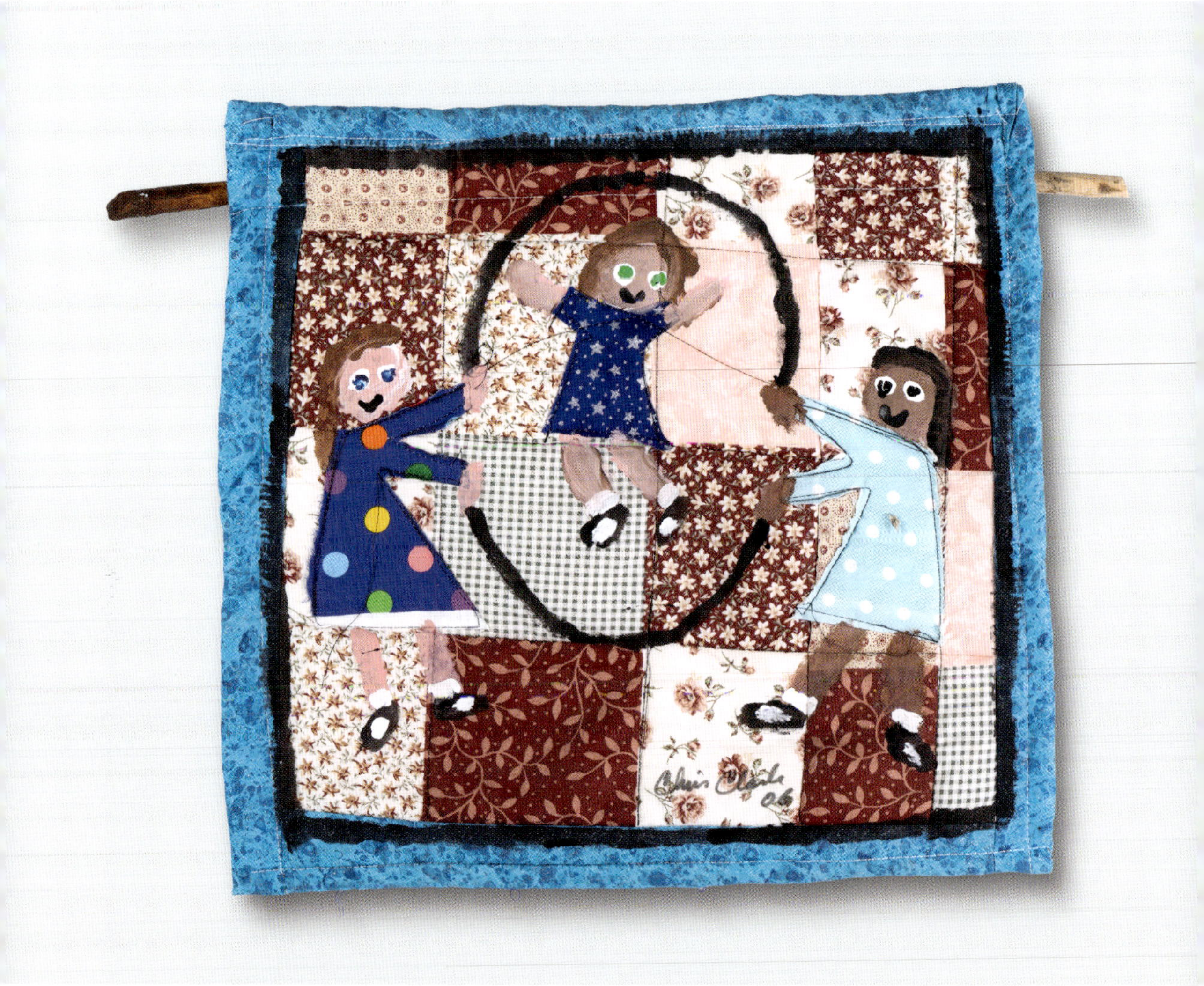

Plate 11. Chris Clark, *Jumping Rope*. Paint on quilted background with machine-sewn dress cutouts. 15 × 15½ inches.

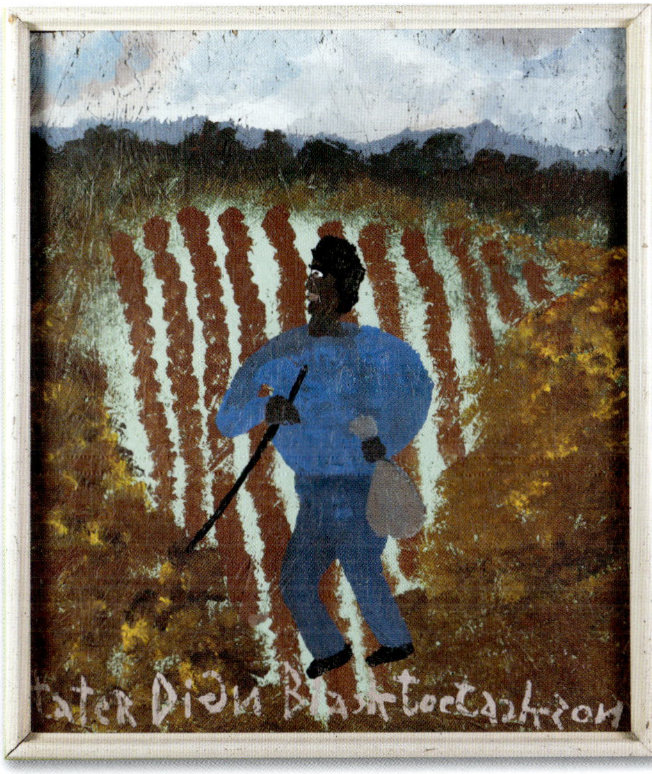

Plate 12. Black Joe Jackson, *Tater Dign*. Paint on composition board. 26 × 21½ inches.

more leaves in one bundle. Then you chose a good golden leaf to wrap and hold the bundle together. (Plate 10) You wanted to show off the best-quality leaves to get the best grade and price. This took weeks of work, but was a time to celebrate because the most brutal summer work was done, and going to tobacco market was a big time.

After school and chores, often as part of chores, the kids would jump rope, swing, play with their pets, or shoot baskets. (Plate 11) "We made that basketball goal with a fruit basket. Everybody played." (Larry Dixon) Fall also was the time to dig potatoes. (Plate 12) Then you repaired equipment that had been damaged or broken during tobacco season. Nothing was thrown away. All the mule collars, harnesses, plows, and planters would be patched and hung up out of the weather. And when work was caught up, Shorty would go hunting. "He had two dogs, Black and Blue, got them from Reed Shuff. Those dogs hunt everything, rabbits, squirrels, coons." (Larry Dixon) Shorty almost never got a turkey. They were rare in those days.

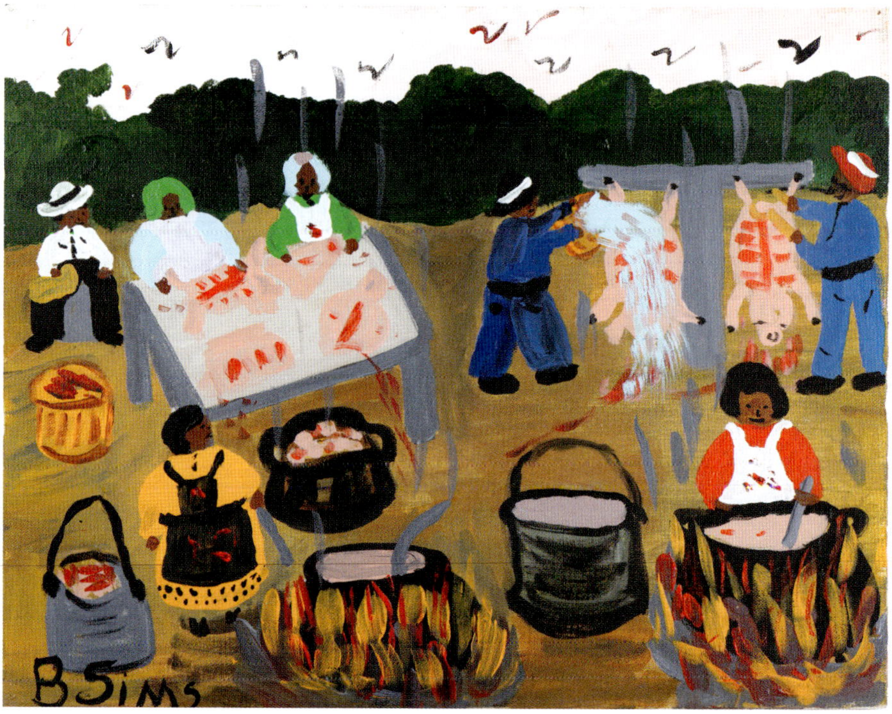

Plate 13. Bernice Sims, *Hog Killing*. Paint on canvas. 16 × 20 inches.

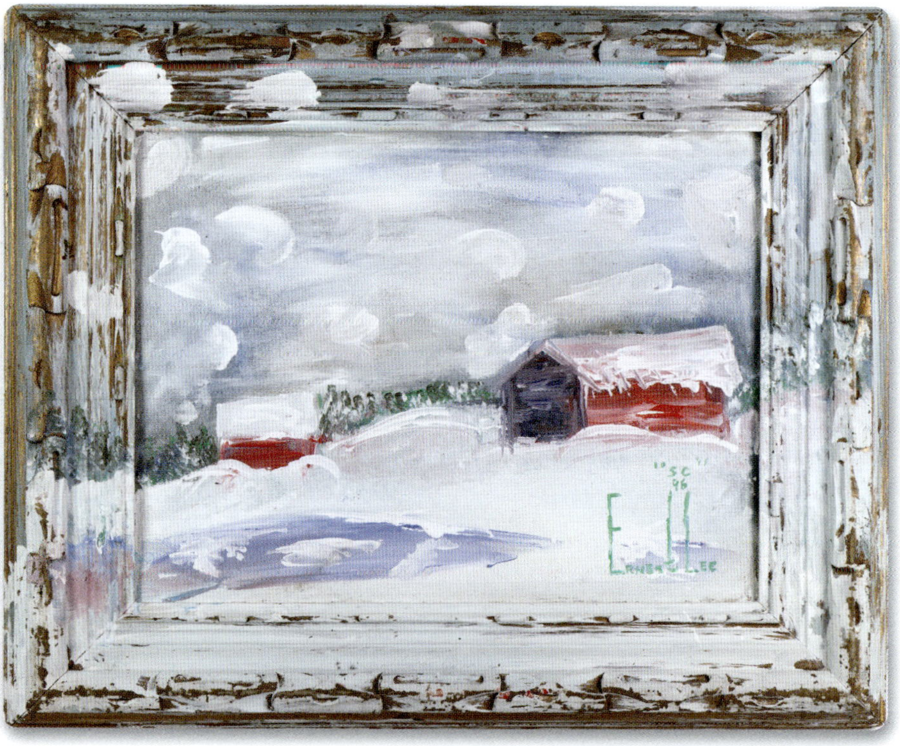

Plate 14. Ernest Lee, *Snow*. Paint on unstretched canvas and frame. 20¼ × 24¼ inches.

Winter

The first really cold spell in December was hog-killing time. (Plate 13) You had to wait for freezing weather so the meat wouldn't spoil. Shorty and Randolph would get a big fire going under the scalder; they would shoot each hog with a twenty-two and cut the throat with a butcher knife to drain the blood. After scalding the hog in boiling water, they scraped the hair off with knives and tin-can tops, washed the hog down, cut up the meat, and salted it down, or ground it for sausage. Randolph and Shorty went halves on the hogs, providing both families pork for a year, but Randolph usually got the choice hams.

Hog killing was an exciting day even though Larry cried when his pet pig was killed. There were jobs for everyone from the youngest to the oldest, and they all knew that supper would be a feast of fresh sausage, tenderloin, and chitterlings. "We had one pig, Arnold, sort of a pet, get out the pen, follow us around everywhere, a nuisance. We'd go squirrel hunting, real quiet-like, hear something rooting around behind us, oink, oink, oink, turn around and there was Arnold. We would have to chase him back to the pen, ruined the hunting. Sometimes Arnold would follow us when we set rabbit gums. That didn't bother us like he did when we were squirrel hunting, because we didn't have to keep quiet, just put an apple in the back of the gum and set the door open on one, leave it and move on to bait another trap, Arnold just behind, begging for an apple. Down at the edge of the woods or around brush piles were good places to catch rabbits. That Arnold was something else. I loved that pig, balled when Shorty shot him, but I still ate the sausage for supper that night." (Larry Dixon)

Most of the house was cold. The kitchen was the warmest room, facing the sunny south, out of the north wind, heated by a fireplace roaring hot and the cookstove full blast. Eventually Shorty got an oil-burning stove in his and Annie's bedroom, but the rest of the house had no heat. The boys' room was icy cold, and snow drifted into the living room, but, in spite of it all, "We loved this little house." (Stella Dixon) But the children still had to go over to the big house to get water, bitter cold, especially on windy days. The Lawsons had one really mixed blessing. They never had to worry about freezing pipes; there was no plumbing.

There were big snows every year. (Plate 14) Schools closed for weeks at a time because the buses couldn't negotiate dirt roads. Most of the roads in the community were not paved, even the main ones. The children had a big time.

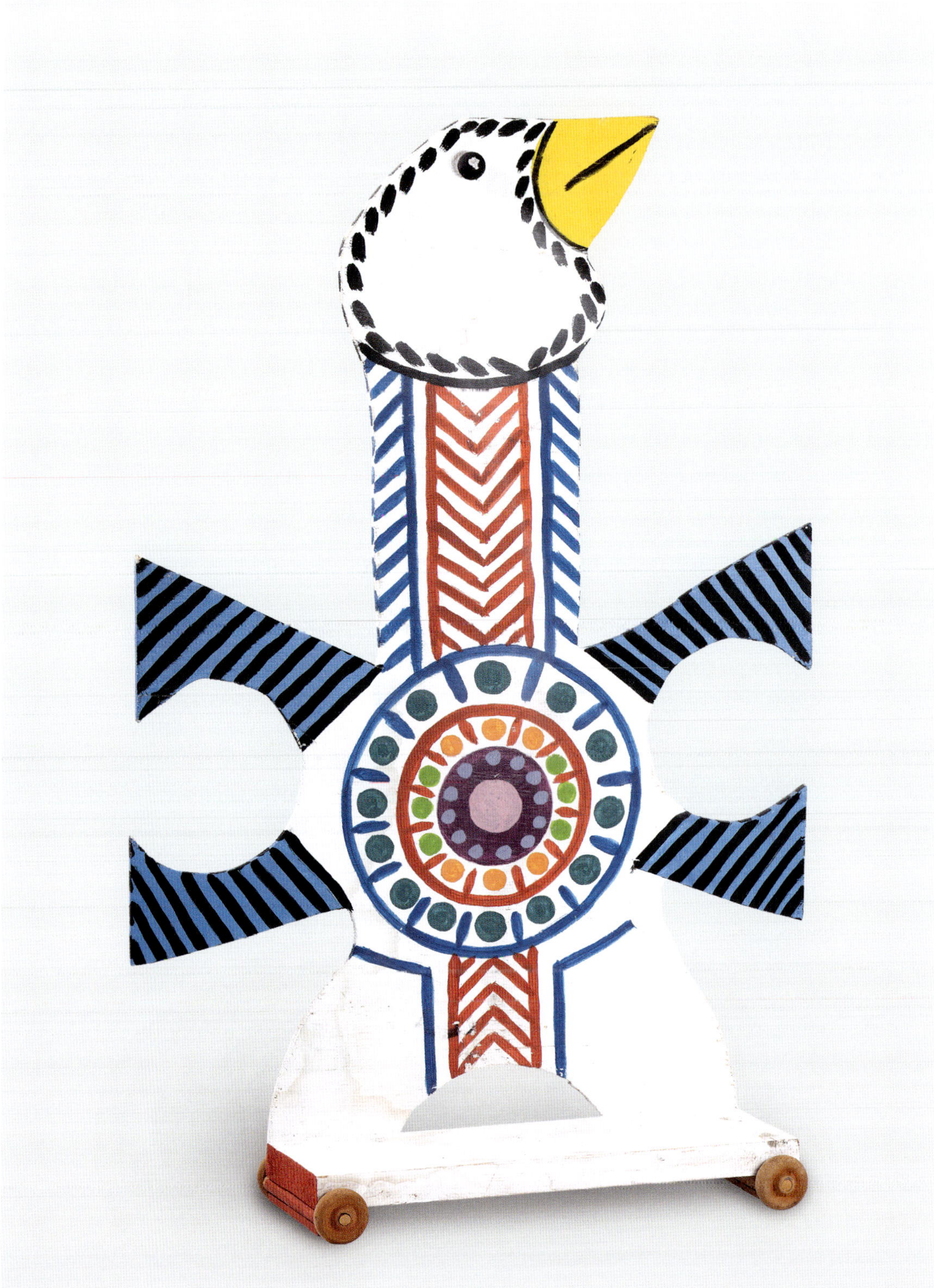

Plate 15. Marvin Finn, *Untitled*. Cut-out and painted wood bird pull toy with wood wheels. 25 × 15½ × 4¾ inches.

Christmas was special for the family. Randolph brought a whole box of apples, oranges, and candy. The little children believed in miracles, the Angels of the Lord, the miraculous birth of Jesus, and Santa Claus. And Santa always brought some small gifts for the children, even in bad times. Toys, store bought or homemade, were scarce. (Plate 15) You might get a pull toy with wheels if your Daddy or Uncle were handy, but "I remember a lot of Christmases when I never seen me a toy." (Marvin Finn)

Winter weather varied from bitter cold one day (minus 9 degrees F) to spring-like the next (80 degrees F). Really cold weeks were best for catching rabbits, but you nearly froze, turned blue when out checking the gums. No matter how cold it got, Shorty still had to tend the mules, cow, and chickens, and the family had to keep getting in firewood. (Plate 16)

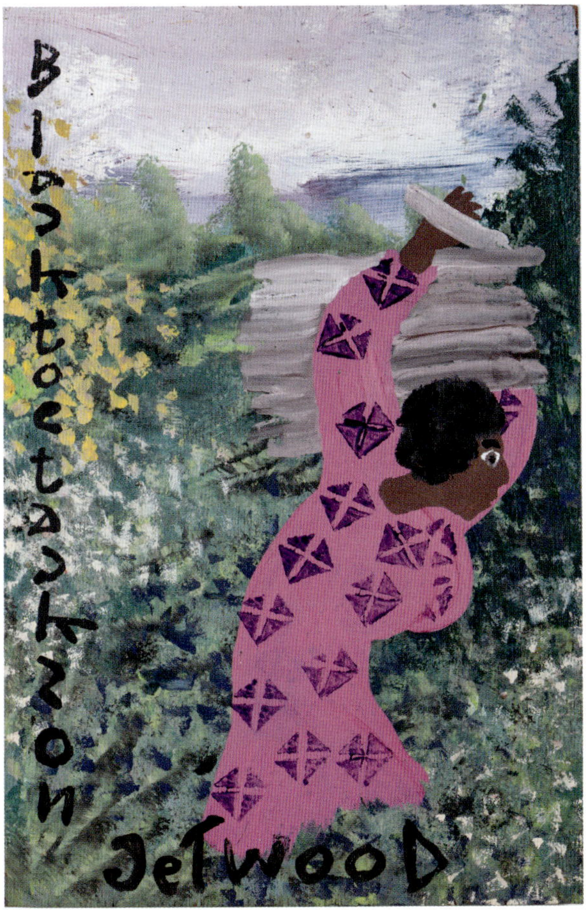

Plate 16. Black Joe Jackson, *Get Wood*. Paint on wood board. 18¼ × 11½ inches.

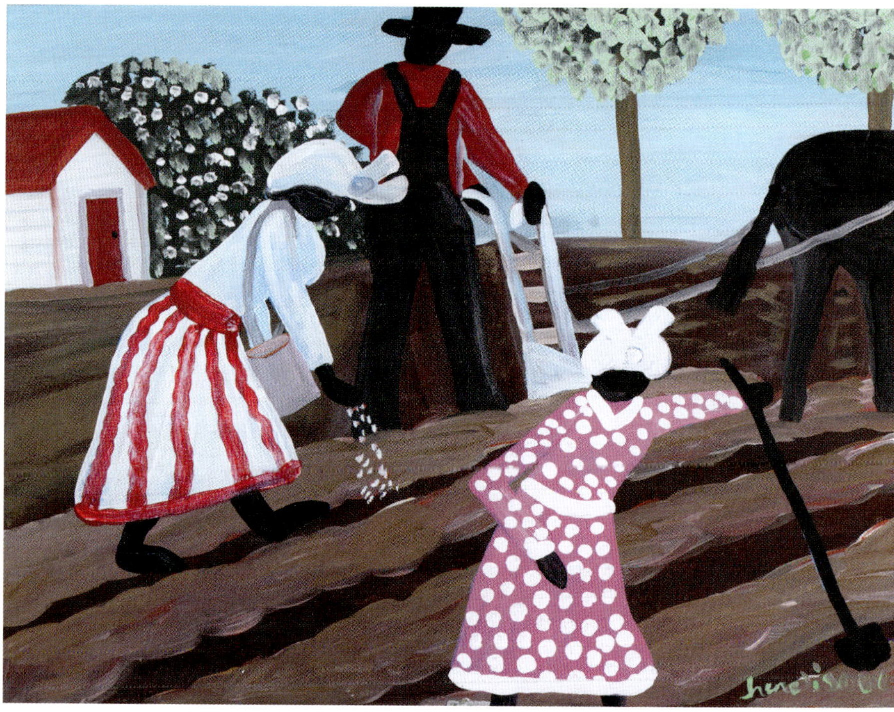

Plate 17. Irene Tison, *Ploughing Time*. Paint on canvas. 22 × 28 inches.

Plate 18. Randolph Hester, *Untitled*. Carved wood tobacco planting peg. 8 × 2½ × 2½ inches. Shorty Lawson Museum Collection, gift of Randolph Hester.

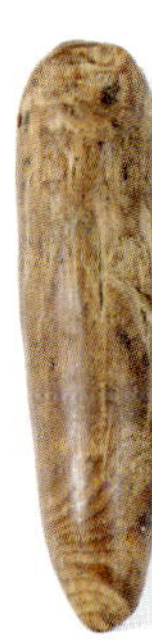

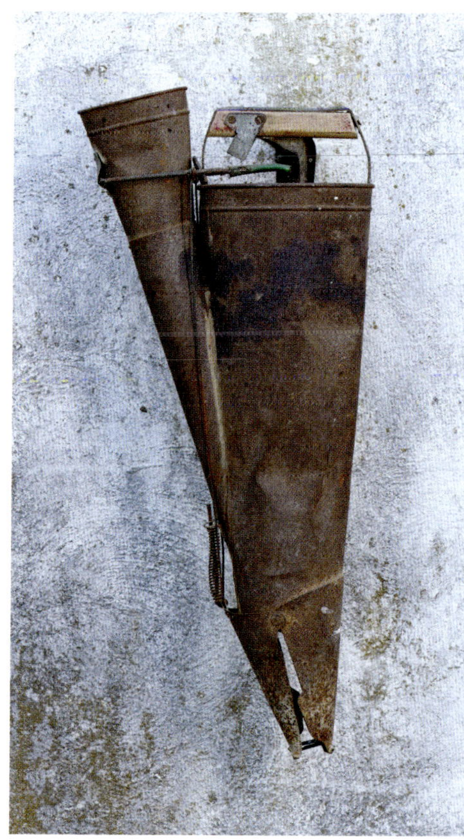

Plate 19. W. B. Owen & Co., *Untitled* PAT NO. 1711612 and 2034536. Metal hand-held tobacco planter. 31 × 12 × 8 inches. Shorty Lawson Museum Collection, gift of Randolph Hester.

Spring

"Give me spring. Give me green fields. Give me blossoms." (Ta-Nehisi Coates) The birds knew it was spring before anyone else did, mocking birds what waked you up before the rooster if the moon was out, red birds, sparrow hawk, that big hawk with the red tail, all kinds of birds, the little wren bird always building a nest in your best tools, singing old songs passed down like church music. That little wren bird had the happiest song, a big song for such a little bird, cheer you up when you were down in the dumps.

If you got a stretch of warm days, the world sprouted to life, turning pink and pale green overnight, flowers popping out the ground, trees coming back to life. "I remember there was a pear tree up about where the power pole is now, a real pretty tree when it bloomed, and good pears too." (Carolyn Lawson)

Soon every creature was having babies. The wood duck laid her eggs deep in a hollow tree late in winter, and the family tested the water at the pond the day after the last duckling hatched in spring. More than half the babies got eaten by raccoons or snakes or something. Mr. Rooster was abandoned by his wife and had to raise nine chicks by himself.

"We got plows out, plant bed started. One year Sylvester got gassed at the plant bed, poisoned, rushed him to the doctor. He got alright." (Larry Dixon) When old enough to manage a mule, the Lawson boys helped their Daddy plow, and the whole family planted the summer garden just north of the house. (Plate 17) But the major work was breaking land for tobacco and other field crops. And that was work that never seemed finished, just like a counted cross stitch.

As a boy Shorty plowed with a mule and wooden plow. But at the Bowes Farm he had metal plow points, and in the last years of his life most cultivating was done by tractor. Weeks of plowing were followed by weeks of planting tobacco. Bending to the ground hour after hour, Shorty learned to plant tobacco with a wooden peg, making holes, then covering the roots with dirt. (Plate 18)

With the acquisition of a metal planter he could stand upright to do the tobacco planting. Shorty and Randy used metal hand-held planters with two compartments, one they dropped a baby plant into, the other holding water. Pushed into the ground, the planter created a hole. With the pull of a trigger both baby plant and water were released into the hole. Then they pushed dirt around each plant with a foot. This invention dug a hole, planted, and watered the tobacco slip with a single pull of a trigger. (Plate 19)

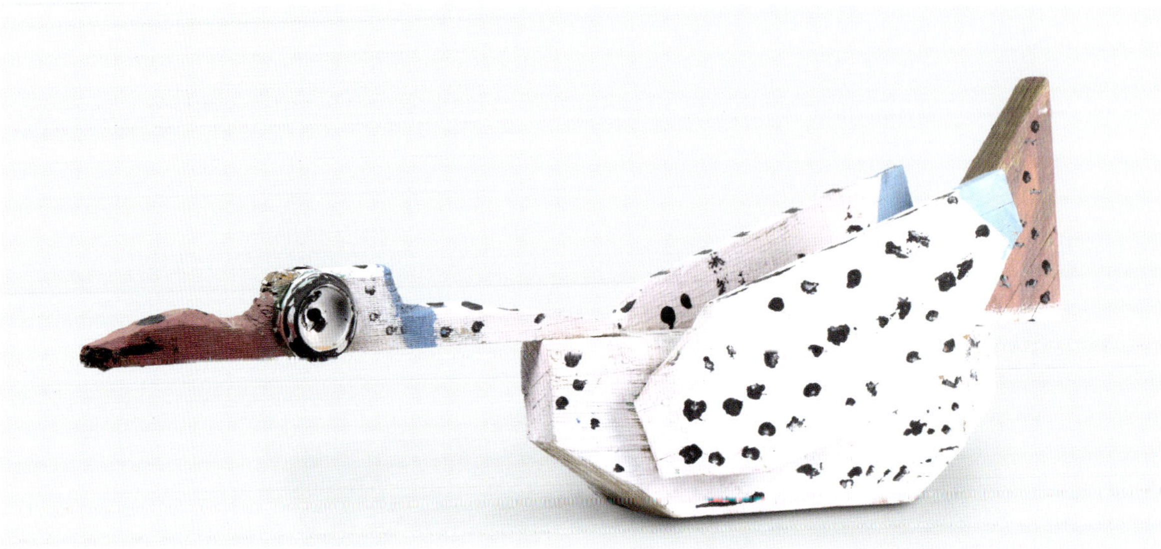

Plate 20. Robert Howell, *Untitled*. Assembled painted wood in goose shape, mixed media. 12 × 35 × 8 inches.

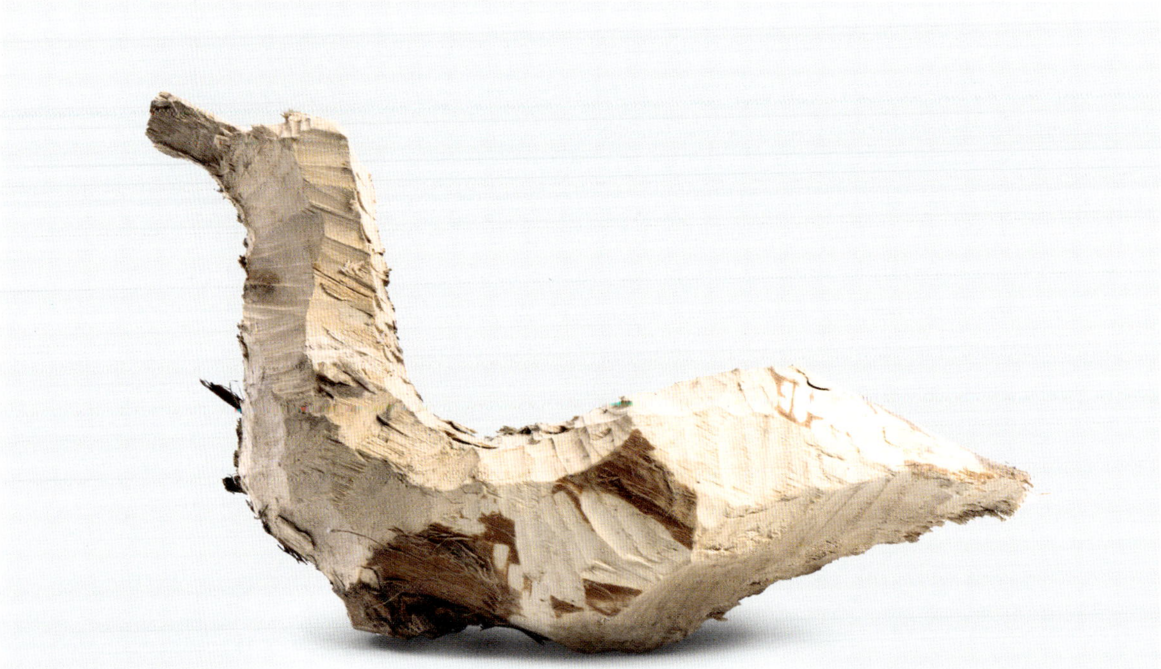

Plate 21. Anonymous Beaver, *Untitled*. Wood carved into bird shape by beaver teeth. 6 × 9 × 3 inches.

Ms. Fox had two frisky pups, one larger and far more adventurous than the other, that played at the edge of the woods, keeping their den out of sight, but close enough so the mother could practice her babies stealing into the chicken house when folks weren't looking. She'd hunt around the pond for the occasional goose nest. (Plate 20) But likely the best bird ever was found swimming on the pond, shaped from wood by a beaver. (Plate 21)

While all this was going on, more plowing had to be done. Early spring plowing was hard work, but days were pretty cool. Late spring it started to get hot, seemed like overnight. Grass and weeds were outgrowing tobacco. Shorty plowed to get the worst grass and weeds. Everybody else hoed around each tobacco plant to kill what grass was left, eight- or nine-hour days. "One real hot afternoon we were drenched with sweat and dead tired. I looked across the field where Shorty was plowing. (Plate 22) A bunch of buzzards were watching us. They were pretty excited, shifting around to get the best view of us like they expected a meal of carrion fieldworkers." (Randy Hester)

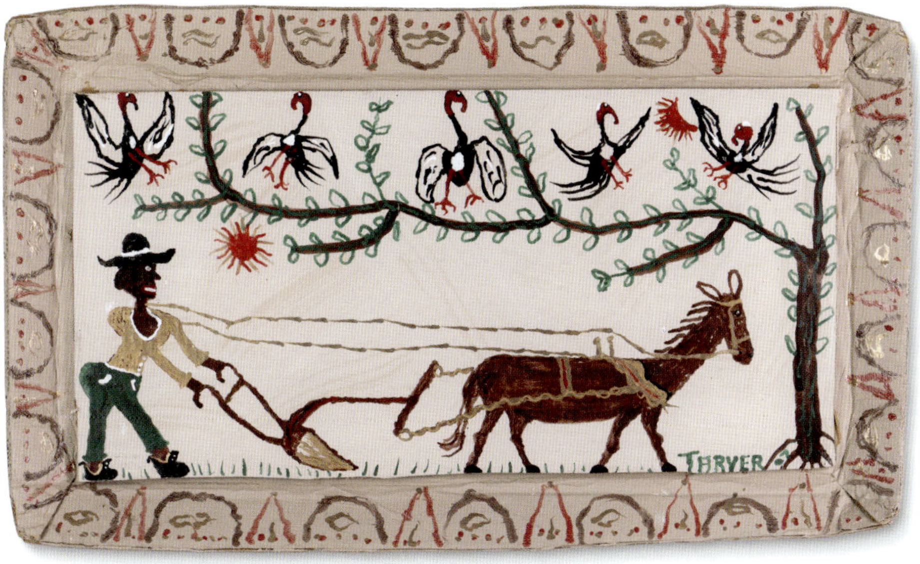

Plate 22. Willie Tarver, *Five Buzzards Watching a Man Plow.* Paint on cardboard. 16 × 26¼ × 1½ inches.

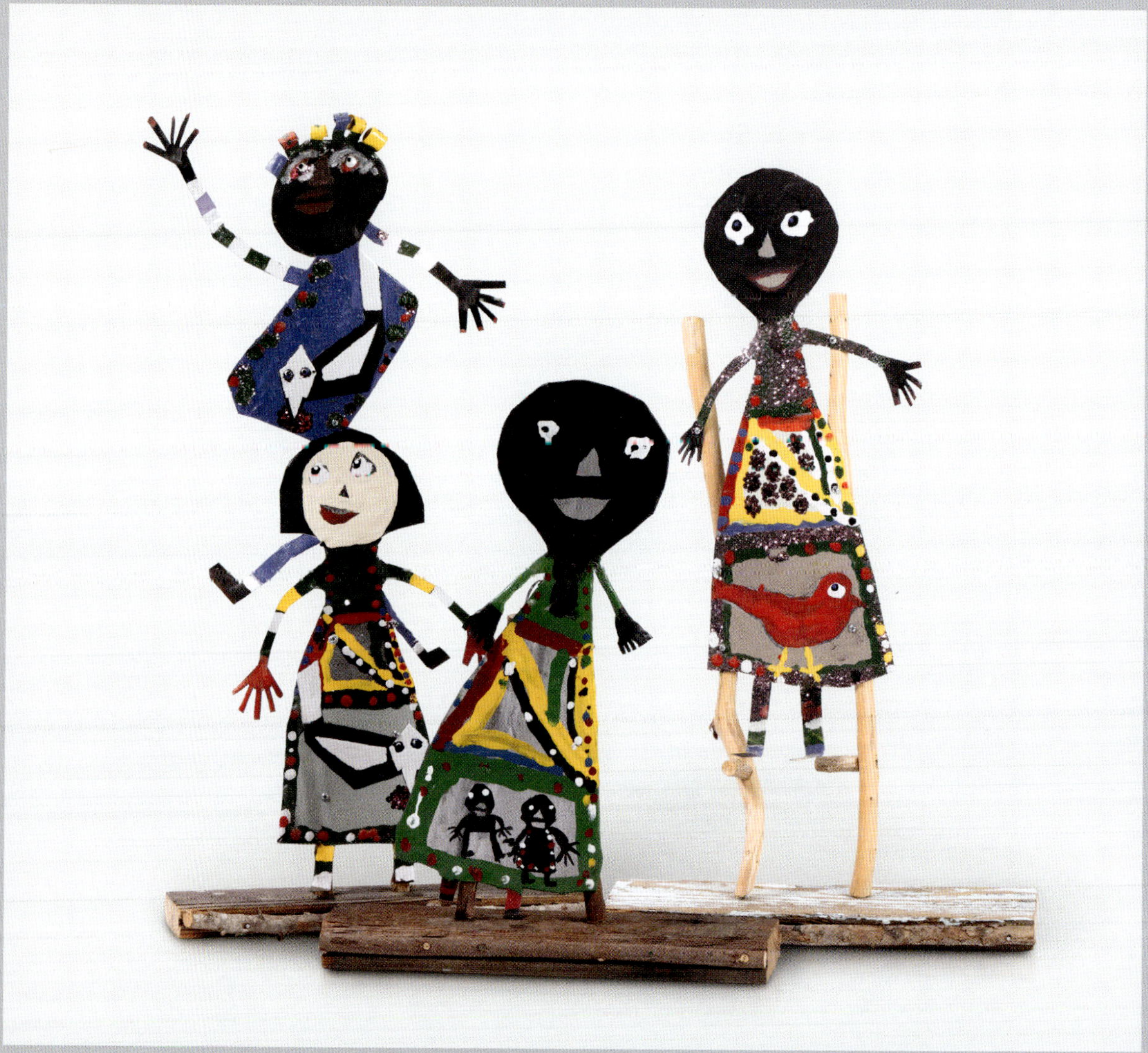

KITCHEN

Cooking, Eating, and Bathing

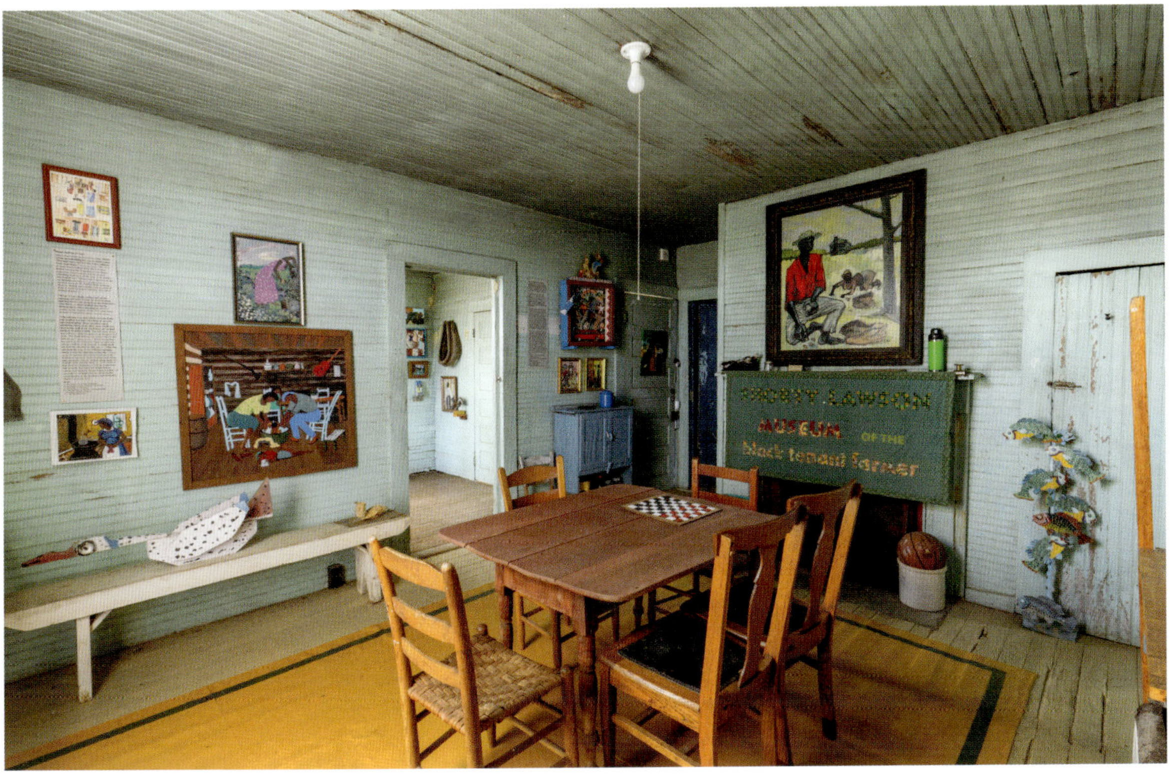

Plate 23 (facing). James Buddy Snipes, *Mrs. Blackberry Pie Lady*. Paint on metal cutout, sticks on wood base. 15 × 11½ × 4 inches. Randy Hester, *Blackberry Pickers after James Buddy Snipes*. Paint on metal cutouts, sticks on wood base. 22 × 11½ × 4 inches, 20½ × 11½ × 4 inches.

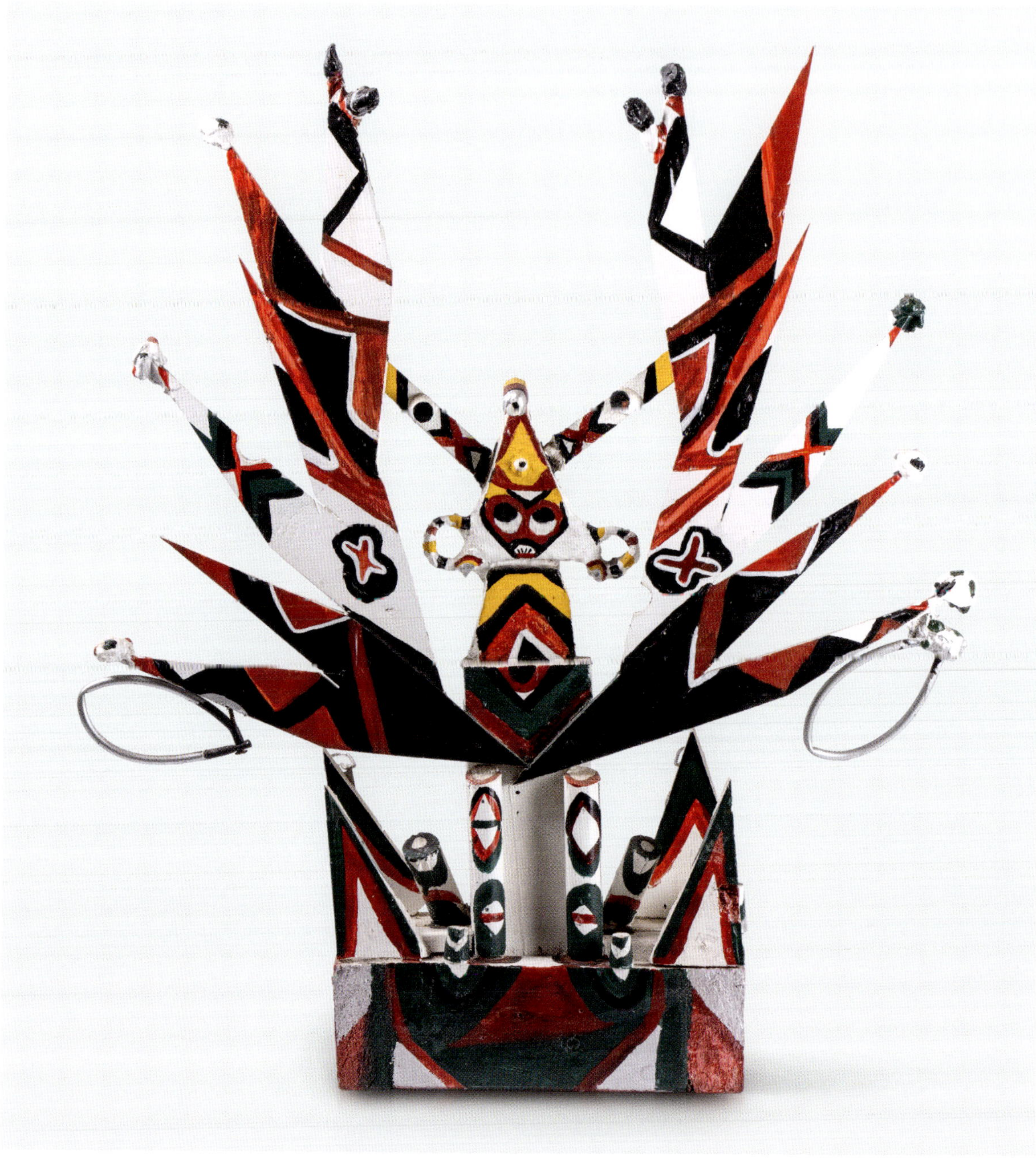

Plate 24. Derek Webster, *Untitled*. Paint on wood cutouts and dowels, tubing, plaster or bondo. 28 × 24 × 4 inches.

A Lot Going on in Annie's Kitchen

When Shorty and Annie married, she was already a good cook. She shaped the family diet with what she had, and they ate well under her direction. "Only once I remember when we didn't have anything to eat." (Stella Dixon) The Lawsons lived modestly by managing the kitchen efficiently, growing almost all of their food, and fishing, hunting, and trapping.

From 1961 and 1968 the household expenses averaged only $528.50 each year. The 1961 expenses included $12.00 for lard in March, $4.75 for a sack of potatoes in April, $25.00 for baby pigs in July, $14.00 for a barrel of flour in August, $2.15 for hog food including grinding in September, $9.47 for school clothes for the children at S. P. Gentry Store, $6.40 for pants for boys, $5.95 for shoes, $13.00 for Christmas presents, and $19.05 for the electric bill for the year.

In 1968 expenses included $17.00 for flour in January, $12.00 for boys' clothes and $9.00 for shoe repair in February, $30.00 for pigs, $25.50 for 300 pounds of flour, $5.00 for potatoes, and $10.00 for lard in March, $7.00 for medicine for Annie, $287.00 for income tax, $22.75 for dresses and $20.00 for children's insurance in September. That year Annie gave herself an allowance of $1.00 per week.

But the kitchen was more than managing the budget, cooking, and eating. It was a concentration of all things domestic. "And furthermo' everything is got tuh have uh center and uh heart tuh it." (Zora Neale Hurston) In the Lawson home the kitchen was unquestionably the center, the heart of family life. The Lawson children were always doing lots of different things besides making and sharing meals: washing up, doing homework, telling stories, playing, or joking around until an adult calmed things down. The kitchen felt like it would explode from the combined energy of so many activities. (Plate 24)

Once Annie sent Fernell to get water; he came back smelling like a skunk. He had run into one at the well. Nobody wanted to drink the water, but the water didn't really taste like skunk. They teased him; he got real mad.

The Lawsons ate a lot of fish; they loved to fish, the ponds were in sight of the house, and fishing put free food on the table. When Shorty, Carolyn, or the boys caught fish, they argued who got the biggest one until it was a lie, then hung around the kitchen waiting for Annie to fry it up.

Like most women around Hesters Store, Black and White, Annie used a lot of lard that made her cooking delicious and dangerous to their health, but that is a matter of hindsight. To make preserves or do

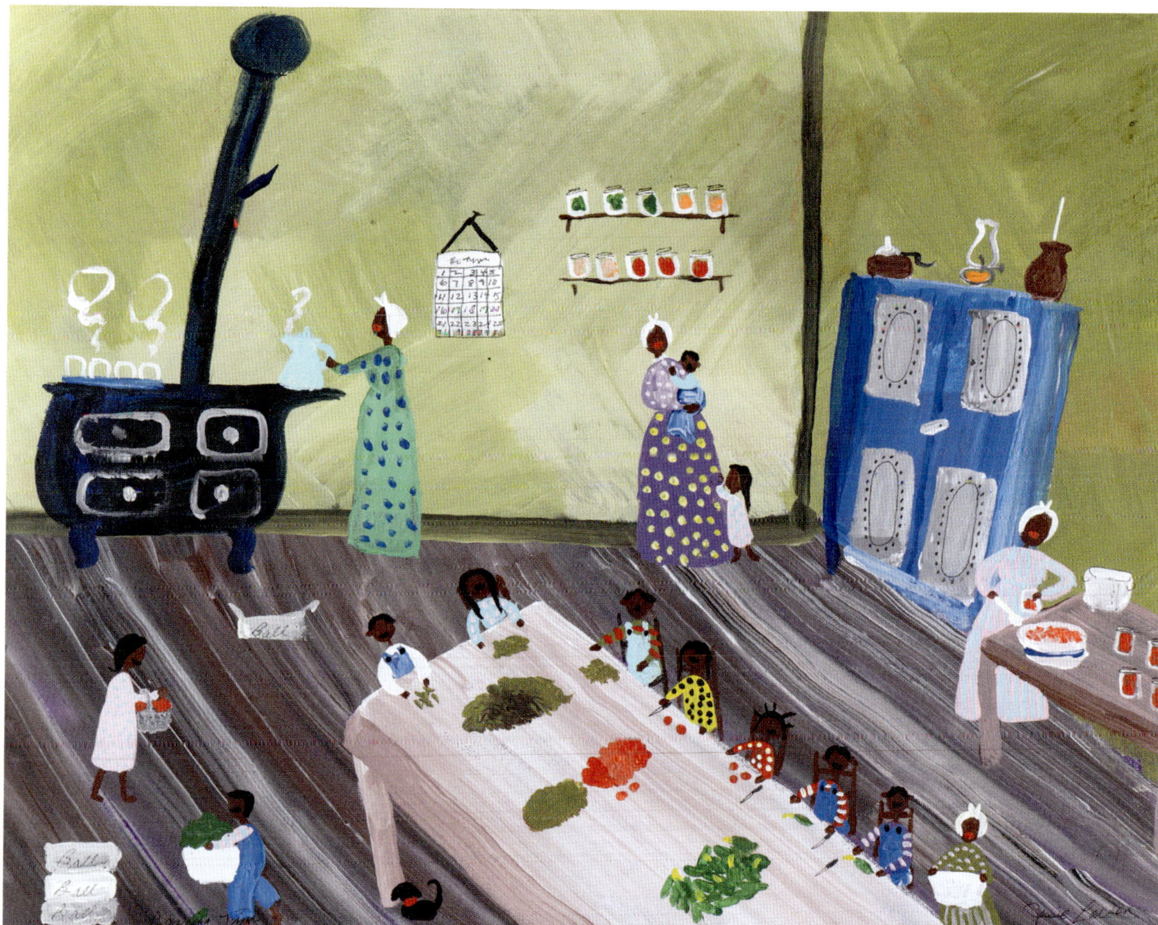

Plate 25. Jessie Lavon, *Canning.* Paint on canvas. 16 × 20 inches.

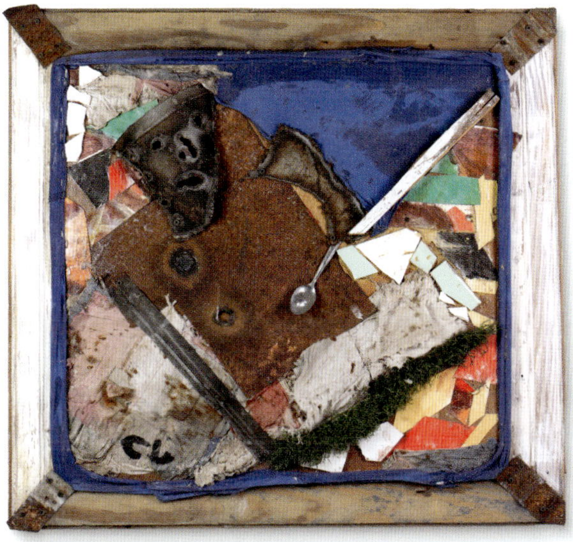

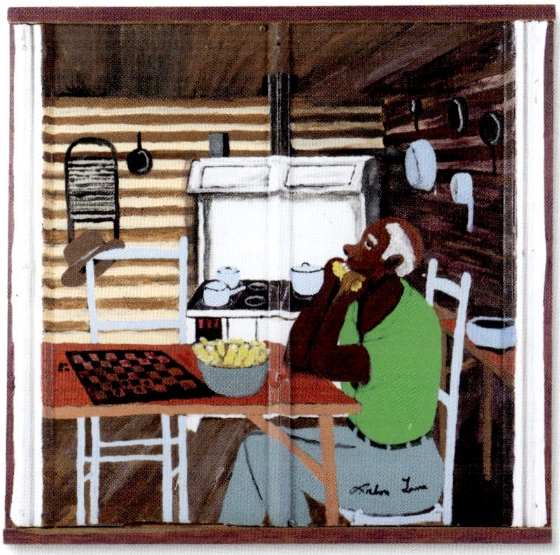

Plate 26. Charlie Lucas, *Feeding the Hungry*. Cut metal, broken pottery, cloth, artificial grass, wood, spoon, tin, paint, paper cuts on wood board. 25 × 26 inches.

Plate 27. Arbon Lane, *Untitled*. Paint on roofing tin. 27 × 26½ inches.

canning, she would get the children into a production line, sort of like a factory, but not so organized. In fact, there was a lot of disorganized fooling around. (Plate 25)

Annie said that they all had to do their parts to put food on the table; it was hard feeding every hungry mouth in a big family. (Plate 26) If she sent a child to get in firewood or feed the chickens, she expected that person to be back directly with wood or feed the chickens without anyone complaining about supper. And there were never complaints about Annie's cooking. Everyone had a favorite. Some said corn on the cob was best. (Plate 27) Others argued for sausage, but nothing matched her hoecakes. Only needed cornmeal, water, and salt. "Annie's hoecakes, whooooo lord, with sorghum 'lasses." (Larry Dixon) Flour and cornmeal were store bought in bulk. Her family ate a lot of both. In 1966 they bought 300 pounds of flour in January for $24.50, 200 pounds in April for $16.00, and 200 pounds in August for $17.00.

In summer she made pies after the children picked berries. Everybody loved Annie's pies. "We competed to find the best blackberry bushes and get the most, the real black fat ones, and those in the tallest bushes. The little kids mostly ate the berries as fast as they picked them." (Carolyn Lawson)

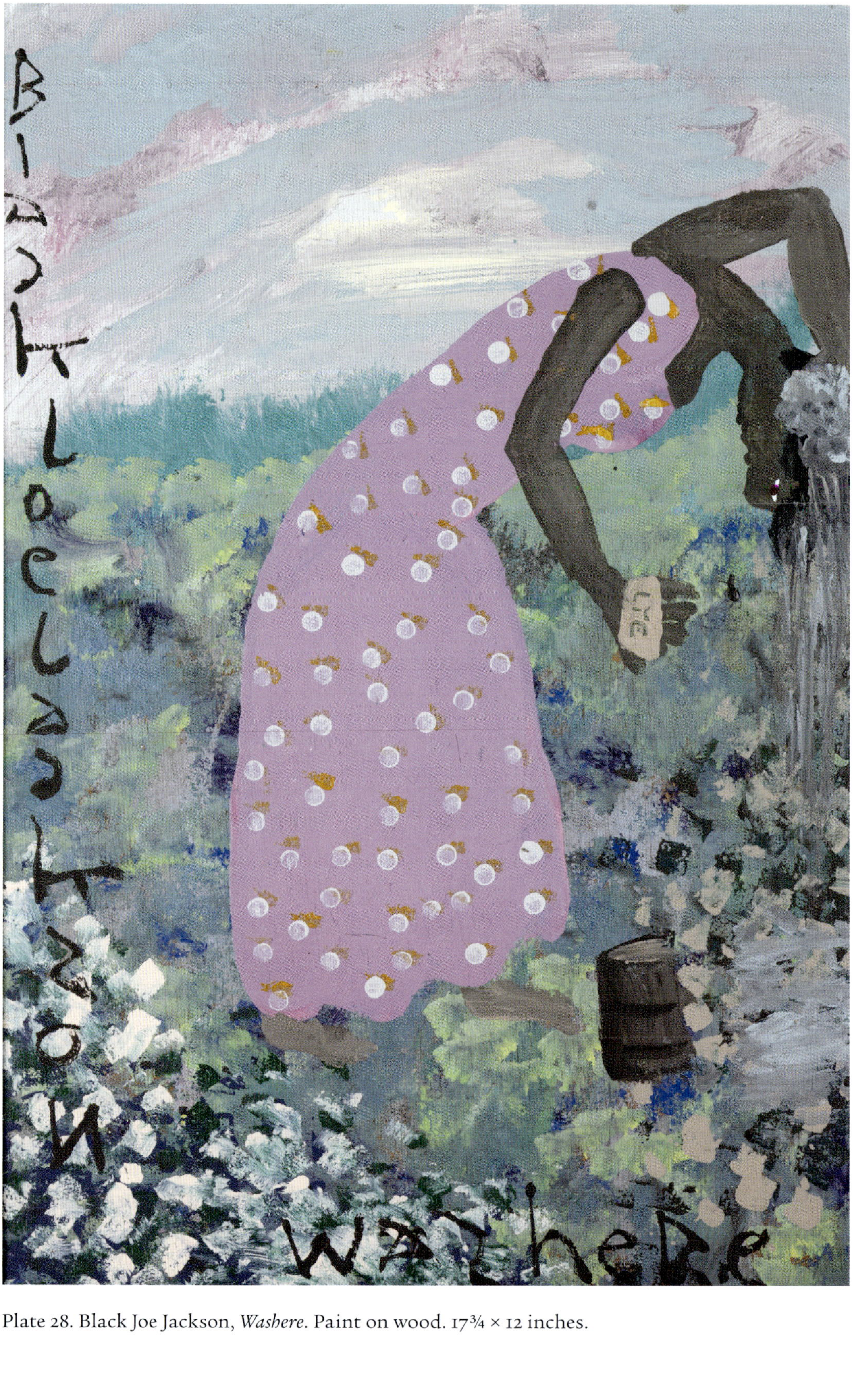

Plate 28. Black Joe Jackson, *Washere*. Paint on wood. 17¾ × 12 inches.

Please Pull Up a Chair

Join us for a while at the kitchen table. We'll warm up something for you to think about. "We'd sit around, Shorty talk about the old times before tractors or regular doctors like it teaches us something. If you got sick or hurt, didn't go to a doctor, just a drop of kerosene oil on sugar cure a cold, rub on for arthritis too. Pinee or kerosene oil cleaned up real bad cuts, kill off infection." (Stella Dixon) Annie used Pinee; but Randolph swore by kerosene oil. "We look back that we may learn wisdom from experience." (Anna Julia Cooper)

Annie's place was the present, extending from here all the way to the garden and clothesline. "Mama wasn't hard on us, but we did what she told us." (Carolyn Lawson) In summer she kept the big children busy helping out, fixing meals or setting the table, the little ones busy swatting flies. During cold weather Annie gathered them to warm up before bedtime; they did so without protest.

"When I was a baby, Mama did all the cooking, but later we got an electric stove, had two stoves, she cooked on the wood stove over there and I cooked too, on the electric stove where the plug is, summer mostly on the electric, winter the wood stove because it heated the room." (Carolyn Lawson)

"The kitchen was also where we took baths and washed our hair. In winter it was the only warm place. Since we didn't have plumbing, some of us older ones would run over to the well at the big house, get enough buckets to make a bath. The little ones would race after us, make it a game even though it was work." (Carolyn Lawson) "The hardest thing was toting water to the little house." (Brenda Lawson)

"Mama would heat the water on the stove. Then we took turns taking a bath in a big foot tub. I would wash my hair in a bucket or tub, too. That was just how life was. Even without running water it was the best time of my life." (Carolyn Lawson) In summer the children bathed in the kitchen or out back with lye soap and without a complaint. (Plate 28)

Older brothers and sisters, and a few times Shorty, helped Annie bathe the younger ones and the baby. "All I claim is that there is a feminine as well as a masculine side to truth; that these are related not as inferior and superior, not as better or worse, not as weaker or stronger, but as complements—complements in one necessary and symmetric whole." (Anna Julia Cooper)

Everybody Had Chores in the Morning

Morning started real early in a frenzy of activity. (Plate 29) All the children, even the little ones, had chores. Get in firewood, set the table, feed the chickens and baby brother, run across the road to the well for water, tend the mules, milk the cow. (Plate 30) "I had to milk the cow, wash up, get dressed in school clothes, eat breakfast, get my books and lunch, then catch the bus. Some years the school bus came down our road; other years the route was just on Gordonton Road so we had to run over half a mile for the bus." (Carolyn Lawson) There was seldom any complaint even in rain or freezing weather because Shorty and Annie made it clear to the children that missing the bus was worth a whipping.

Although the kitchen was the women's place, Annie relied on Shorty and the boys to make repairs to broken windows, mice holes, and leaks in the roof. She expected them to build cabinets, shelves, add rooms when

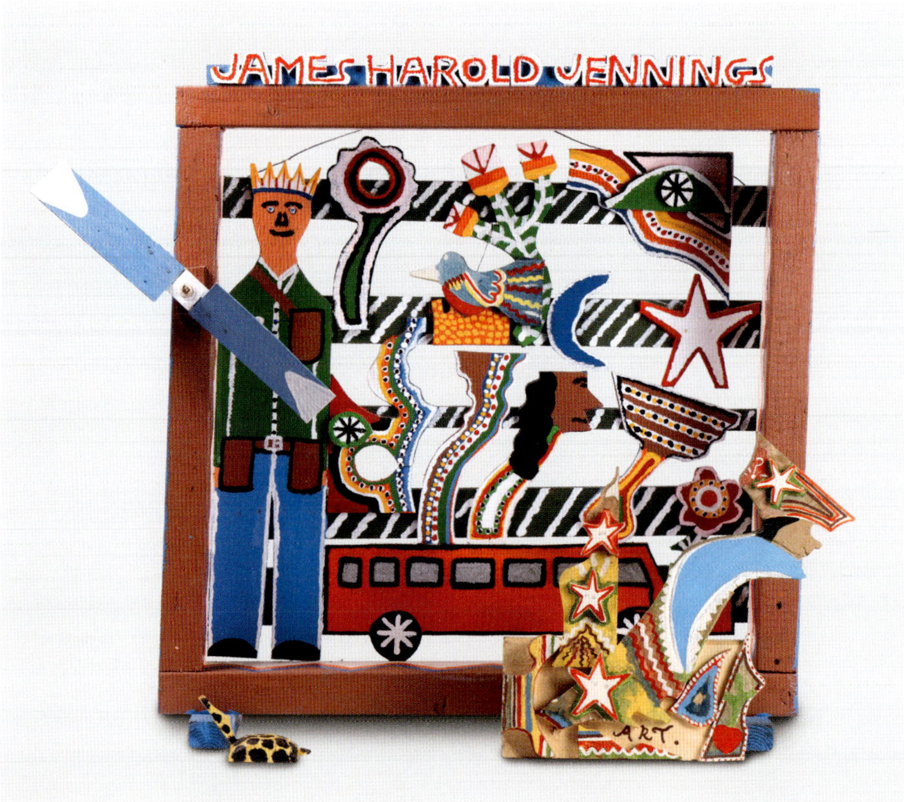

Plate 29. James Harold Jennings, *Self-portrait with School Bus.* 2 × 4 and 1 × 2 wood, painted wood cutouts, wooden propeller. 22 × 28 × 7 inches.

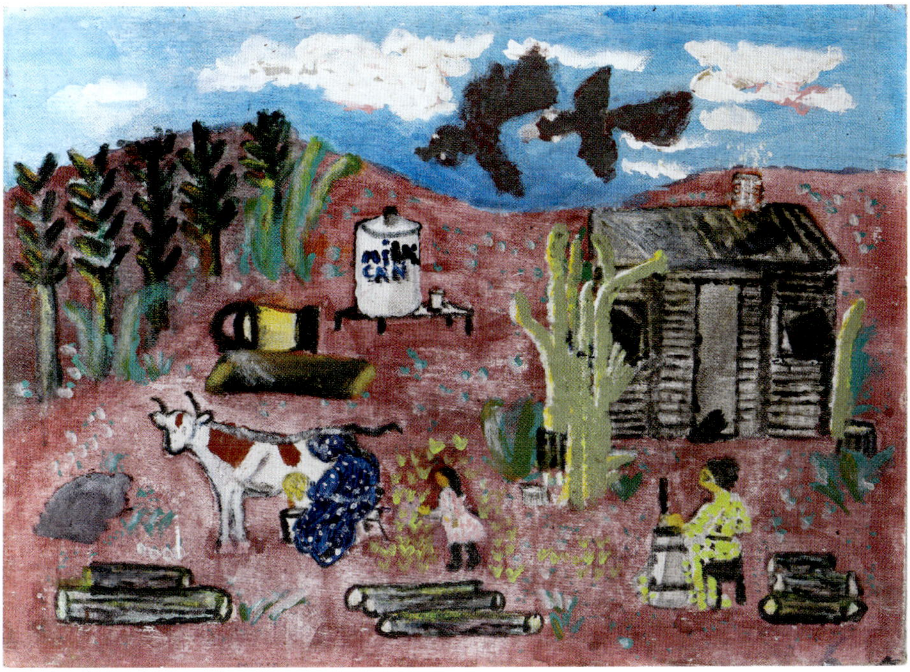

Plate 30. Eula Parris, *Milking.* Paint on canvas board. 18 × 24 inches.

she ran out of space, and all sorts of things like that. Shorty was creative in making things from scraps and stuff he found. And the boys helped and learned from him.

Every once in a while something Annie needed didn't get done; she would get short and raise her voice if Shorty or the boys didn't fix a broken drawer or bring in the stove wood. "The feeling of slighted womanhood is unlike every other emotion of the soul." (Anna Julia Cooper) You might hear Annie call out, "I can't cook until you split up the wood, old man." "A lot of this stuff my people want to forget." (Richard Roebuck)

The Lawsons were farmers, gardeners, hunters, and gatherers. Everyone did their part, but the children knew that Shorty and Annie would always try to find a way to take care of them no matter what. There was certainty in that. The garden provided for the family in summer. "We grew snaps, potatoes, peas, and butter beans." (Brenda Lawson) Tomatoes and corn filled many working bellies. There was plenty of hog meat to fry and old chickens to stew, and, if need be, they could catch things from the woods or pond. Rabbits, squirrels, bullfrogs, big fish and small fish provided many a meal when meat was scarce. There were wild grapes and berries in season and the great pecan tree. It usually provided a gracious abundance of nuts waiting to be picked up.

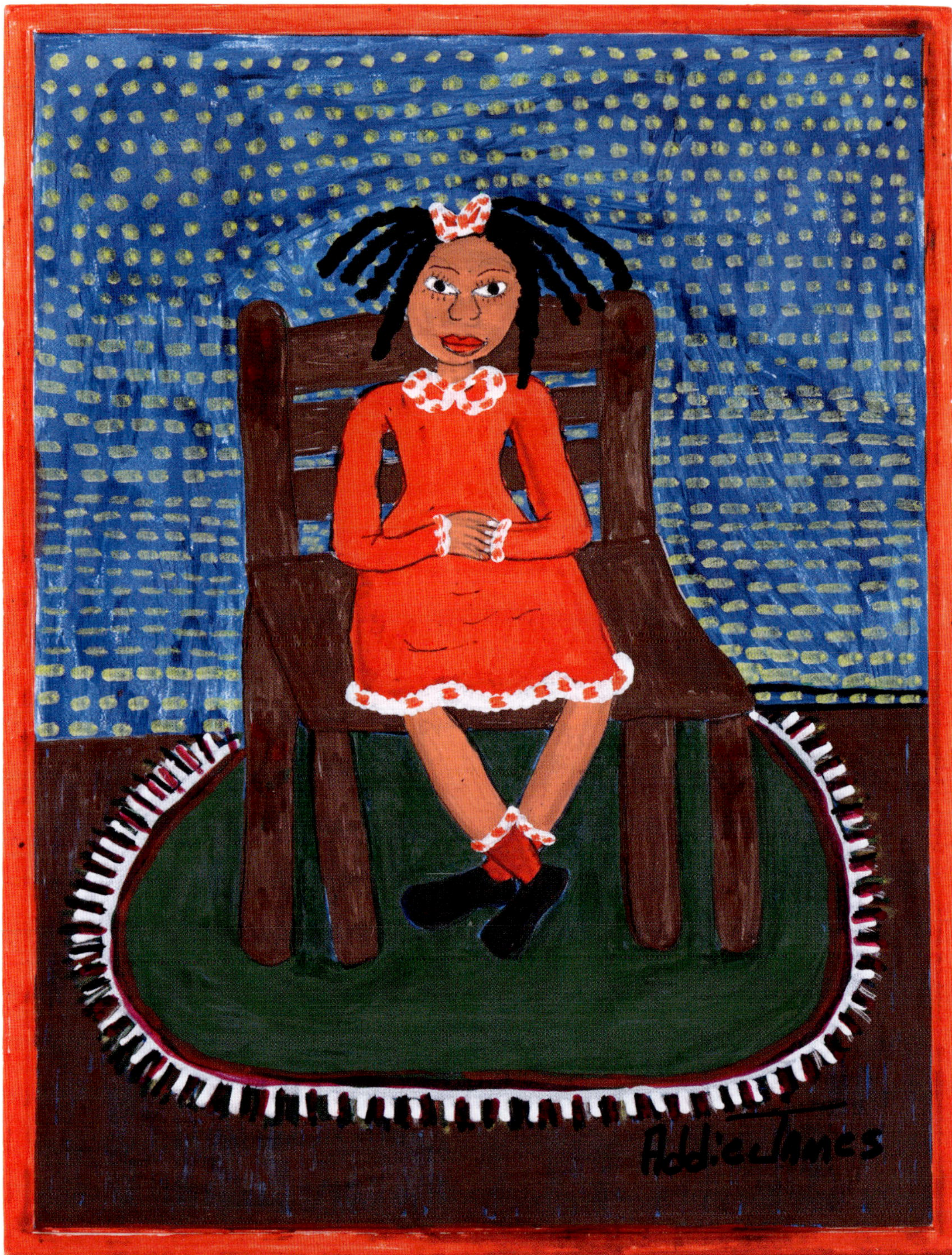

Plate 31. Addie James, *Portrait of a Girl.* Paint on board. 13½ × 10½ inches.

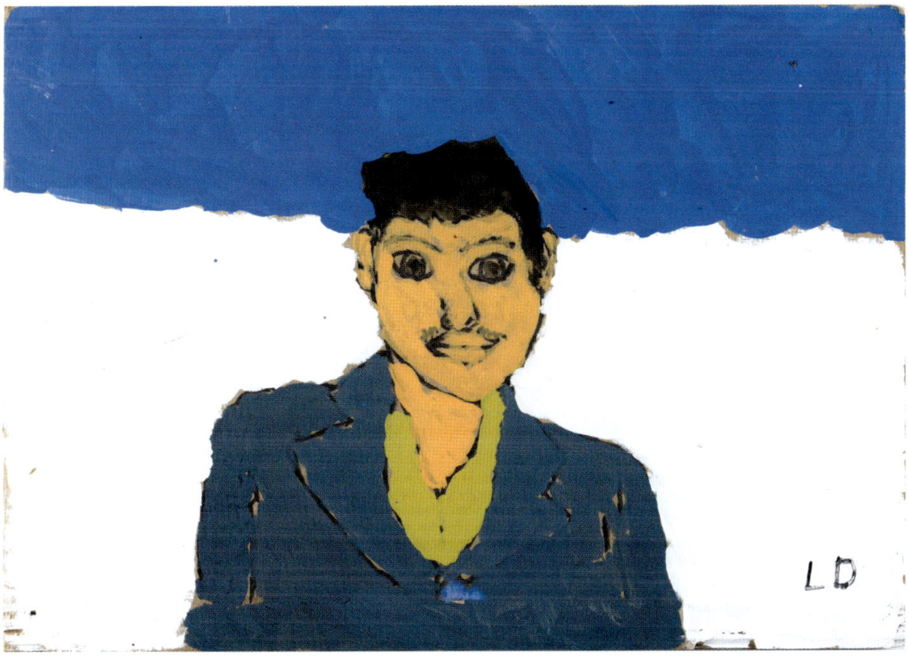

Plate 32. Larry Dixon, *Man*. Paint on cardboard. 12½ × 17 inches.

They tended the land. In turn, the land took care of them, granting them symbolic ownership and a sense of certainty. Land gave the Lawsons most everything they needed from satisfied stomachs to grounded, robust identities. "We didn't think we were so poor, never felt sorry for ourselves. That, too, was the way life was." (Carolyn Lawson)

They likewise tended each other and their community. And their community tended them. If some family needed help, the community pitched in, whether an emergency or everyday matters. Everyone wore clothes passed from older brothers and sisters or from people in the community. (Plate 31) "Other families gave us hand-me-downs. That's what I mostly wore, but you could look real nice in hand-me-downs. We always had what clothes we needed." (Carolyn Lawson) Secondhands and patched hand-me-downs was what most people, Black and White, wore out here, even families that had more money. You needed something real nice for Saturday night or Sunday church, but as long as it was fresh washed and you were too that was alright. (Plate 32)

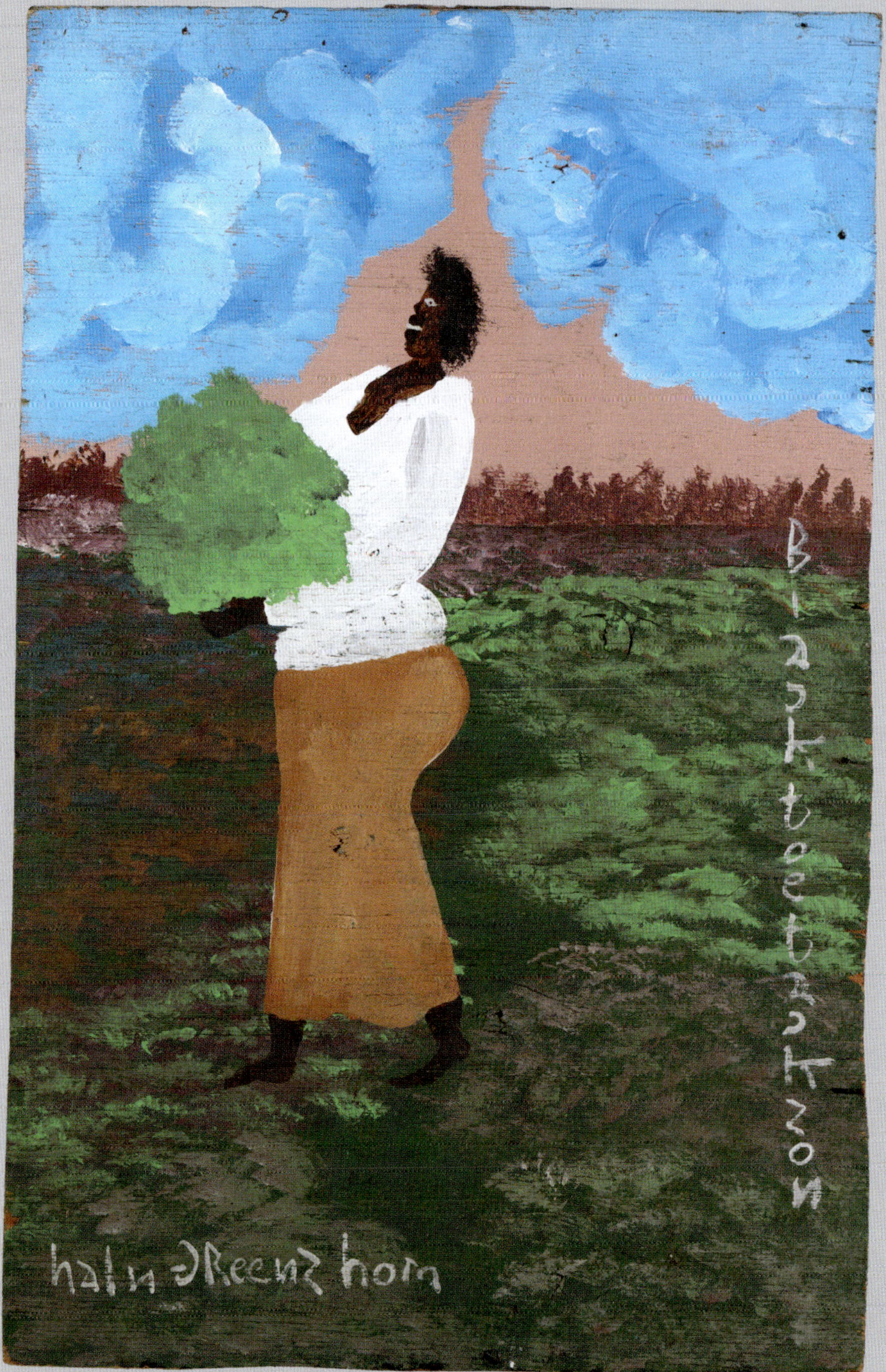

ROOM OFF THE KITCHEN

Processing, Washing, and Fixing

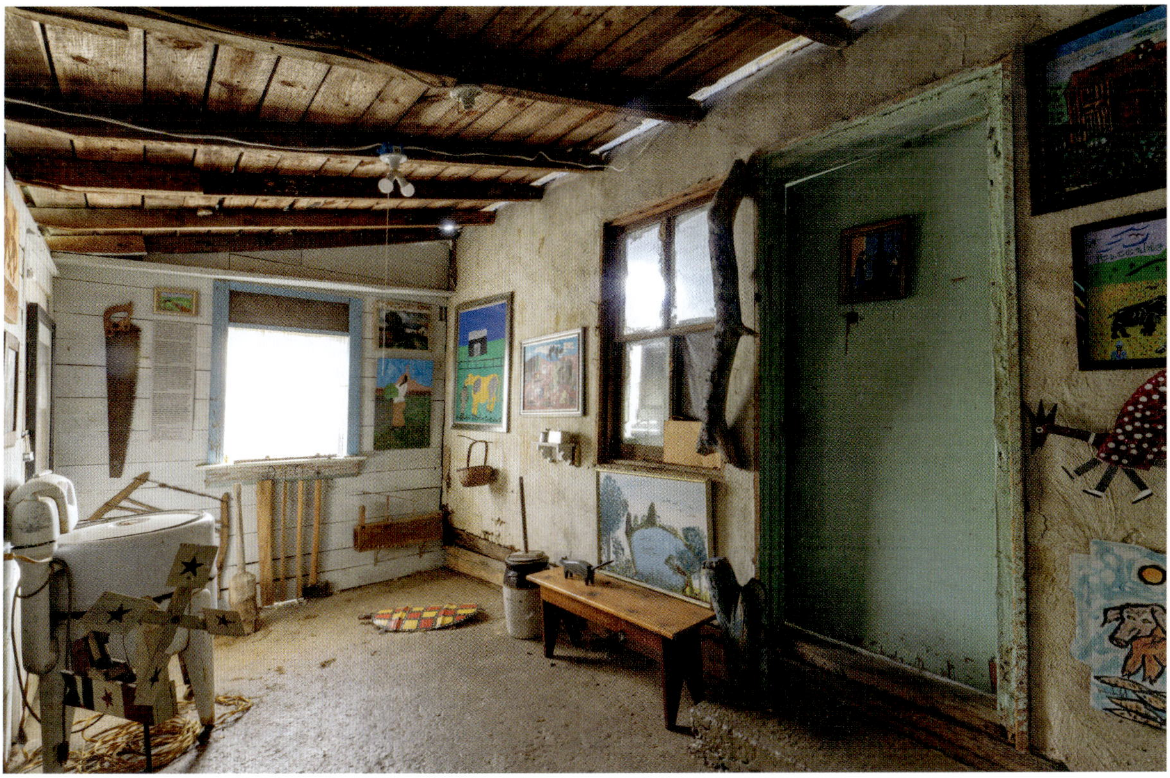

Plate 33 (facing). Black Joe Jackson, *Haln Greenz Hom*. Paint on plywood. 28½ × 17¾ inches.

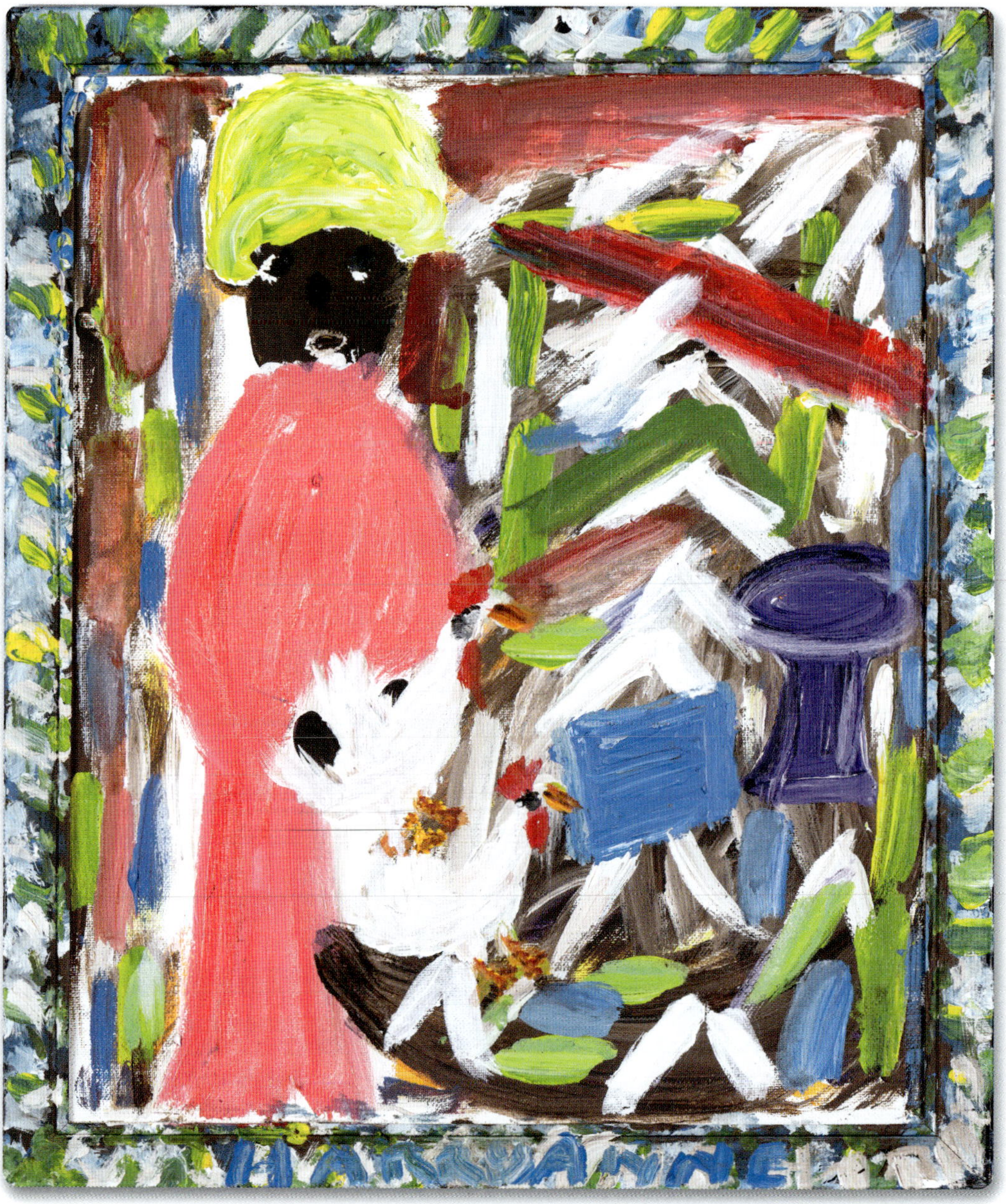

Plate 34. Alyne Harris, *Two Cocks Fighting.* Paint on wood panel and frame. 18 × 15 inches.

Add-on

As the family grew the kitchen simply couldn't hold all the activity. The house had been built before electricity came to the area and designed to accommodate only the newly married Bowes son and his wife. The kitchen had no space for anything but cooking and eating for two. So the first room added to the little house was an all-purpose space that made room for some of the activities overflowing from the kitchen. The men poured a concrete floor and sided the room with rough-cut lumber from Walter Bowes' sawmill just up the road. The room served as both expanded kitchen and pantry and transition from outdoor to indoor functions. They moved the churn, big containers of flour, water buckets, and firewood out of the house, making the kitchen far more livable.

In time the add-on room accommodated kitchen appliances. One purchase with tobacco profits was a deep-freeze. That was a joyful day when Shorty and Annie got that deep-freeze, sat it right in the add-on room. It fit perfect. Annie had always canned, but freezing food expanded what could be saved for winter. With the deep-freeze, she could keep both vegetables and game the boys got hunting and fishing, although most times what got caught was eaten up right away. And there were plenty of rabbits and squirrels in the brush and woods, fish, bullfrogs, and turtles in the pond, sometimes more than they could eat at one meal. Bullfrogs were a delicacy, legs jumping around in the frying pan. Their family didn't eat turtle, but a relative did so they'd freeze snapping turtles until he came by.

They also grew vegetables, always enough for themselves, extra to can and freeze and share with others. Randolph, Shorty, and his brother Sam would load the truck full of corn, tomatoes, watermelons, whatever was in abundance, and deliver food to shut-ins. "I always thought Mr. Randolph was a smart man, but I don't know why he grows all that food just to give it away." (Sam Lawson)

Annie raised chickens. They weren't supposed to be pets, but the children fed them and played with them anyway. Annie would kill fryers for special occasions, old hens for chicken and dumplings. She'd wring their necks, snap off their heads; they'd run around, well, like chickens with their heads cut off. (Plate 34)

Outside seemed all peaceable, animals living in harmony with the family. Reality was everyone was trying to eat somebody else up; opossum after the rooster what wouldn't go up, she just providing for her babies. Folks do the same to others.

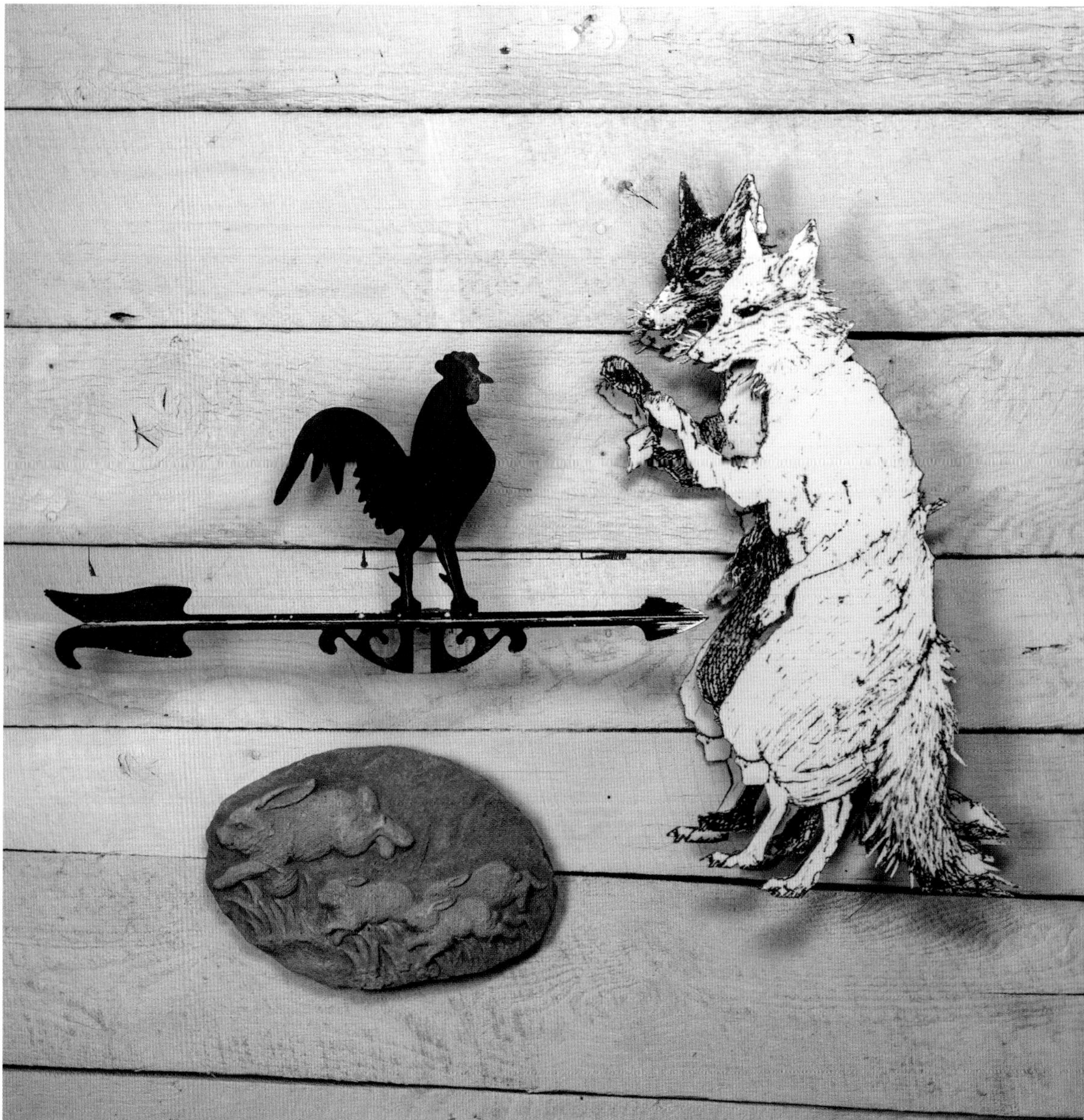

Plate 35. Wayne Roberts and Randy Hester, *Fox Be Smart.* Black-and-white and color decals of fox after A. B. Frost on tin, wood spacers, aluminum rooster weathervane, water-based paint over cast concrete rabbit. Fox 24 × 17 × 2 inches, rooster 11¼ × 23 × 1 inch, rabbit 9½ × 12½ × 2 inches.

Every so often a fox would steal a chicken. Raccoon the worst; he'd bite off the heads, just leave dead chickens everywhere, somebody have to clean up after the slaughter unless the buzzards did.

Once a rat snake got a biddy, had him in his mouth. Randy grabbed that snake round the neck, choked him until he gave up the chick. The chick lived. Had to let the snake go because you needed a good rat snake to keep down the rats and mice even if he did get a chick sometimes. Randy didn't get bit that time.

Shorty and Randolph grew a lot of food together. Randolph would buy a bunch of little pigs, "Daddy fatten them up with slop, kitchen scraps, anything going to waste, butcher them up in winter, live high on the hog." (Carolyn Lawson) Folks had a saying about pigs that you ate everything but the squeal.

Everybody hunting and killing, using their skills to feed themselves and their families. The fox was scary bad and not very smart in bedtime stories, but Shorty thought different. "Fox eats plenty rabbits and a chicken if he can, but if rooster doing his job, he'd make a fuss, we'd chase old fox away. A smart rabbit stay close to the briar patch. Natural, good or bad I don't know. Old fox kills only what he eat, he plenty wise, most like a ghost, you see him but you don't." (Plate 35)

Every animal had a purpose, even those old roosters, just strutting around, not only kick up a racket after the fox but also eat worms (Plate 36), make babies in eggs, and teach men folk pride. (Plate 37)

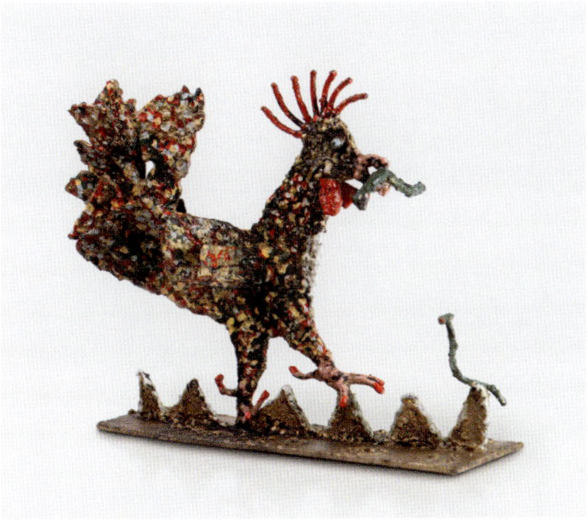

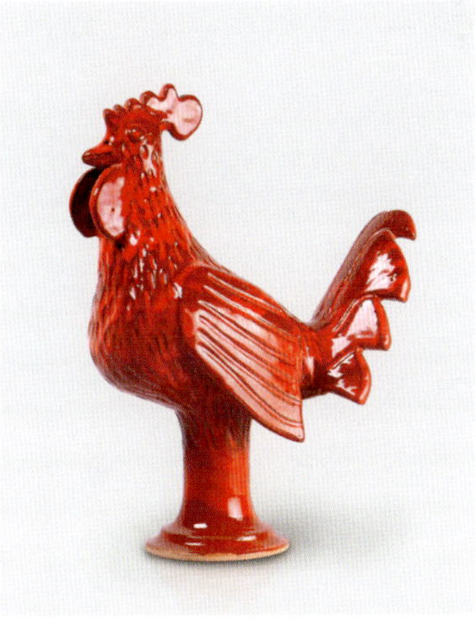

Plate 36. Willie Tarver, *Pharaoh*. Welded and painted metal. 12 × 17 × 4½ inches.

Plate 37. Larry Moore, *Untitled*. Red glazed rooster pottery. 12¾ × 9 × 4½ inches.

Clean Clothes and Fresh Milk

Some chores started in this room and finished in the yard, or the other way around, often back and forth from outside to inside. In the first years of marriage washing clothes was done with a tub and washboard. Annie had to do it all by herself. (Plate 38) If there was an especially heavy load to wash, Shorty might help Annie, but not often. To him that was women's work. But he realized it was dreadful hard. "The washing was not easy work. We spent the first hour drawing up water . . . filling our caldrons . . . With the fires going and the black caldrons heating, we held up the garments and bedding and beat the soiling out of them . . . And then for the next few hours we scrubbed, rinsed, and wrung, and then scrubbed, rinsed, and wrung twice more. Our arms and backs were sore. Our hands were raw." (Ta-Nehisi Coates)

When the girls got old enough, they helped out with the back-bending, arm-tiring, and hand-rending chore even after fieldwork occupied them all week. Getting clothes out to dry was a happy event, most things on the line, work overalls hung over the fence, smiles all around. Plus everybody loved the smell of drying clothes. (Plate 39)

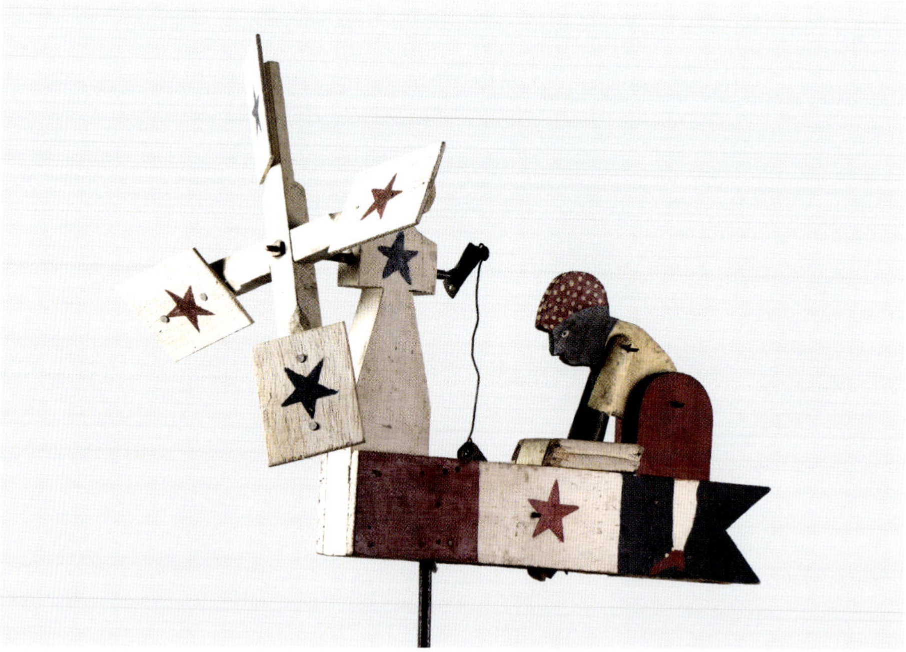

Plate 38. Unknown, *Untitled*. Painted wood cutouts of woman washing, metal, whirligig mechanics. 42 × 18½ × 12 inches with base.

In 1965 the Lawsons purchased a washing machine for $70.00. Getting a wringer washer was cause for an even bigger celebration than the deep-freeze; but remember, the Lawsons didn't have running water. Shorty had to figure something out. "He set up three 55-gallon drums right outside to catch rainwater off the roof, one for cooking, one for bathing, one for Annie to wash. If we got no rain, we hauled water from the pond." (Larry Dixon)

She filled the washer with clothes, then brought in rainwater from the barrel, added soap; plugged into the electric outlet; and the washing machine did the back-bending, arm-tiring, and hand-rending work. She rinsed in the basin with fresh rainwater, then ran clothes through the wringer to squeeze out excess water. It worked sort of like a spin cycle does today. The clothes were more or less ready to air-dry. Praise the Lord.

Never weathertight, the add-on room kept rain out but not heat and cold. Birds came in, but the children coming and going scared them away. Blue racers came in and out as they pleased, eating insects. Dirt daubers would build a mud village and set up house in a day or two if you didn't keep an eye out for them.

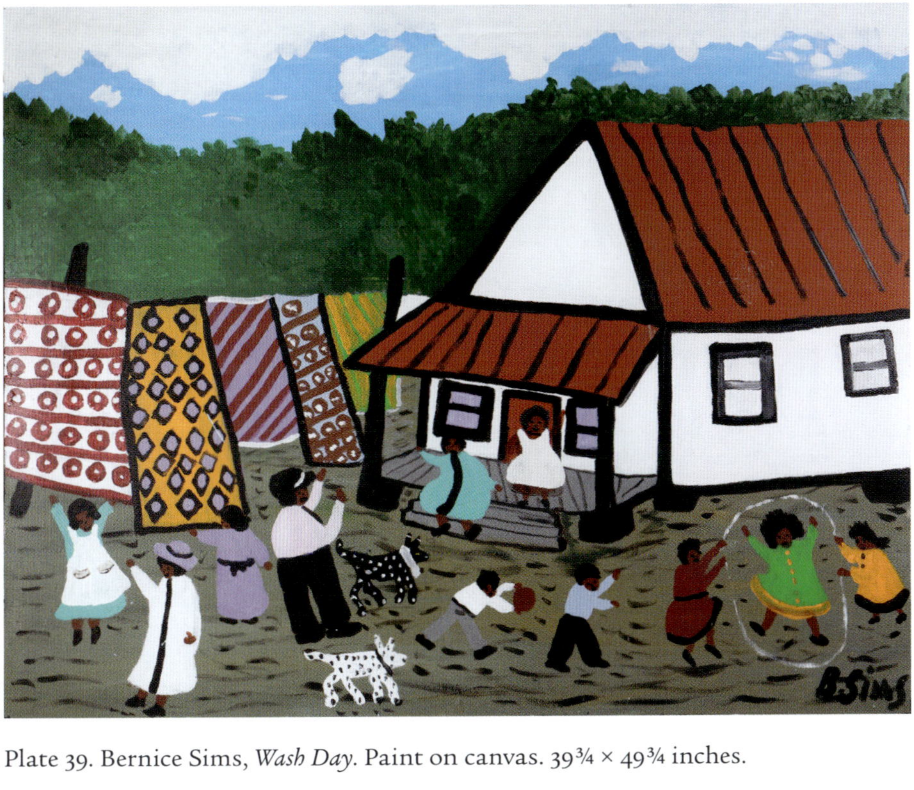

Plate 39. Bernice Sims, *Wash Day*. Paint on canvas. 39¾ × 49¾ inches.

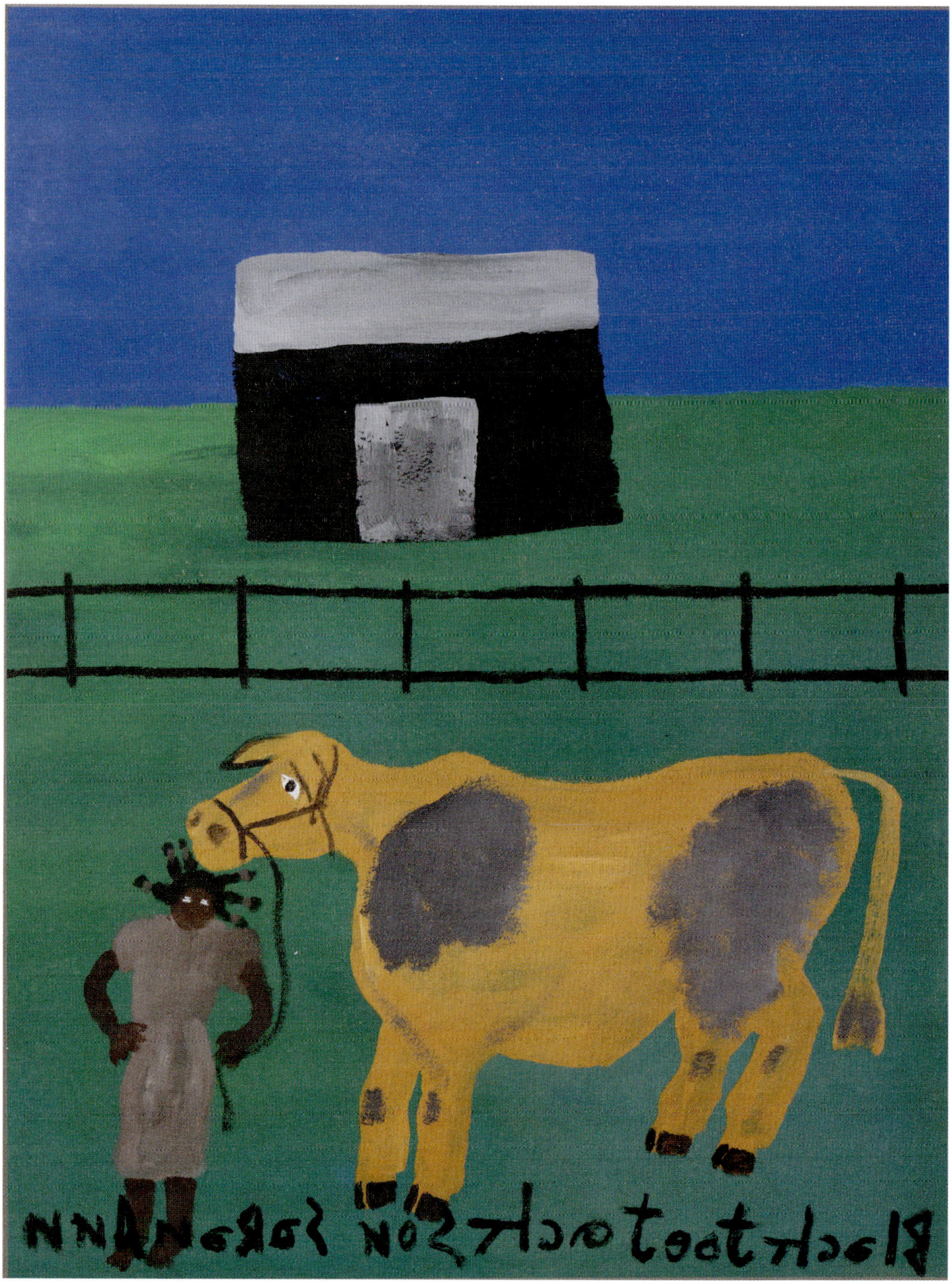

Plate 40. Black Joe Jackson, *Sara n Ann*. Paint on paper. 35 × 26 inches.

And flies, all kinds of flies. House flies, blow flies, green flies, fruit flies, crane flies, those with long legs like mosquitoes but bigger, deer flies, robber flies, May flies, sometimes more flies than folks at church.

Horse flies. "Lord, they were the worst. They bite through your skin and suck your blood. And that was a screaming hurt. They liked cows and horses best, but they just as soon feast on you or me." (Larry Dixon)

The Lawsons also used the add-on room in making butter and buttermilk. Jasper milked his cows, and Carolyn volunteered to help, then share the milk between the families. "You had to get the cow used to you else she wouldn't stand still, kick over the milk pail, all sorts of trouble. I liked milking." (Carolyn Lawson) A slew of kids drinks a lot of milk. (Plate 40)

Later the Lawsons had their own cow, kept her out beyond the outhouse. "One cow so calm we just milked her in the pasture." (Larry Dixon) When done, they brought the milk to the add-on room. Sweet milk had to be kept cool. The girls would churn some of the milk to make butterfat and buttermilk. Up-and-down work, churning tested your endurance unless you could make it a game and get the boys to play, but they only churn a little then go out and play with the dog or something. (Plate 41) To make stick butter Annie set the butterfat into a mold, squeezed out the liquid to get the butter to set up.

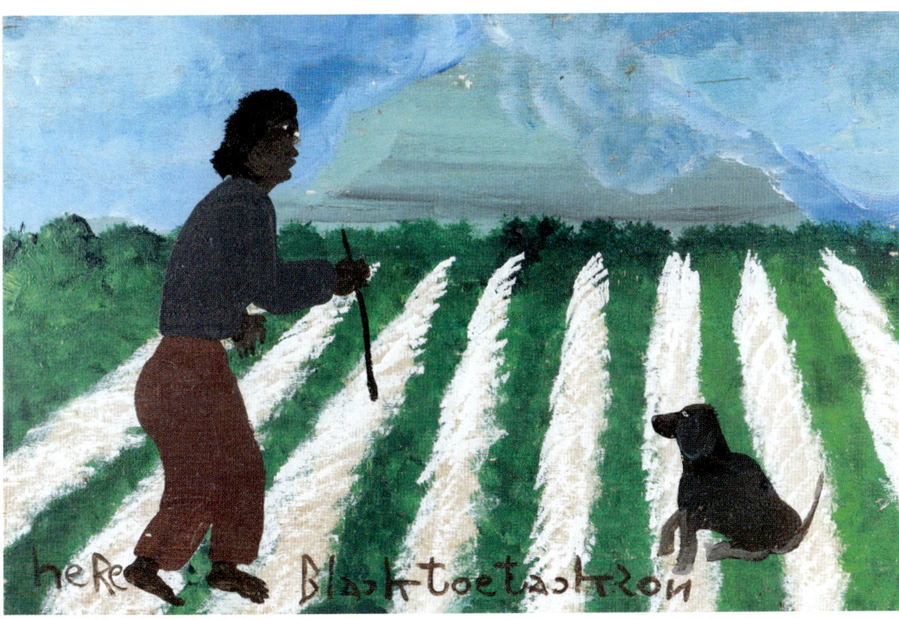

Plate 41. Black Joe Jackson, *Here*. Paint on wood board. 16 × 24 inches.

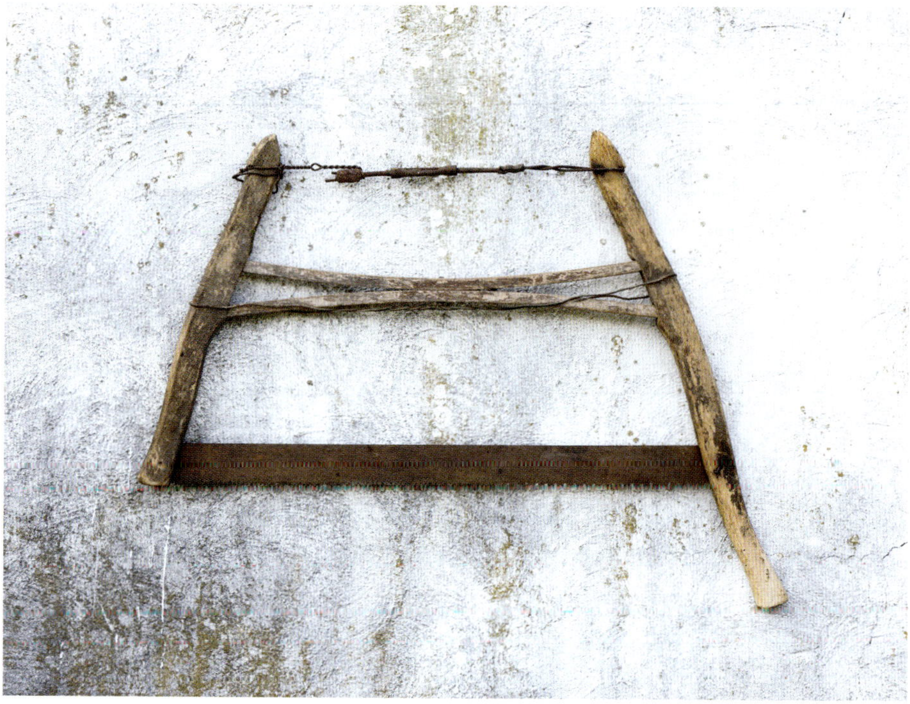

Plate 42. Randolph Hester or Shorty Lawson, *Untitled*. Saw with wood handle, wire repairs. 23 × 34 × 2 inches.

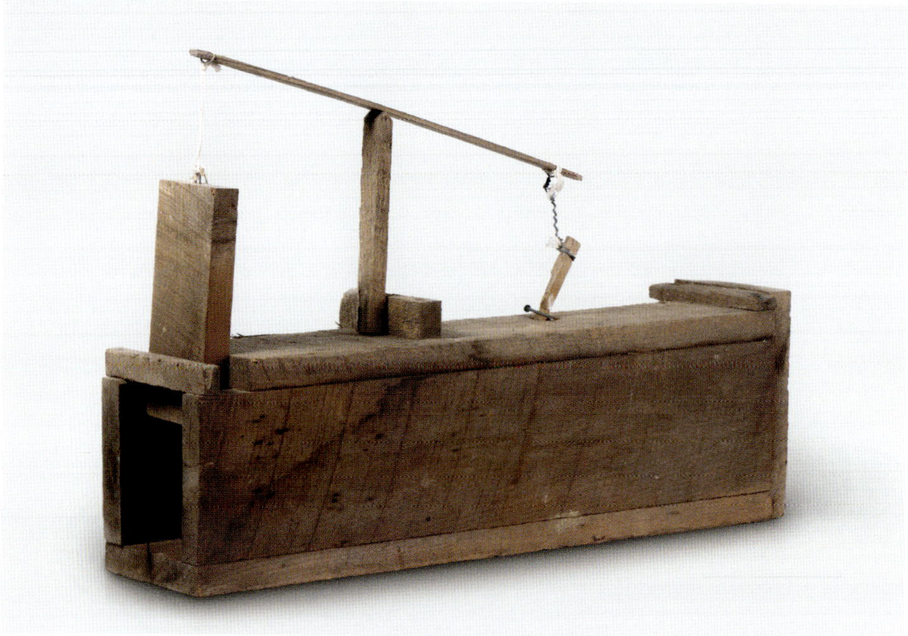

Plate 43. Unknown, *Untitled*. Wood, nails, and string rabbit gum. 17 × 25 × 5½ inches when set.

Shorty didn't consider himself an artist. That was and still is Larry's world, but Shorty was creative in practical ways. He could adapt or repair anything he needed from what was at hand. He made compactors and saw handles from wood, extended the life of an expired tool or made a new tool.

It was important to improvise on the spot. When something broke, you didn't call a repairman or go to town for a replacement. A whole day of work would be lost, plus there wasn't money to pay somebody else to fix it or buy a new one. Shorty's creative genius was repairing things immediately with integrity using scrap wood, leather, a piece of old metal, wire, nails, nuts and bolts, put together in unconventional form. (Plate 42) Most people could only imagine using materials how you were supposed to.

Shorty knew that a repair had to last. How it looked wasn't his primary interest, but, most of his homemade items possessed genuine craft. "Shorty's ability to create something beautiful from found objects made a lasting impression on all of us." (Randy Hester) Consider an ax handle. Shorty and Randolph found a perfect ash or hickory tree, a foot diameter, quartered the green wood with the grain, roughly shaped each handle to size. Then with a draw-blade and sharp pocketknife, they smoothed a tree into a fine ax handle to last longer than a store-bought one.

When all farm work was caught up, they turned to "improvements" like repairing a broken door or window, adding a shelf Annie needed, or adding to the house. Most years a new room, shed, or outhouse would be built. In 1995 Randolph paid Larry $235.00 for a new woodshed from used materials saved for such projects. The Lawsons' house was always clean and right nice. "We called it the Little House because it was smaller than the Big House where the Bowes lived, later the Furges family and then Sam and Brenda Lawson lived. Don't judge people by where they live. Sometimes there's more love in a little house than you would find in a mansion." (Stella Dixon)

Shorty made his own rabbit gums, using a time-honored design. The hard part was getting each detail exactly right so that the rabbit would trip the trap door when he went to get the apple in the back for bait. (Plate 43)

The women in the community also crafted things for domestic work, made things you needed or were likely to. The youngsters might need a new fly swatter, a school book bag, or something to tote the food crops from field to home. There was usually someone who could make whatever you needed from what they got.

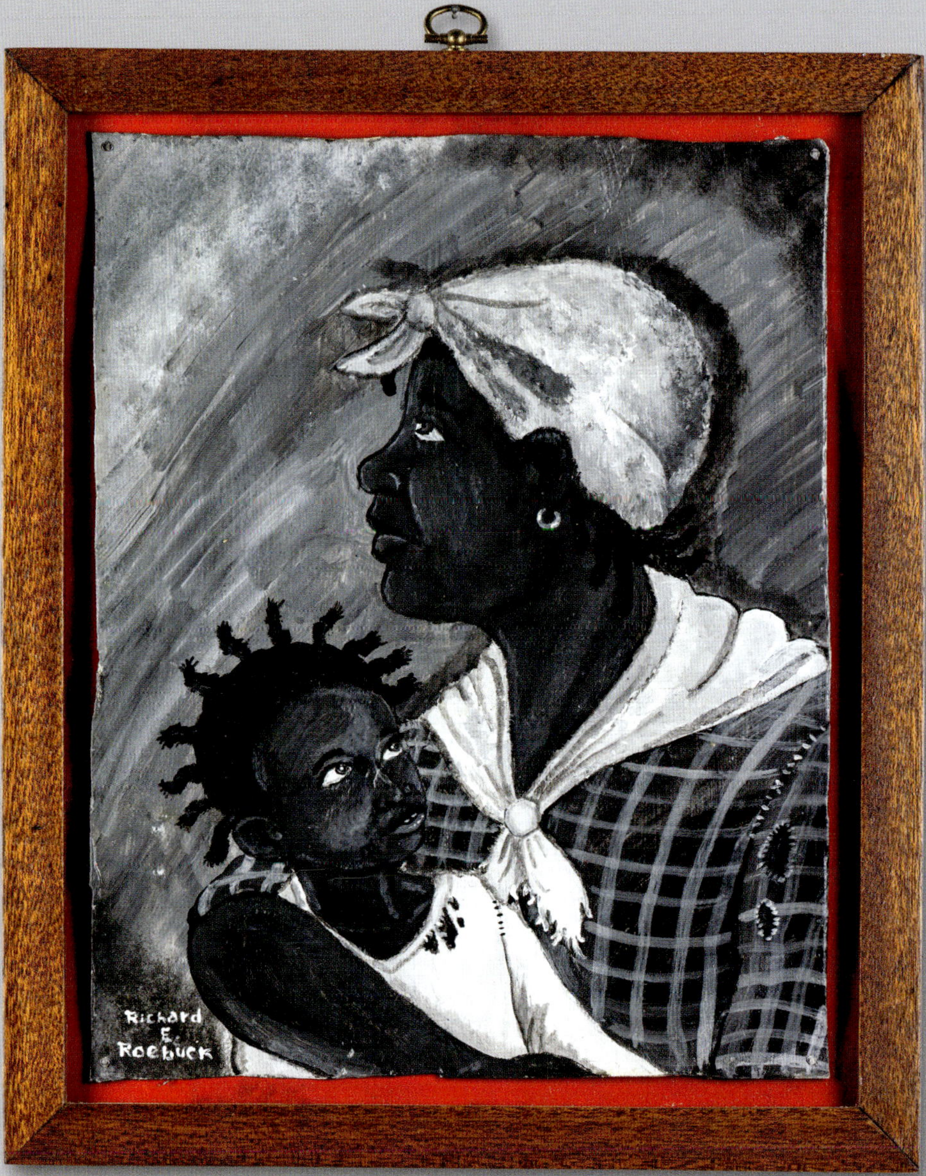
Richard
E.
Roebuck

SHORTY AND ANNIE'S BEDROOM

A Shared Crop of Values

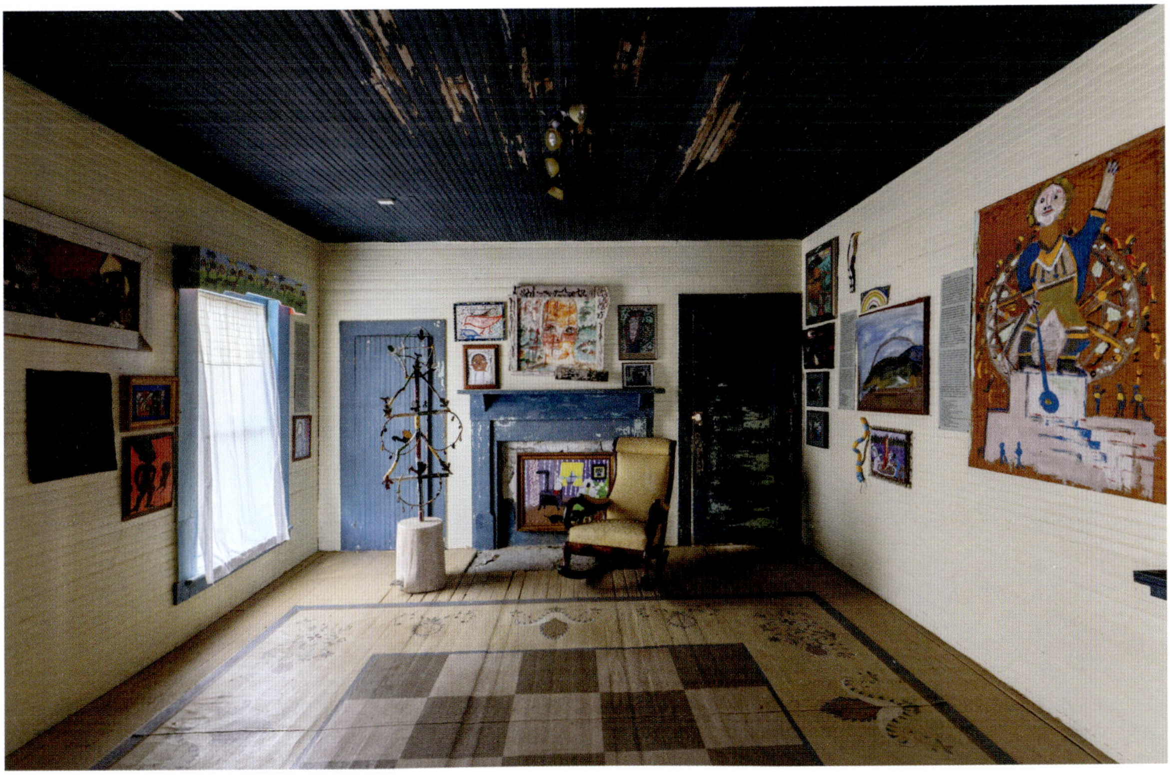

Plate 44 (facing). Richard Roebuck, *Mother and Child*. Paint on metal. 11 × 8½ inches.

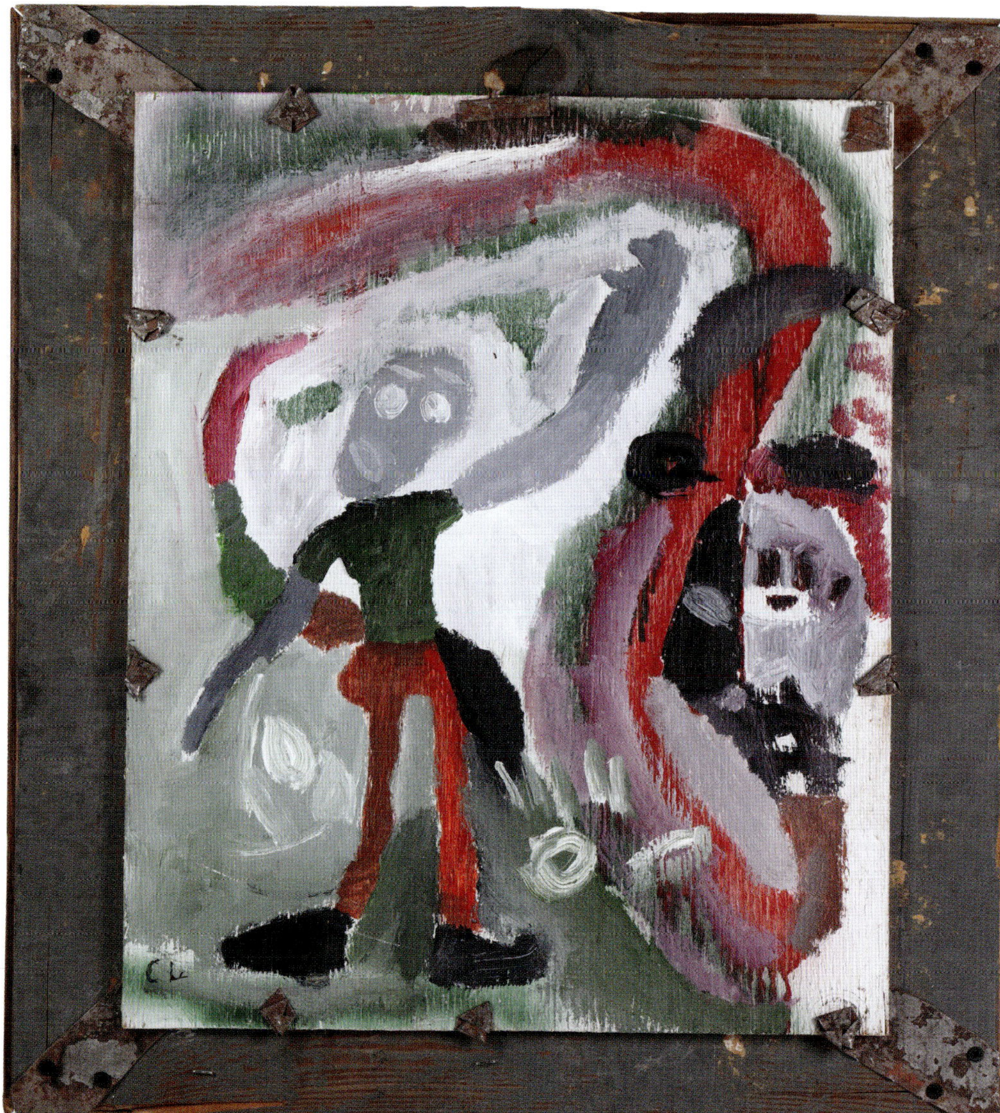

Plate 45. Charlie Lucas, *Half Brother*. Paint on wood, folded metal. 19 × 16 inches.

Family Values

Shorty and Annie were newly married, very practical love birds when they moved into the house that is now the Shorty Lawson Museum of the Black Tenant Farmer. Very practical, very young, and determined to make a good family. Annie was from here, the Bradsher family, the most respected of families, Black or White. Annie's family was related to Wiley Bradsher, the founding preacher of the Church of the City of God in the Wilderness, and the moral authority in the Black community for miles in every direction.

Annie and her family were active members of Preach Bradsher's church and, although poor, were blessed by his teaching and by his name. The Bradshers were held in high regard throughout the community.

Shorty was from a complicated family over near Leasburg. His daddy died young, his mother remarrying in the Dixon family. "I knew all those generations of Lawsons and the half-brother, Larry Dixon. His daddy and mine worked together. All hard workers, Shorty more so." (Donald Hester) Most people around here said the same thing about Shorty that Donald did. "My father knew his reputation and wanted Shorty to work for him. They were a good match. They shared fundamental values." (Randy Hester)

Larry Dixon's childhood memory is important to understanding the family values in the Lawson home. Shorty and Annie were already married when Shorty and Larry's mother took ill. She knew she was facing death. She called Shorty and Larry to the hospital in Danville with explicit final instructions. "When our mama was dying, she worried about me being so little, prayed on it, told us she had nothing to leave me, but she didn't want me stay with my sister. Mama worried that the Dixons wouldn't love and take care of me or raise me up right. She wanted me to live with Shorty and Annie. She thought they would be the only ones would treat me good." (Larry Dixon)

And, indeed they treated him good. They took him in and made him part of the family. Larry grew up like one of Shorty and Annie's children, nurtured by their love and their values. (Plate 45) After he was grown and married, Larry and his wife, Stella, raised their own family in the same little house with the same, deep commitment to family.

Annie

Annie was the nurturer. Everybody tells how hard Shorty worked. Only her children knew her capacity to work crops hour for hour with him and still have the will to do kitchen work and put them to bed. Women "give love and care, and they also give strength and power. But you got to listen. I always paid attention to what the women was saying, even when I was a little fellow." (Thornton Dial)

She was like a mama bird, teaching her babies little things and to obey. (Plate 46) "Reading wasn't easy for her, but she read them a little from the Bible at bedtime, waited for them to say prayers." (Stella Dixon)

In their bedroom Annie birthed her children. (Plate 47) "She worked slap up to the baby coming, almost had Sylvester in the field. I guess she just wanted to be there in the field with Daddy. Whoever was the baby slept in the cradle next to their bed so Mama could nurse him. I remember little Cisco sleeping in that cradle. He is dead now." (Carolyn Lawson)

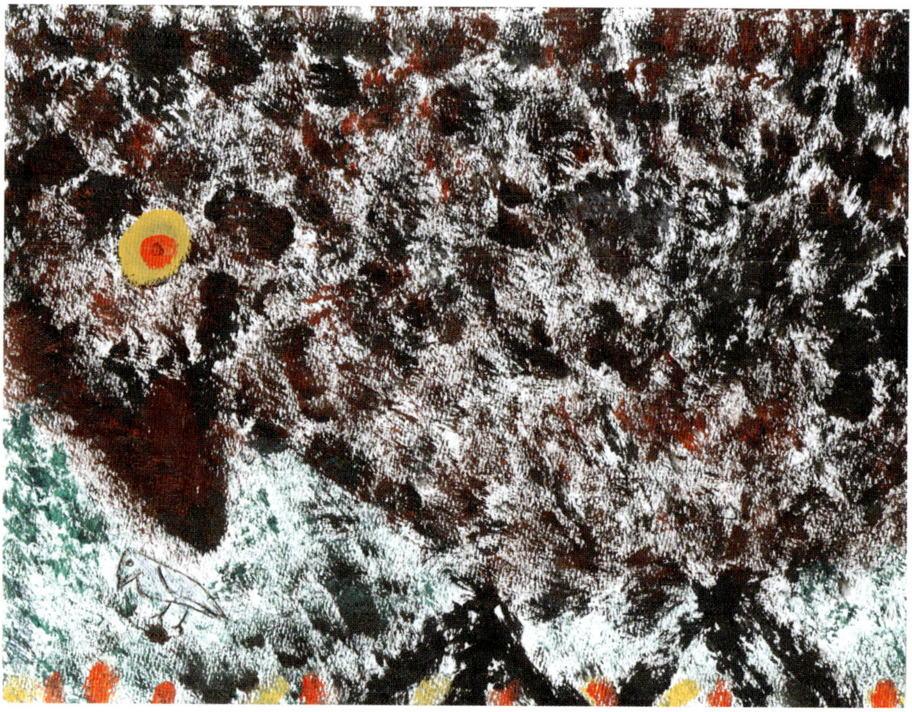

Plate 46. Mama Johnson, *Mama and Baby Teaching Her Little Things and to Obey*. Paint on paper, possibly ink pen. 10¼ × 13 inches.

Annie wanted a good life for her children, and paid special attention to her daughters. "We might as well expect to grow trees from leaves as hope to build up a civilization or a manhood without taking into consideration our women and the home life made by them, which must be the root and ground of the whole matter. Let our girls feel that we expect more of them than they merely look pretty and appear well in society." (Anna Julia Cooper)

Lacking much schooling themselves, Annie and Shorty were strict about the children working hard and going to school to make something of themselves. And the children paid attention to the lessons, got good jobs, bought single wides or stick-built homes and made good lives for themselves and their children and grandchildren. "Millions of white Americans, for the first time, had a clear, long look at Negroes engaged in a serious occupation . . . The stereotype of the Negro suffered a heavy blow." (Martin Luther King Jr.)

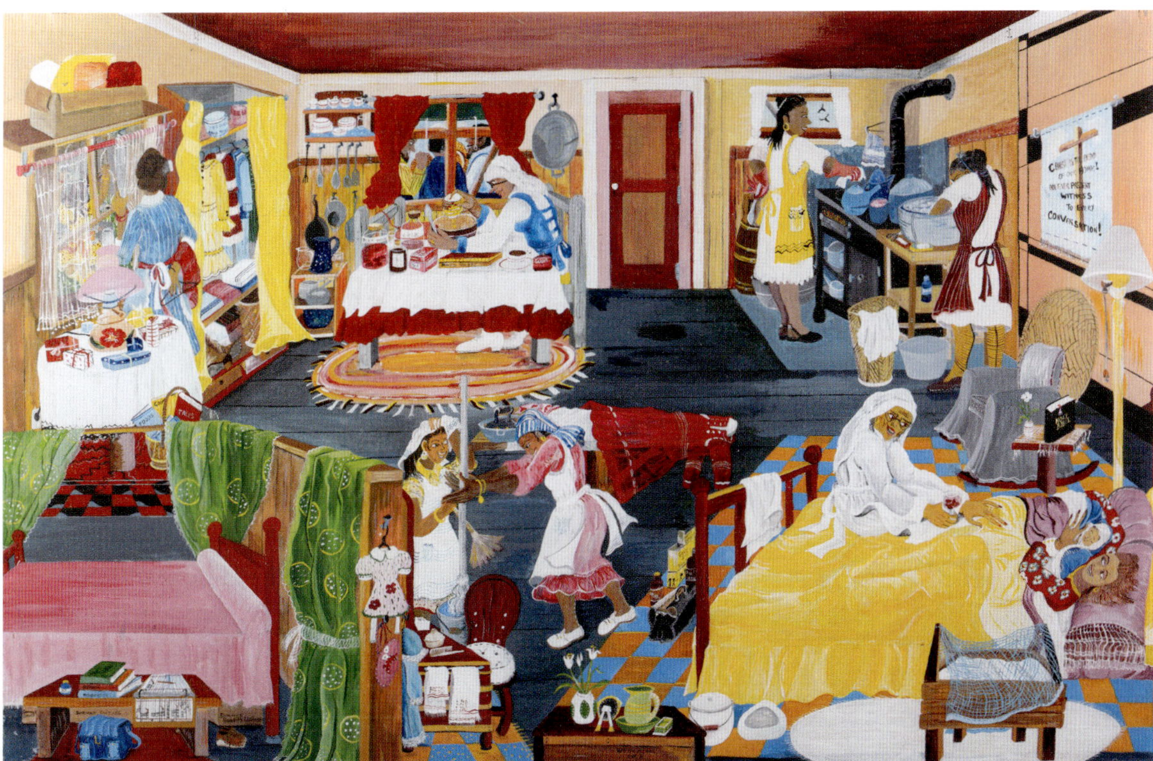

Plate 47. Ruth Mae McCrane, *Birth in a One-Room Shack*. Paint on plywood. 32 × 48 inches.

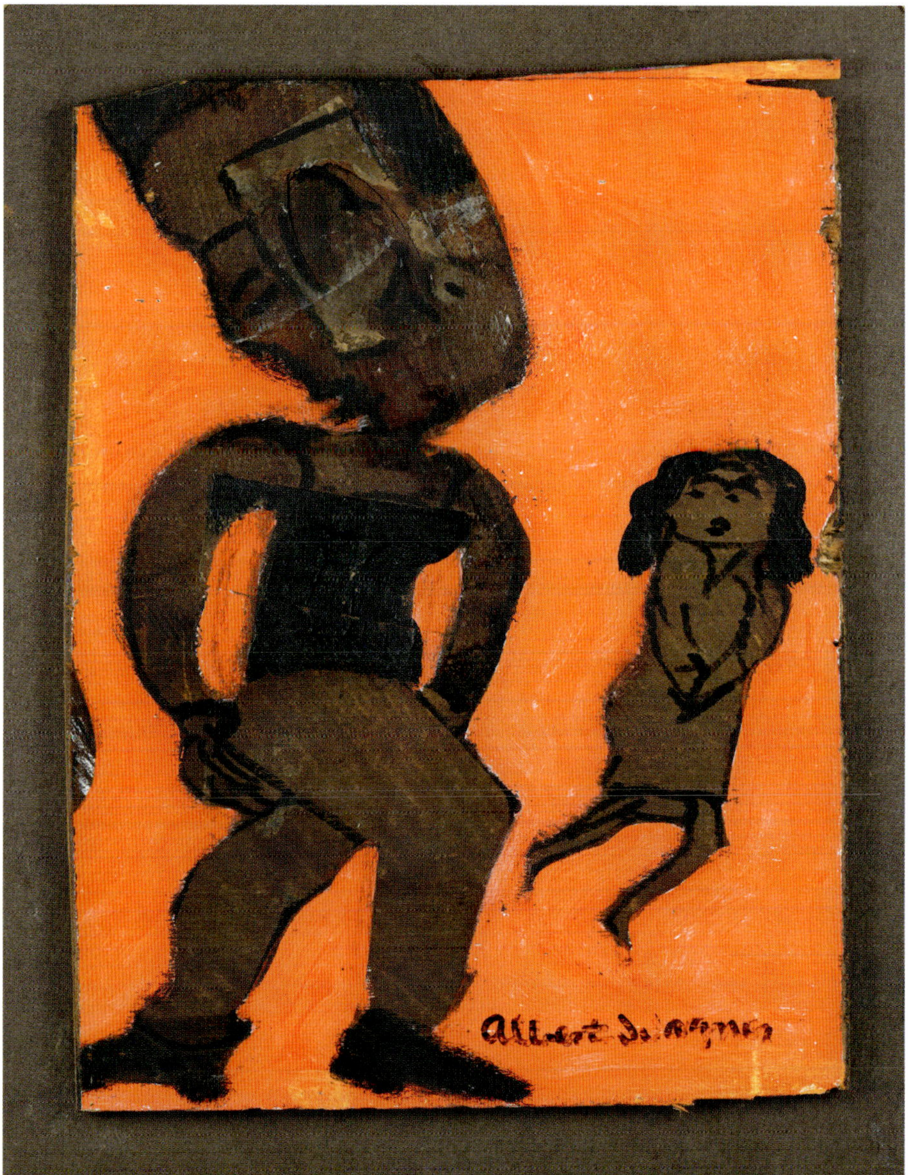

Plate 48. Albert Wagner, *Untitled*. Paint and marker on board. 13½ × 10 inches.

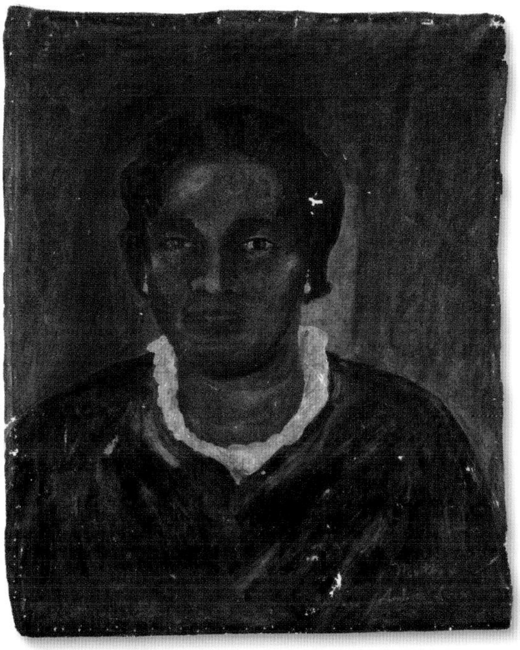

Plate 49. Arbon Lane, *Mother*. Paint on canvas. $17\frac{1}{2} \times 13\frac{3}{4}$ inches.

Annie was gentle, but she disciplined the children if necessary. She might call them out, but Shorty doled out the harshest punishment. "I remember one time the boys went skating on the pond one real cold spell. That was against Daddy's rules. It wasn't completely frozen over, and the boys fell in, came home soaking wet. It was hard to hide what had happened. All of them got a serious whipping." (Carolyn Lawson)

Rural Black womanhood of Annie's generation was complex; women were often equal partners in making a living in tobacco, honored by some, molested by others, a sexual object when a powerful man forced himself on her. Albert Wagner described that outcome thusly, "Mamma's baby, Pappa's maybe." (Plate 48)

> My little woman, she had a baby this morning Haa!
> My Little woman, she had a baby this morning Haa!
> He had blue eyes, Lawd, Lawd, he had blue eyes
>
> (Zora Neale Hurston)

In contrast Black women were respected within their families. Arbon Lane painted his mother with reverent darkness, likely admiration for her stoicism facing hardship. (Plate 49)

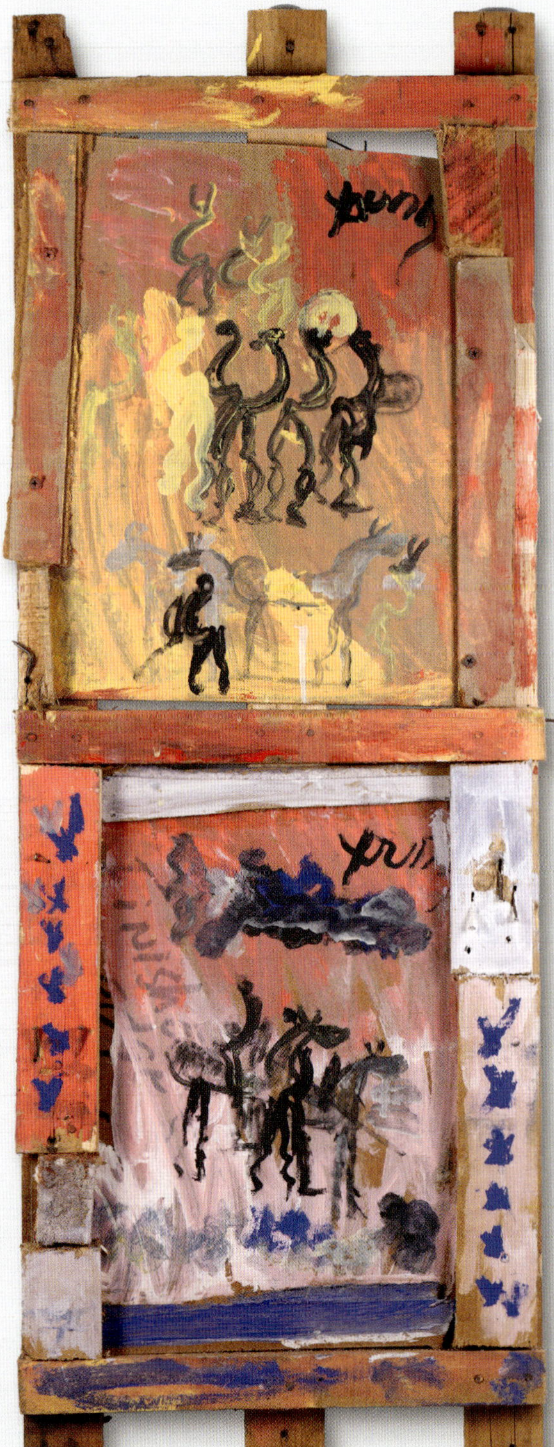

Plate 50. Purvis Young, *Leaders and Warriors*. Paint on wood crates, Masonite and pieces of wood, nails. 42½ × 16 inches. Shorty Lawson Museum Collection.

Shorty

Shorty was a leader, first to start a job and last to quit, strong, powerful. Purvis Young must have had him in mind. (Plate 50) Shorty expected his boys to pitch in from an early age, without foolishness. And they all did what Shorty instructed, usually without foolishness but with plenty of playfulness when Shorty wasn't within earshot. They learned to do things by helping and careful attention to how their daddy went about each task. They knew practical things like harnessing the mules, clearing land, plowing, planting, hoeing, tending the garden, laying by, harvesting and curing tobacco, getting up hay, repairing fences, dressing a hog, castrating a bull calf, making firewood, and collecting rainwater. They also knew how to fish and swim. They certainly knew that farm work was never done. (Plate 51) Shorty told them not to let their shadows catch up with them, but they weren't sure what that meant.

Shorty schooled the children by actions spoken louder than words. "He taught Larry how to be a good man." (Stella Dixon) The children were nurtured by their parents and the idyllic natural world of rural childhood; domesticated and wild animals filled each playful spirit.

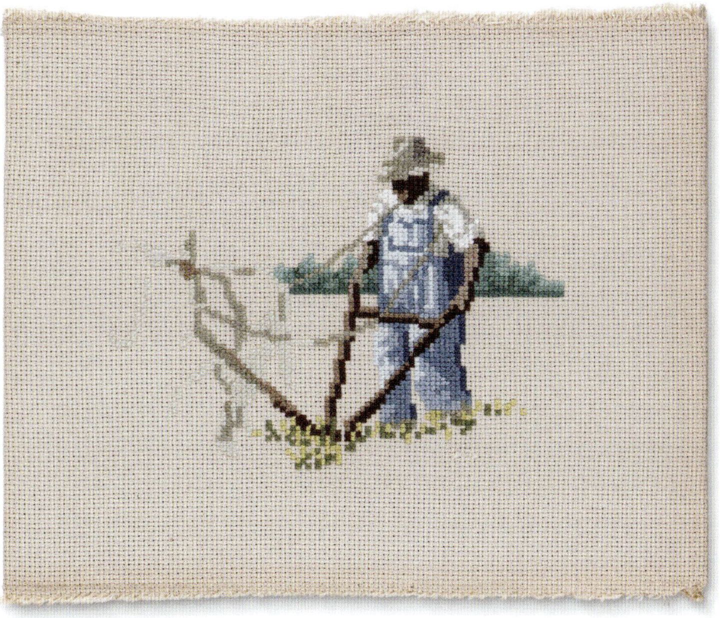

Plate 51. Unknown, *Untitled*. Counted cross-stitch of man plowing with unfinished mule outlined. 10½ × 12½ inches. Shorty Lawson Museum Collection, gift of Nate Hester.

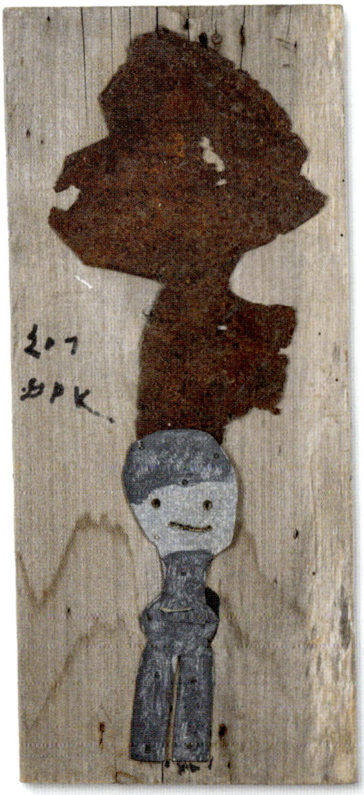

Plate 52. George Paul Kornegay, *Figure with Shadow.* Cut-out tin on wood. 18½ × 8 inches.

Not knowing the rising racial strife in the big cities, the children were delighted, challenged, and taught by the woods and creeks. They were relatively isolated from society's prejudices in the daily life of early childhood. "I don't remember any." (Brenda Lawson) This was due in part to their parents' high standing in the community, partly because the White landowner lived in town and entrusted the place to Shorty, and partly because the Lawsons seldom left the Hesters Store area. Shorty had taught them the racial delineations that existed sans posted signs at Hesters Store.

The children had to grow up fast. When they went to town, they were confronted with "Whites Only" signs and restaurants that didn't serve them. Civil Rights tilted rural. Their daddy died when the children were young. Annie said to the little ones, "This is the last piggyback ride because you are big kids now." That's when they knew one meaning of outpacing their shadows. They hadn't considered their daddy a wise prophet until then. (Plate 52)

The Lawson family had much to weep about. But they knew that if one was crying about troubles, someone in their family or the Hesters would be there to help. Paternalism cut two ways. "The Hesters took care of us, and my brother Kenny took care of Mr. Randolph, too, take him home when he was drunk. Miss Virginia say, 'There he goes again.'" (Carolyn Lawson) "The nebulous 'white man's world' wasn't as free as it looked . . . many white individuals' problems surpassed my own, often by a lot." (James McBride) Humanity stretched thin. Whiteness sometimes covered despair.

Plenty folks imagined a world of racial harmony; artists painted Black and White children playing together, almost like family, emphasis on the "almost." "Almost" was the operative word.

"There is certainly more outspoken racial prejudice in the South than elsewhere, but it is also the place of the strongest inter-racial attachment. The situation is so contradictory, paradoxical and what not, that only a Southerner could ever understand it. The North has no interest in the particular Negro, but talks of justice for the whole. The South has no interest, and pretends none, in the mass of Negroes but is very much concerned about the individual." (Zora Neale Hurston)

Renowned artist Charlie Lucas made a most realistic Lawson family portrait, a gift for the museum, from reused materials. He sculpted the family from metal, adding tiles salvaged from a fine antebellum home in Selma. He depicts individuals within the family, each tough as steel. (Plate 53)

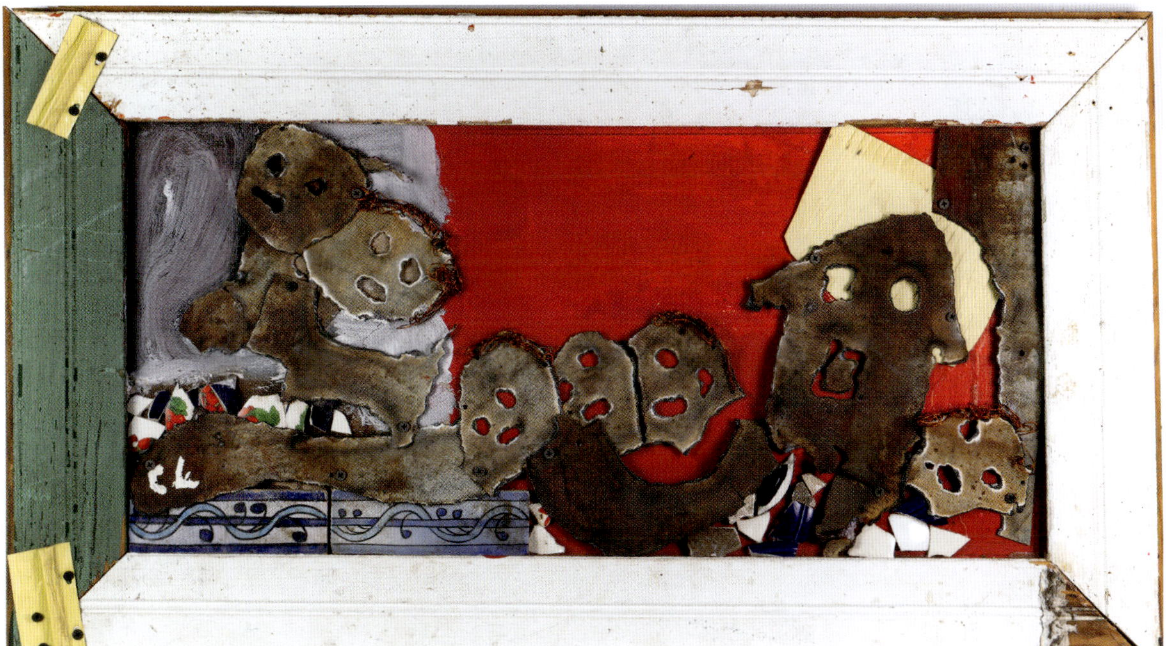

Plate 53. Charlie Lucas, *Lawson Family Portrait.* Painted wood, metal faces, wire, broken pottery, tiles, wood-textured metal siding. 20 × 34½ × 1½ inches. Shorty Lawson Museum Collection, gift of Charlie Lucas.

Nature's Lessons

The children learned matters of life and death from the natural world around them. Watch out for snakes. Water moccasins in wet spots, copperheads camouflaged in the woods. Protect black snakes. Swat horse flies. Amidst these dangers they also learned where and when to find the best wild grapes, blackberries, and honey trees, and where different birds made their nests. They learned the best spots to catch fish, hunt squirrels and rabbits. "Parents don't teach kids that stuff nowadays, just keep them inside, don't let them play in the woods. That's a shame." (Carolyn Lawson) The children made rabbit gums, built basketball goals and most anything they wanted for recreation. An old tire was about as good a playground as any, living in hilly country. Sort of dangerous. Good for big belly laughs when your brother crashed.

There were lessons in the weather. If it came up a purple cloud, a bad thunderstorm was coming. (Plate 54) Everyone better get in a safe place. Jasper and Irene saw a man killed by lightning over at Turbeville; lightning rightly scared the Lawsons. Just a shower, someone had to run to the

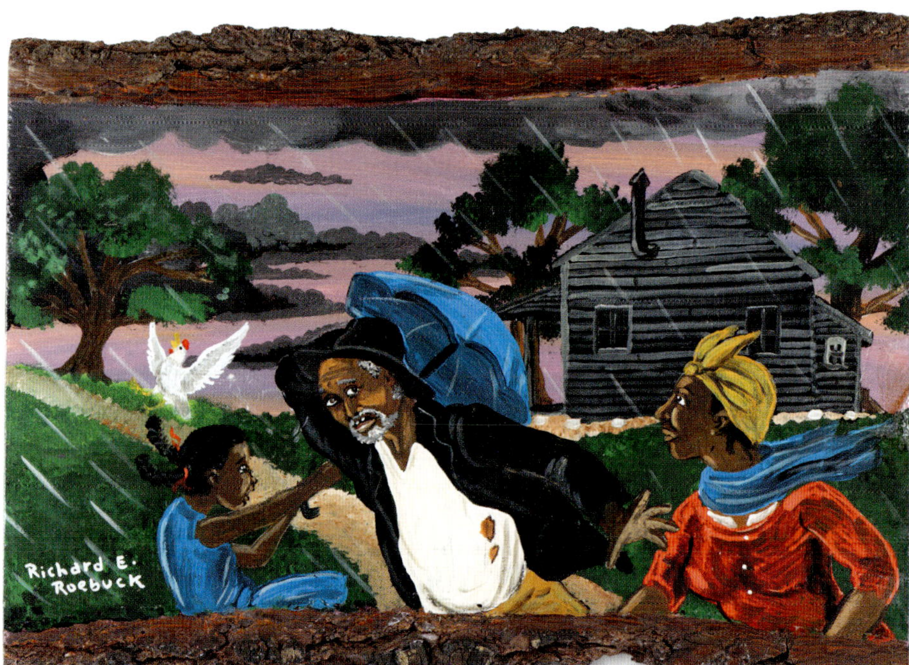

Plate 54. Richard Roebuck, *Storm Coming! Get in the House*. Paint on live edge wood. $13\frac{1}{2} \times 18\frac{1}{2} \times \frac{3}{4}$ inch.

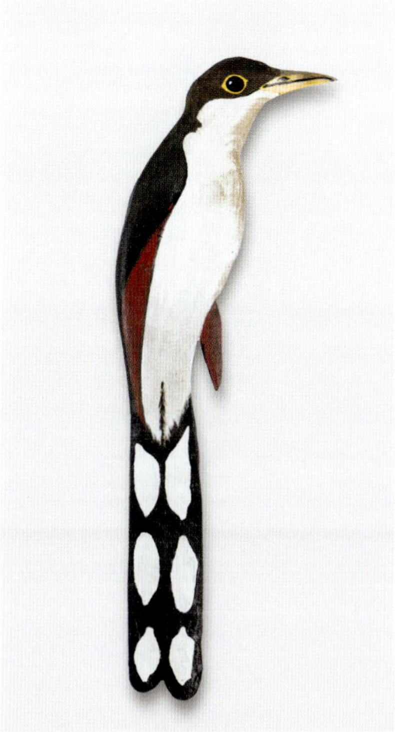

Plate 55. Randy Hester, *Rain Crow*. Sculpted and painted wood. 17½ × 5 × 1 inch.

house to get the clothes in. Worst for most folks was getting caught in a Sunday downpour and ruining their best clothes after preaching.

Good weather the Lawsons worked, but kept an ear out for the rain crow. "Daddy told us if we heard a rain crow, it was going to rain, and it almost always did." (Carolyn Lawson) (Plate 55)

> Oh don't you hear them
> A coo coo bird a keep a hollerin Haa!
> Oh don't you hear them
> A coo coo bird a keep a hollerin Haa!
> It looks like rain, Lawd, Lawd, it looks like rain.
>
> (Zora Neale Hurston)

By knowing clouds, the children could tell when it was safe to play in the rain and wait for a happy rainbow. They believed there was gold at the end of the rainbow, chased after many a one, never found gold, but learned a lot from the adventures. Maybe the gold was just for White people what owned the land. Shorty taught them to deal with those folks too.

If the weather turned hot and dry for several weeks, crops suffered something terrible. Vegetable gardens burned up. Livelihood and food

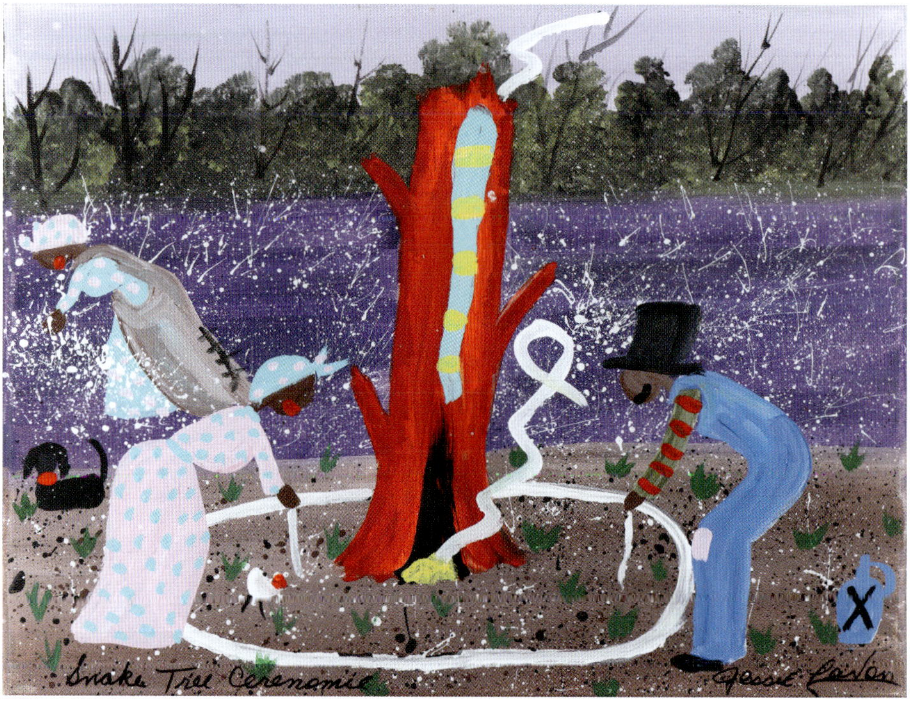

Plate 56. Jessie Lavon, *Snake Tree Ceremonie*. Paint on canvas. 11 × 14 inches.

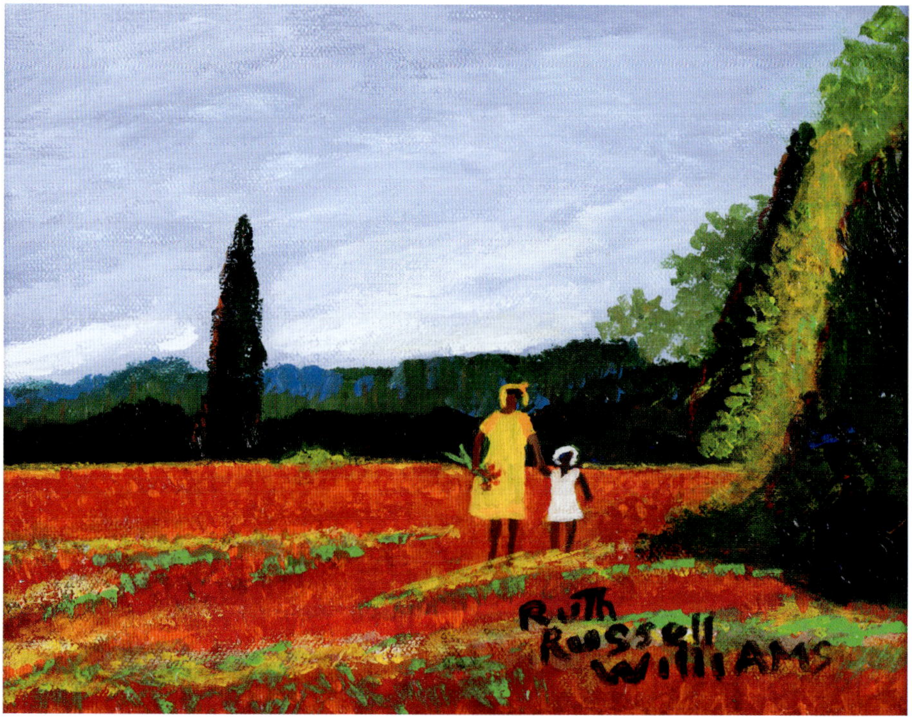

Plate 57. Ruth Russell Williams, *Untitled*. Paint on canvas. 8 × 10 inches.

supply were threatened. "We need an inch of rain a week." (Donald Hester) If the drought continued, the community got desperate; it was time to kill a snake and hang it in a tree. Around here you had to kill a bad snake, not a good one. Shorty was adamant about protecting rat snakes. Some folks did a real elaborate ritual, snake in a hollow tree with a fire in it, a circle of salt marking the sacred ground. (Plate 56)

If you begged forgiveness for sins, repented, performed the correct ritual, and prayed hard to God, that usually was enough to bring rain. When He did make rain, even if the rain didn't come for weeks, you had to remember to thank God for saving the tobacco. You could hear tobacco, corn, and tomatoes shouting after the rain. A thunder shower cooled things off; it was a good time to check the crops and enjoy summer wildflowers. (Plate 57) A few days after a rain was a good time to fish, not right after, let the mud settle out, but the water still high. The children would head for the pond or Crooked Creek to catch knotty heads, having a big time. (Plate 58)

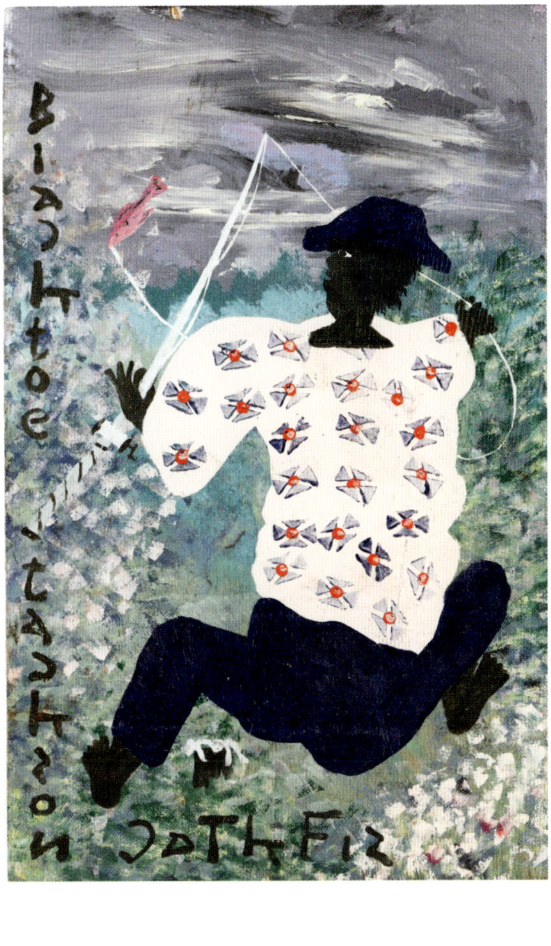

Plate 58. Black Joe Jackson, *Cath Fiz*. Paint on wood board. 20 × 12¼ inches.

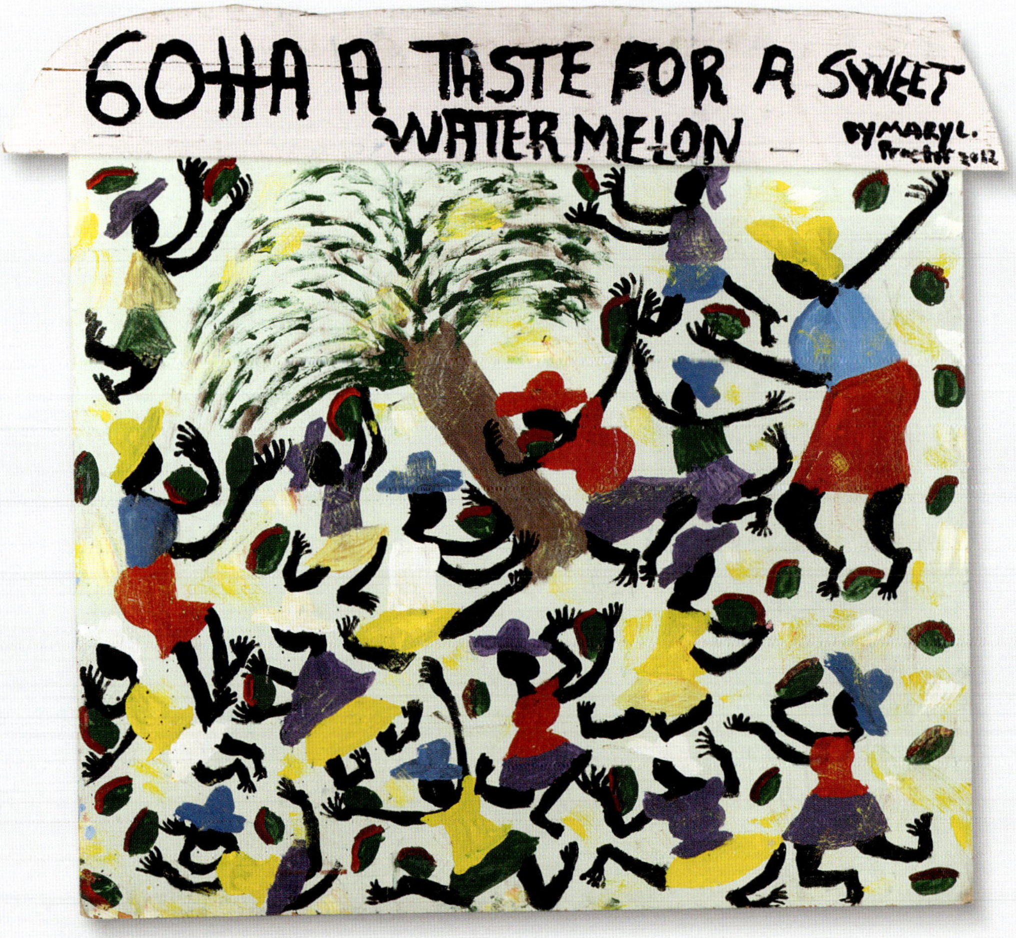

Plate 59. Mary Proctor, *Gotta a Taste for a Sweet Watermelon*. Paint on wood panel and reused plywood. 24½ × 24 inches.

A Lot of Fun

The Lawson children's pleasures sound too good to be true. Most were free. Skipping stones on still water, playing marbles, hopscotch, foot races, jump rope counting, who could pick the most watermelons, or watermelon seed spittin' contests. (Plate 59) Actually, any contest of speed, the most, or strength, even lifting a sack of fertilizer or a heavy foundation rock, was a satisfactory game. Throw small rocks up in the air at dusk to see bats chase them. Chimney swifts didn't chase rocks. On summer evenings the children caught lightning bugs, kept them overnight in jars, evoking twinkling dreams of magical creatures.

There were wild things everywhere on the farm to chase, catch, or befriend and learn about. And there were imagined monsters that hid in the moonless darkness or thick bushes or morning fog or your brother's pocket. (Plate 60) City people thought the country folks, especially Black tenant farmers, were deprived, went wanting, but Shorty and Annie were certainly not wanting or down and out. The Lawsons do not remember life on the farm as disadvantaged.

Most Black people in the community were afraid of big water, didn't know how to swim, feared drowning as much as water moccasins. Water was treacherous. "That was a sentiment of almost all Black people in the area. But not the Lawsons. Shorty was a powerful swimmer, swam like a catfish. He saved several people from drowning. He loved to swim and taught all the children. But he had rules. If we went swimming, one of us had to stay on the bank and watch out for the others. Daddy would come

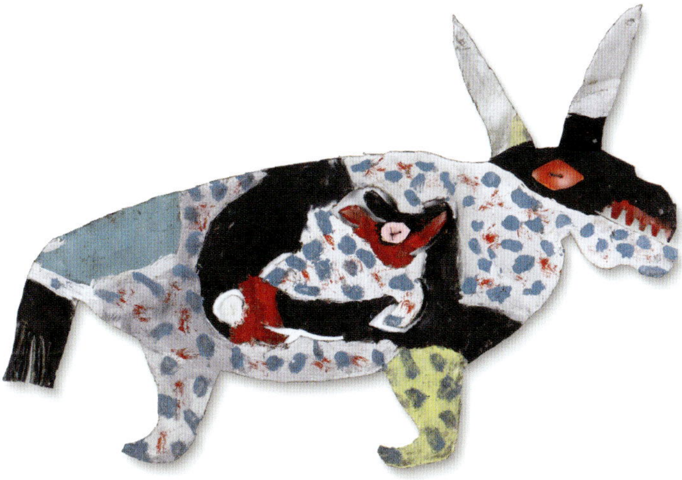

Plate 60. David Butler, *Mother with Baby Fantasy Creature*. Cut and painted metal, plastic eyes. 14 × 21 inches.

down to the pond, and hide in the bushes to be sure we were following his rules." (Carolyn Lawson)

Shorty and Randolph gigged bullfrogs, made Randy get in the water to scare the frogs up on shore. Randolph took to shooting them with a twenty-two, he and Shorty laughing all the while because Randy was afraid of getting shot or bit by a snake. The adventure always seemed better if someone was scared by it.

Bulls made the scariest adventures. Once Carolyn and Diane were playing down in the pasture. They teased the bull. He started chasing them. They ran toward the house fast. Carolyn was faster, climbed the gate, and escaped. Diane fell down, and the bull ran over her. She blamed her sister for stirring him up. But they still went fishing together later that day.

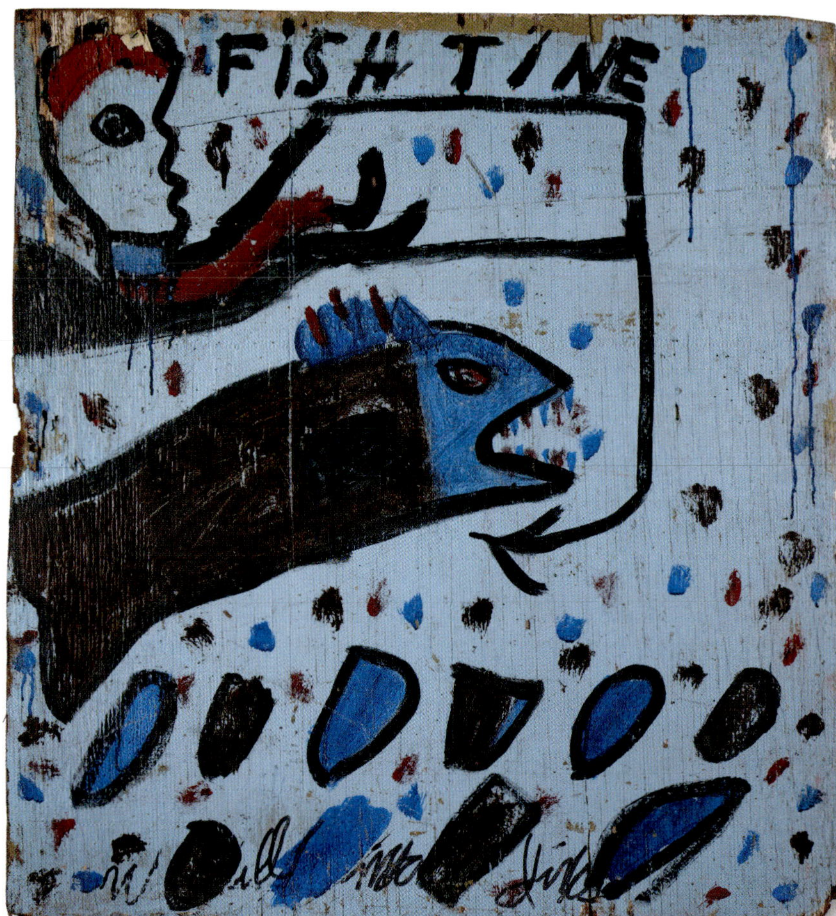

Plate 61. Willie Jinks, *Fish Time*. House paint on plywood. 36¾ × 33¼ inches.

There was nothing like fishing. And fishing wasn't scary unless you caught a snapping turtle. "They bite, won't let go until it thunders." (Larry Dixon) Carolyn became an accomplished bank fisher, caught more fish than people with fancy equipment. The wild creatures often told her where to fish and how deep. These days Carolyn only gets off work July 4th. Fishing time! (Plate 61) She'll teach her grandson if he pays attention to what she tells him like in school. Most all the Lawsons fished as kids and still do, but Carolyn claims to be the hands-down champion.

Elongated fish stories make you laugh and get better with time. Some tell of a granddaddy catfish in the old pond over four feet long. And there is the one about a frog that rode a catfish like a bucking bronco. Even had a cowboy hat. (Plate 62)

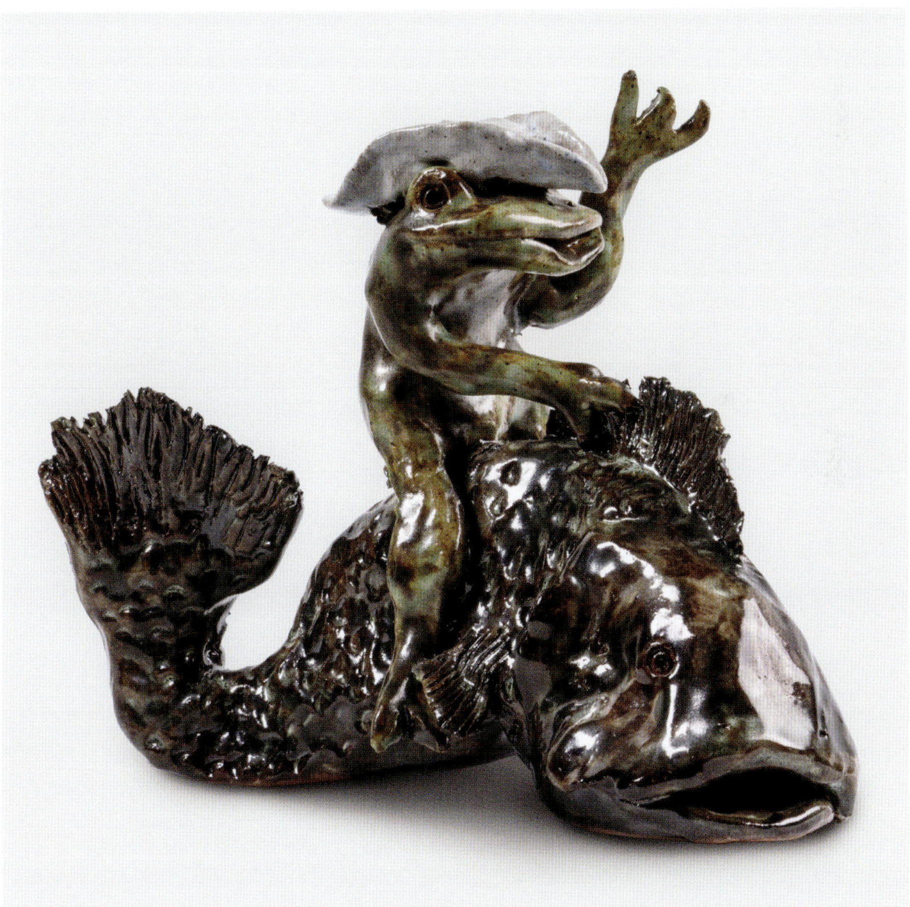

Plate 62. Jim Harver, *Cowboy Frog Riding a Catfish*. Glazed pottery. 5½ × 7¼ × 3¾ inches.

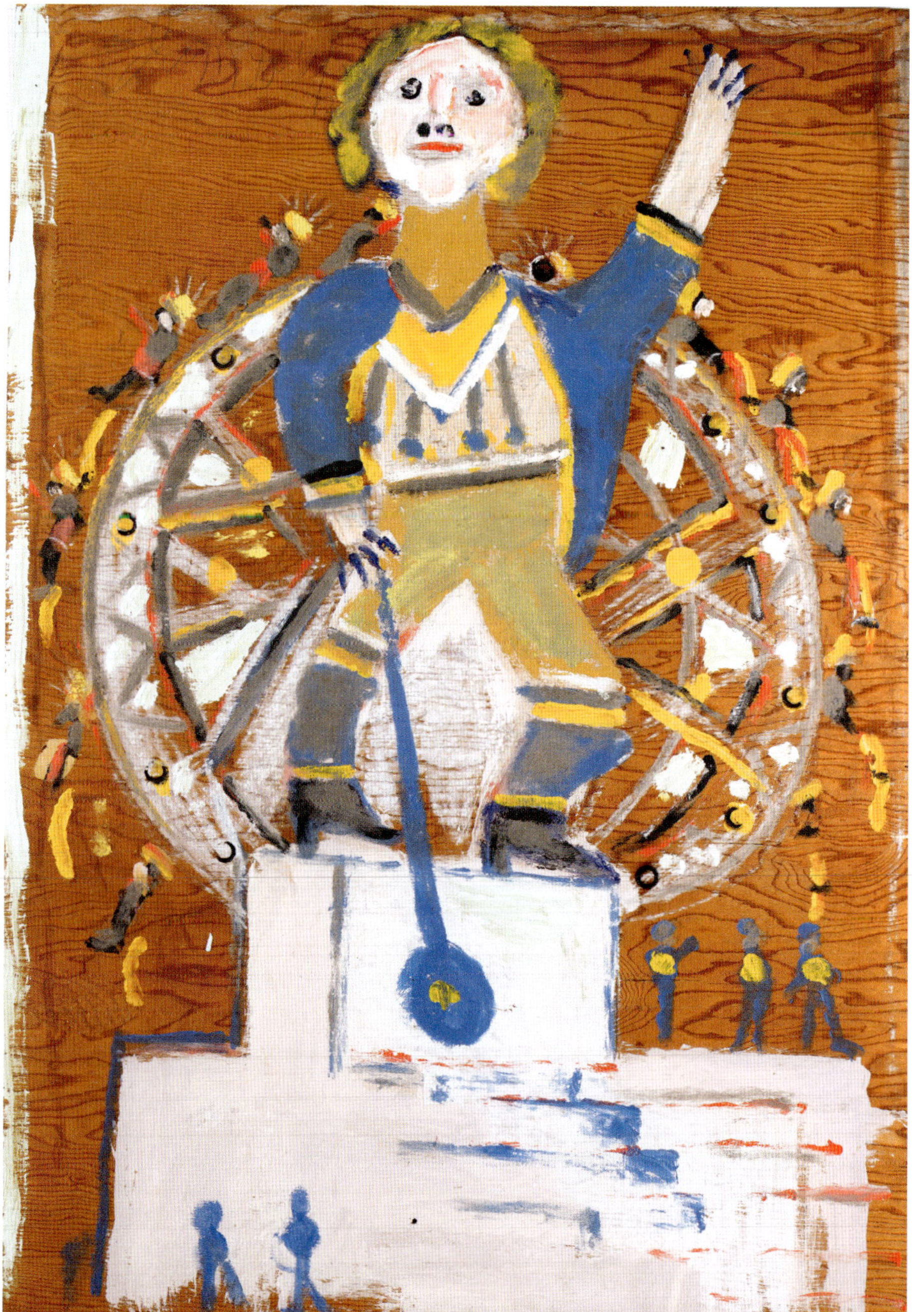

Plate 63. Jim Sudduth, *Carnival Barker*. Paint on plywood, exposed plywood. 48 × 30 inches.

Most pleasures were God-given or homegrown, but as an adult Shorty did have a few adventures with his brothers. Likely the farthest they ever went away from Hesters Store was to the state fair in Raleigh. And Shorty only went that far once or twice in his life. Carolyn knows he went because she has a photograph of him taken there. The fair was in the fall. Tobacco was all sold so Shorty had extra cash. He won all the tests of strength, but lost his money to a carnival barker. (Plate 63) It was a big-time adventure, but he didn't feel a need to stray from his known world where there was little to fear and no one would take advantage of him.

Bulls terrified some folks. Even Shorty was careful around bulls. Nobody but Brenda could charm them. "Randolph bought some bulls, one name Jed, forget the other, couldn't get them out the trailer. He called for help. I whispered 'y'all come on out.' They came on out, no trouble, went on down in the pasture." (Brenda Lawson) Somebody said it was because she was bull-headed. (Plate 64) Others agreed she was a bull charmer, but most denied her story about Jed and the other bull altogether.

Brenda was married to Shorty's brother Sam, and they lived in the Big House cross the road, and continued working on the Bowes Farm after Randolph stopped growing tobacco. They turned tobacco fields into fenced pastures. Randolph paid her $114.00 for helping with the bulls. That was in 1992. The Lawsons' profit from cattle in 1992 was $4,420.00. In 1993 they made $920.00 haying and $4,680.00 from cattle. It paid to be fearless around the bulls.

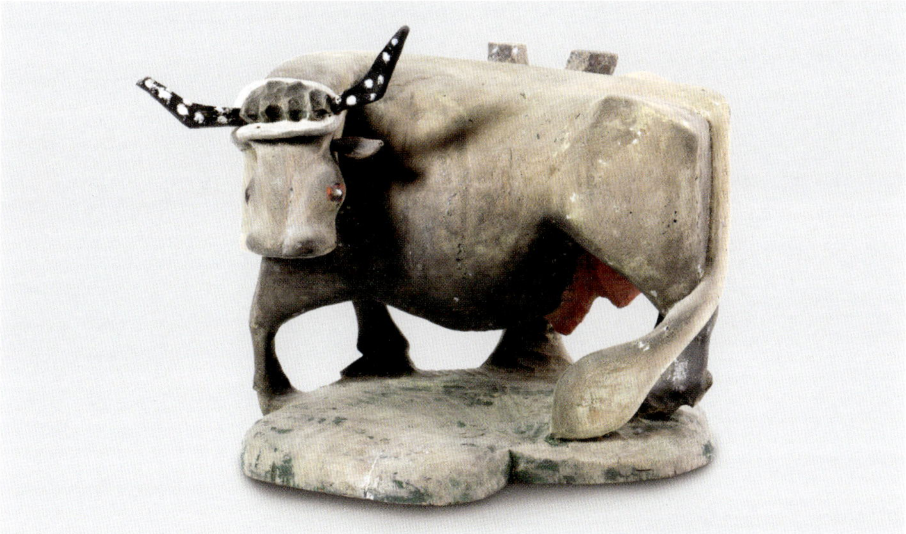

Plate 64. Unknown, *Untitled*. Carved and partially painted bull. 9½ × 12 × 10 inches.

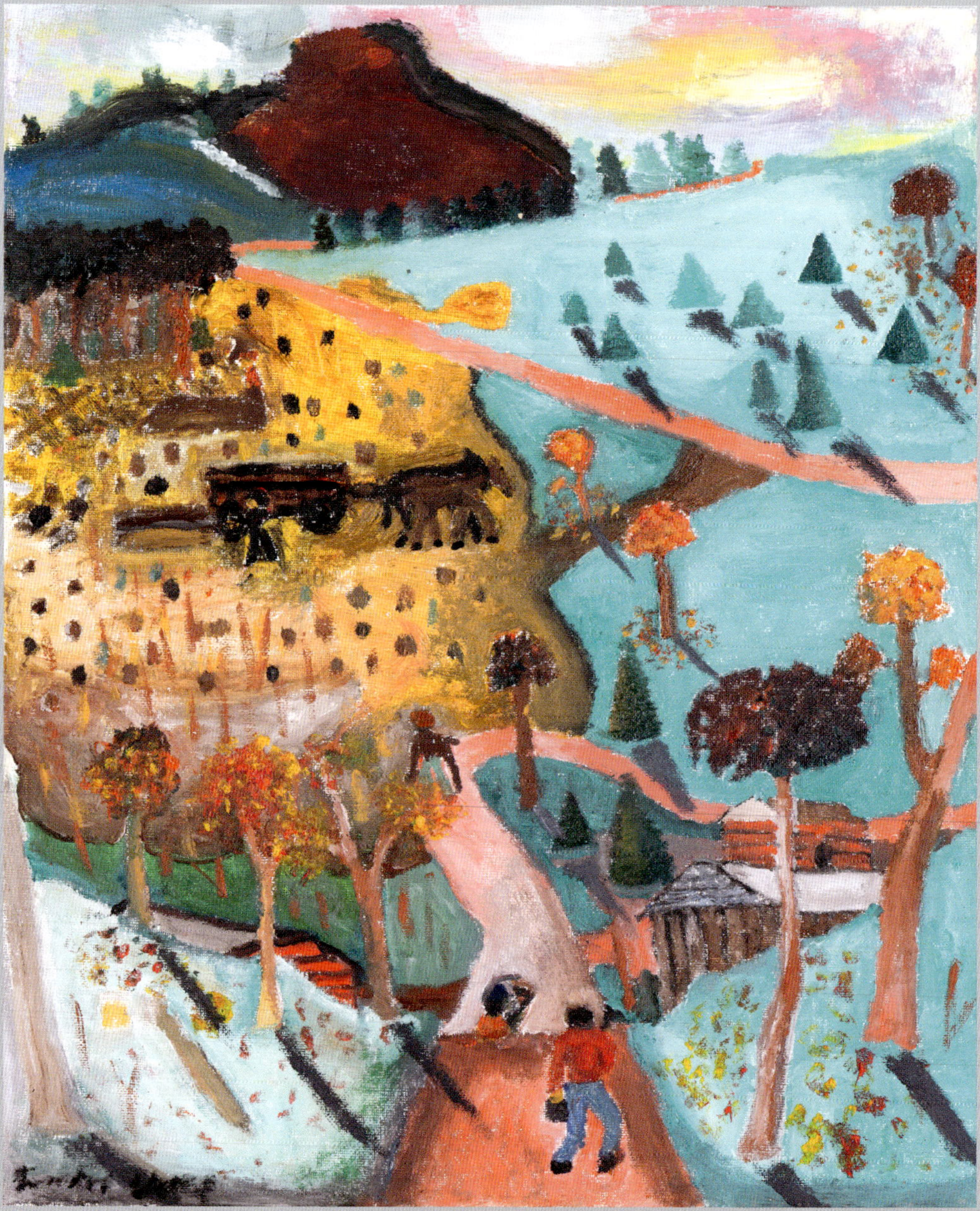

BIG ROOM

Work and Prejudice

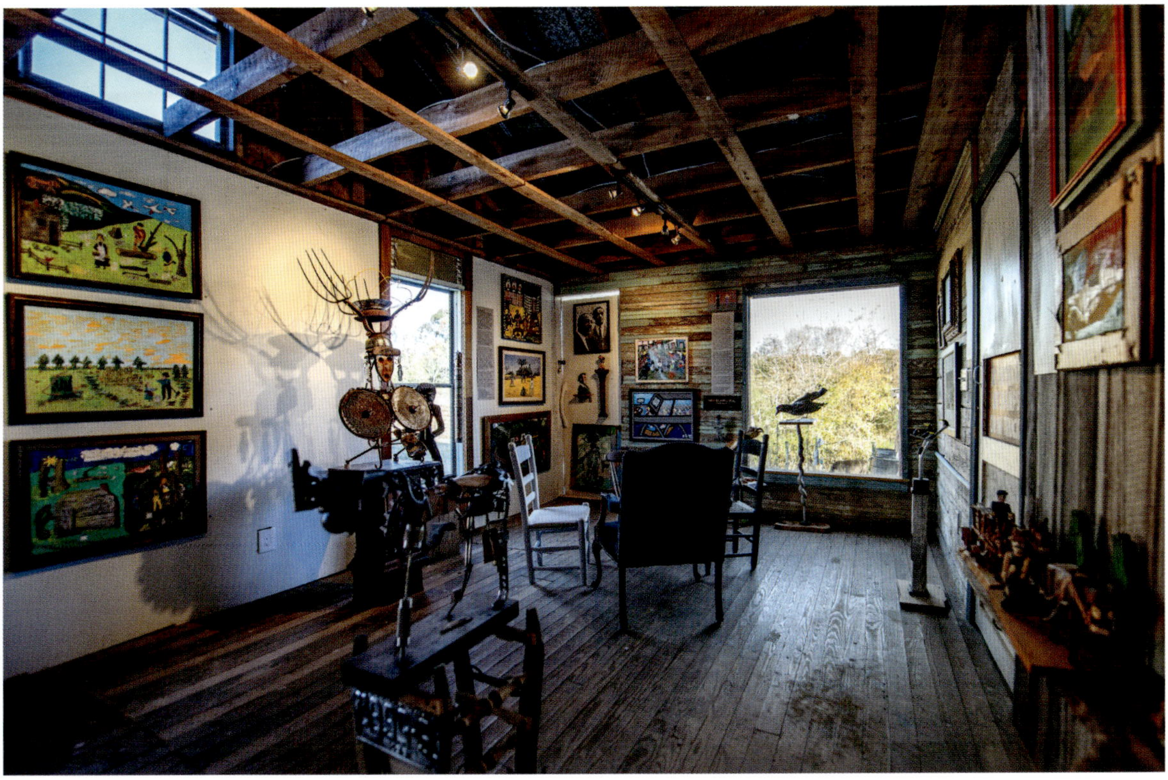

Plate 65 (facing). Frankie Lane, *Untitled*. Paint on canvas board. 20 × 16 inches.

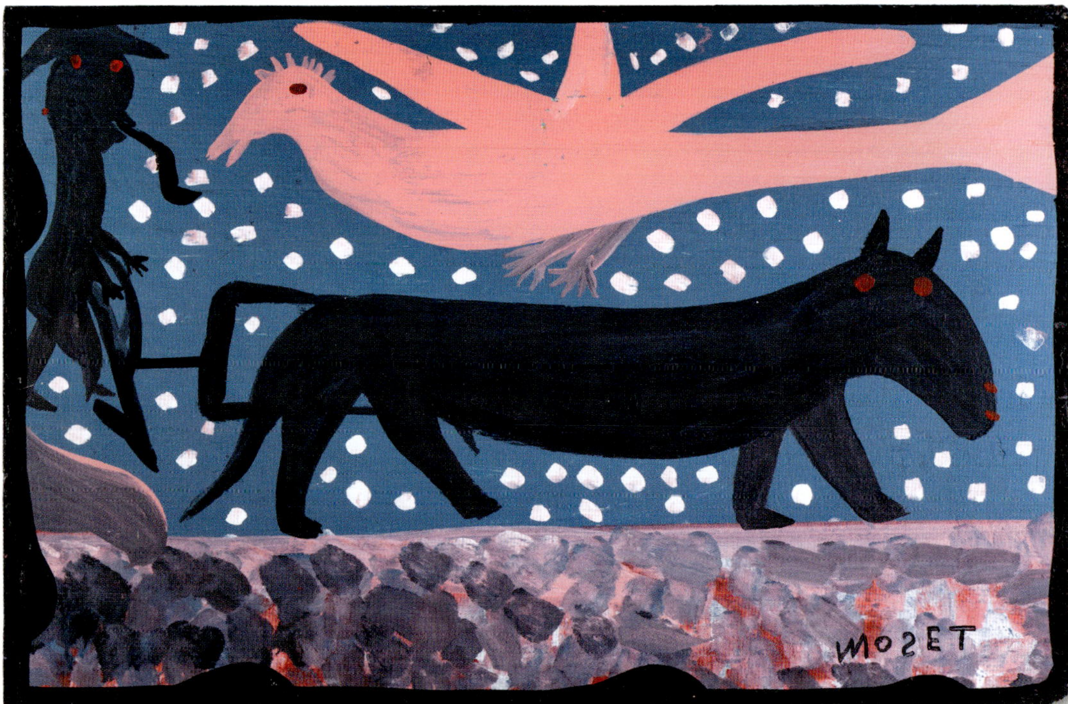

Plate 66. Mose Tolliver, *Plowing at Night.* Paint on plywood. 21¼ × 32 inches. Shorty Lawson Museum Collection. © 2024 Estate of Mose Tolliver/Artists Rights Society (ARS), New York.

Work

Ask people to describe him, they say right off, "Shorty was a hard worker, had to be." (Brenda Lawson) Do more than his part, urge others on by silent example. "Strongest man ever seen, could deadlift a 200-pound bag of fertilizer with his teeth." (Donald Hester) His feats of endurance and strength were legendary, the stuff that created local myths, except they were true.

When he broke these hilly fields under a brutal sun, he and his mule were one with the earth. There was no "quit" in him, plowing all day and until the moon came out, sometimes under the stars. Mose Tolliver could have been thinking of Shorty Lawson when he painted *Plowing at Night*. It depicts the exhaustion and determination that Shorty and his mule possessed. (Plate 66) There were plenty folks that would swear that Shorty and one mule could do the work of half a dozen men and mules. Whether it was working tobacco, haying, plowing, or hauling, Shorty was faster and better than anyone in the community, even better than anyone in all of these parts.

And he could make mules do things others couldn't; he could snake logs, never getting hung up. (Plate 67) He wasn't exactly a mule whisperer, but he knew every mule inside and out, which direction one swished his tail to chase flies or what the mule really meant when he snorted and nodded his head three times. Shorty knew the mule's pace reflected the man, so mules plowed right along the contour, faster and straighter for him than for others. He had to do little geeing and hawing to get the most out of a mule.

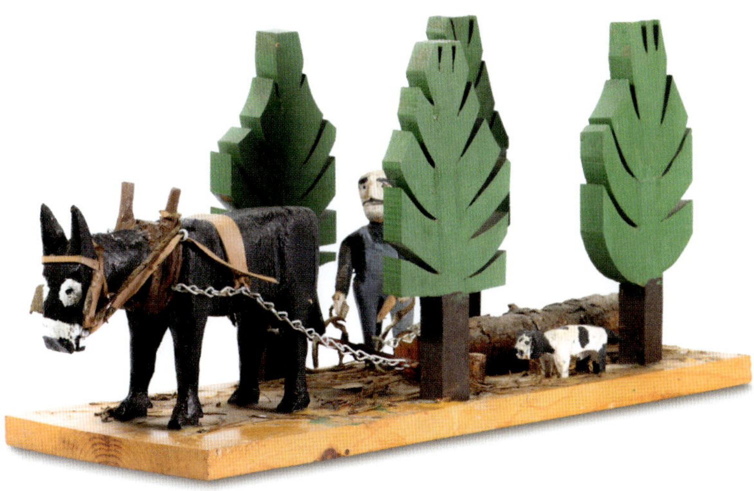

Plate 67. Bennie Grinstead, *Snaking Logs*. Carved, cut-out, and painted wood, cut tree twig, metal chain, leather, pine needles, milled wood base. 10 × 22 × 7¼ inches.

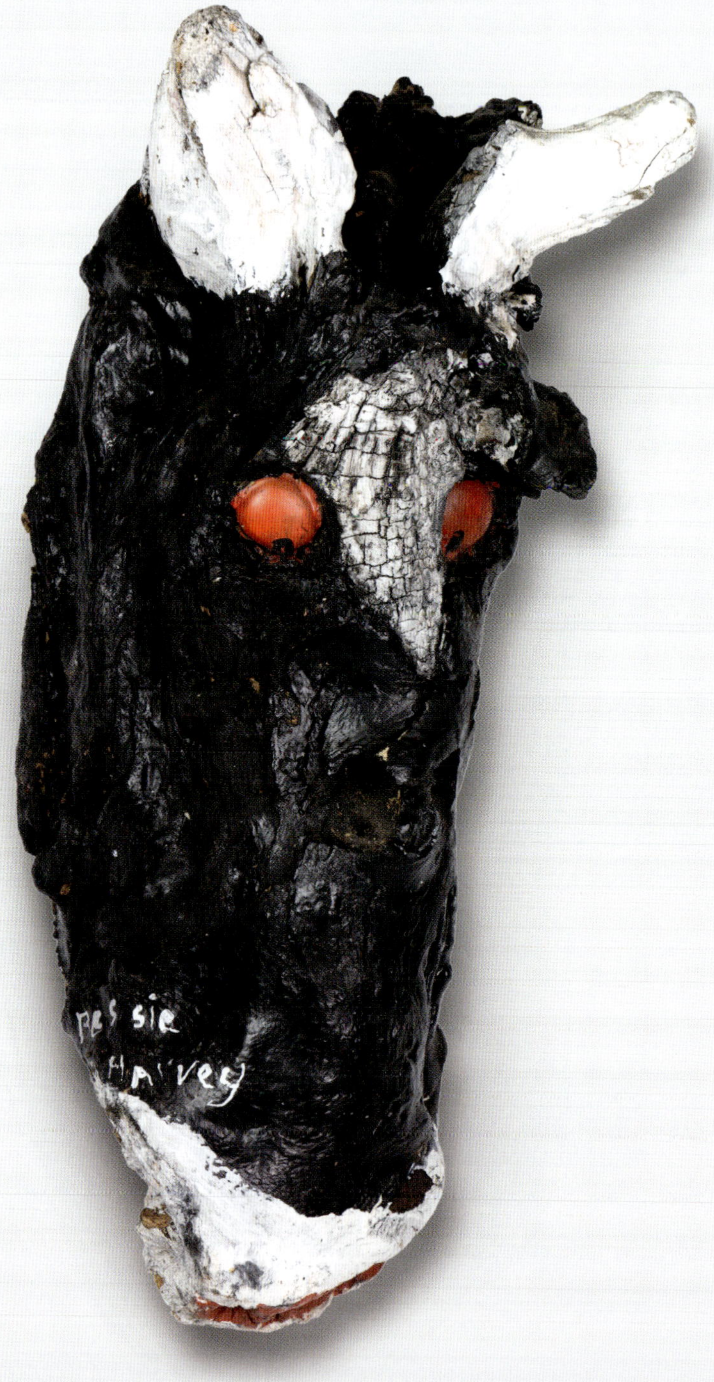

Plate 68. Bessie Harvey, *Devil Mule*. Paint on found wood, plastic eyes. 12 × 5 × 5 inches. Shorty Lawson Museum Collection. © 2024 Estate of Mary T. Smith/ Artists Rights Society (ARS), New York.

There is an exchange in *The Known World* between Caldonia and Moses that describes how Shorty felt about work and mules. Caldonia asks Moses, "Why do you work so hard when you are the one in charge?" Moses answers, "Wouldn't know how to do it any other way . . . there's horses that you can work and work and they keep on workin' till they drop dead. Your average mule won't really do that, but your average horse will. The mule be smarter." (Edward P. Jones) "Some folks argued that a horse was smarter, mules got a devil streak in them (Plate 68), but I never saw any of Shorty's mules act devilish with him." (Randy Hester)

Maybe the mules minded Shorty because he took good care of them and every once in a while let them run wild, him riding bareback. (Plate 69) Shorty loved to celebrate the completion of work well done, leading an impromptu jubilee when a tough week of pulling tobacco was finished by Saturday noon. "We'd race our mules to the pond, strip naked, and go for a swim while the mules drank." (Randy Hester) But come Monday morning any celebration was forgotten; it was back to work.

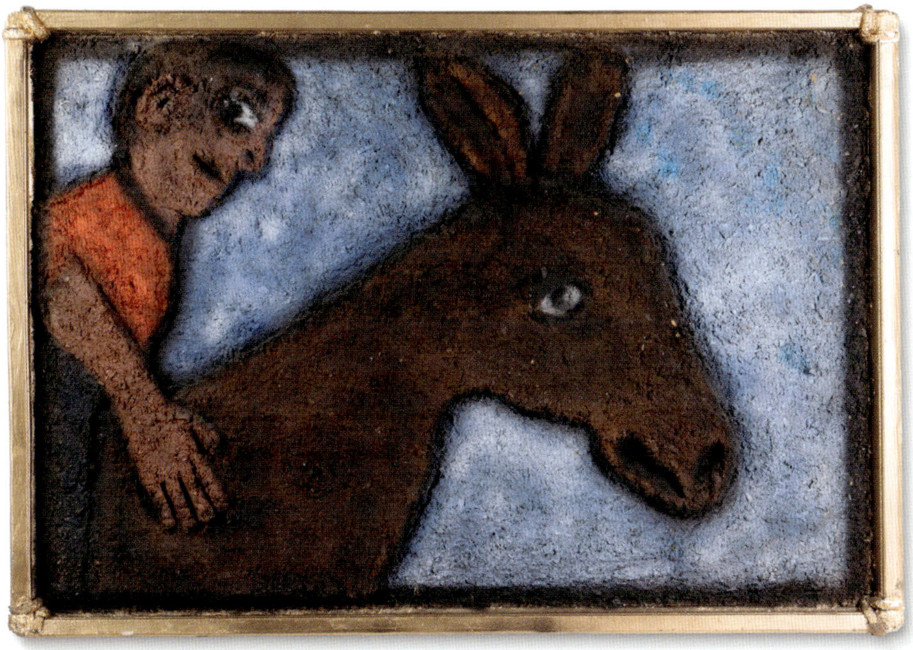

Plate 69. Archie Byron, *Horseback*. Painted sawdust and Elmer's glue mix, bas relief, overpainted gold wood frame, sawdust mix corners. 25 × 36 × 1 inch. Shorty Lawson Museum Collection. © 2024 Estate of Archie Byron/Artists Rights Society (ARS), New York.

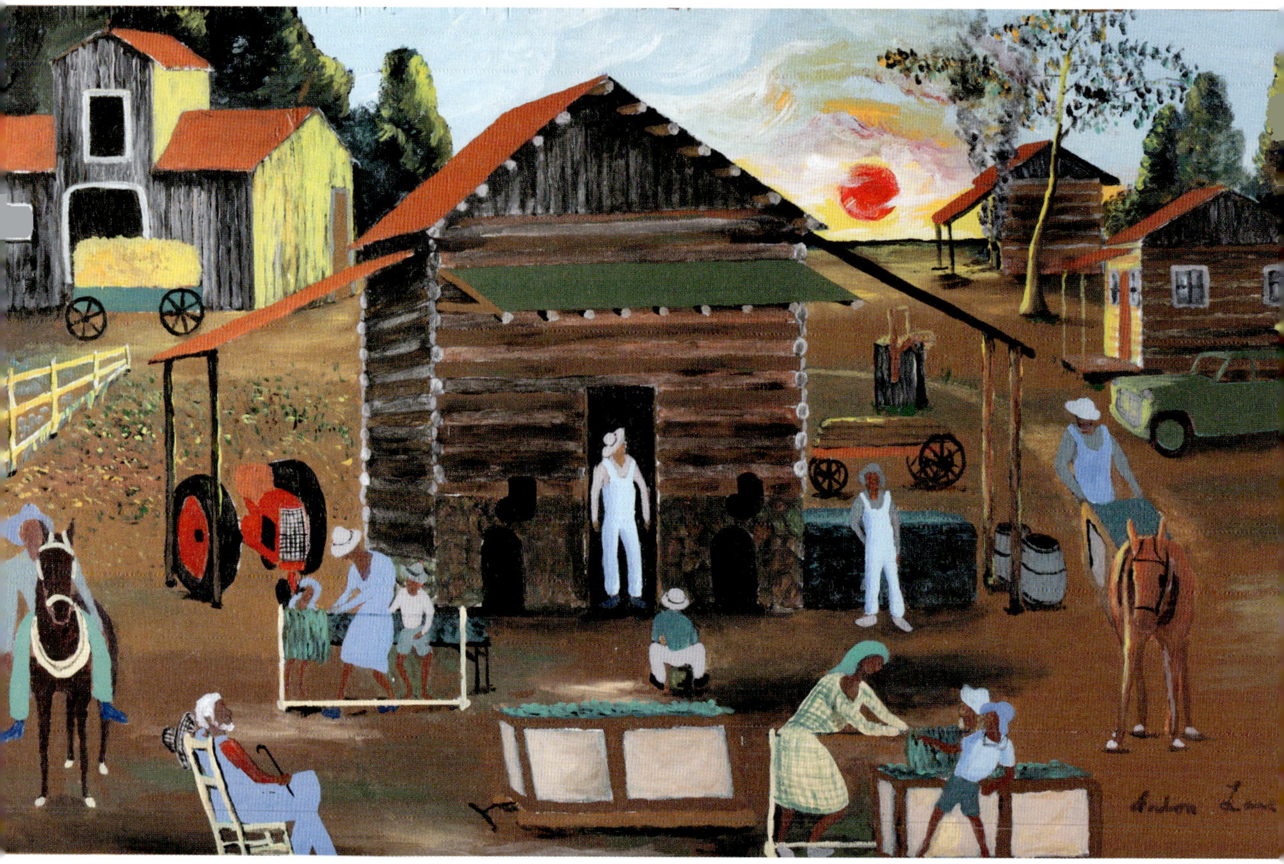

Plate 70. Arbon Lane, *Untitled*. Paint on wall paneling. 28 × 43½ inches.

Shorty loved hard work. He thrived on it. He knew it distinguished him. He got pleasure from outdoing all others, especially lazy and uppity White boys. Hard-working White boys were okay. "For a few years, early 1960s, there was a White tenant farmer who oversaw Shorty and me, always assigned himself the easiest job or no job at all, and he just loved to boss us around. (Plate 70) Shorty and I shared a disdain of him so I adopted Shorty's values. From Shorty I learned the joys of working hard, being attentive to the world around you, and keeping a positive outlook." (Randy Hester)

No one who worked with Shorty could avoid "catching" his ethics, his optimism, his endurance, the power of his authenticity. He never boasted, no need to. He simply was who he was, unspoken lessons commanding. "He won't stop until the job is done." (Larry Dixon)

Surely, he worked to provide for his family. He knew plenty of families, Black and White, so poor that beggar's lice wouldn't stick to their pants. Others nearly got eaten by landowners or banker vultures. (Plate 71) Getting his family ahead was important, but he resisted every endless cycle of status-seeking materialism. "The Negro stood in danger of being dazzled by the shimmer and tinsel of superficials." (Anna Julia Cooper) Not Shorty. Hard work was its own reward, all the shimmer and tinsel he needed.

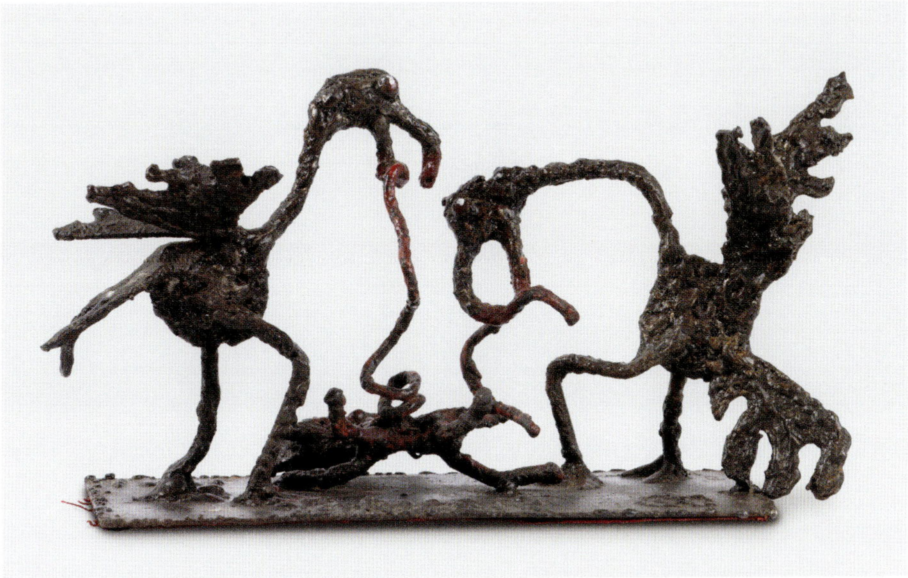

Plate 71. Willie Tarver, *Two Buzzards Eating Dead Animal.* Cut and welded metal, soldered texture with painted highlights. 8 × 14 × 5½ inches.

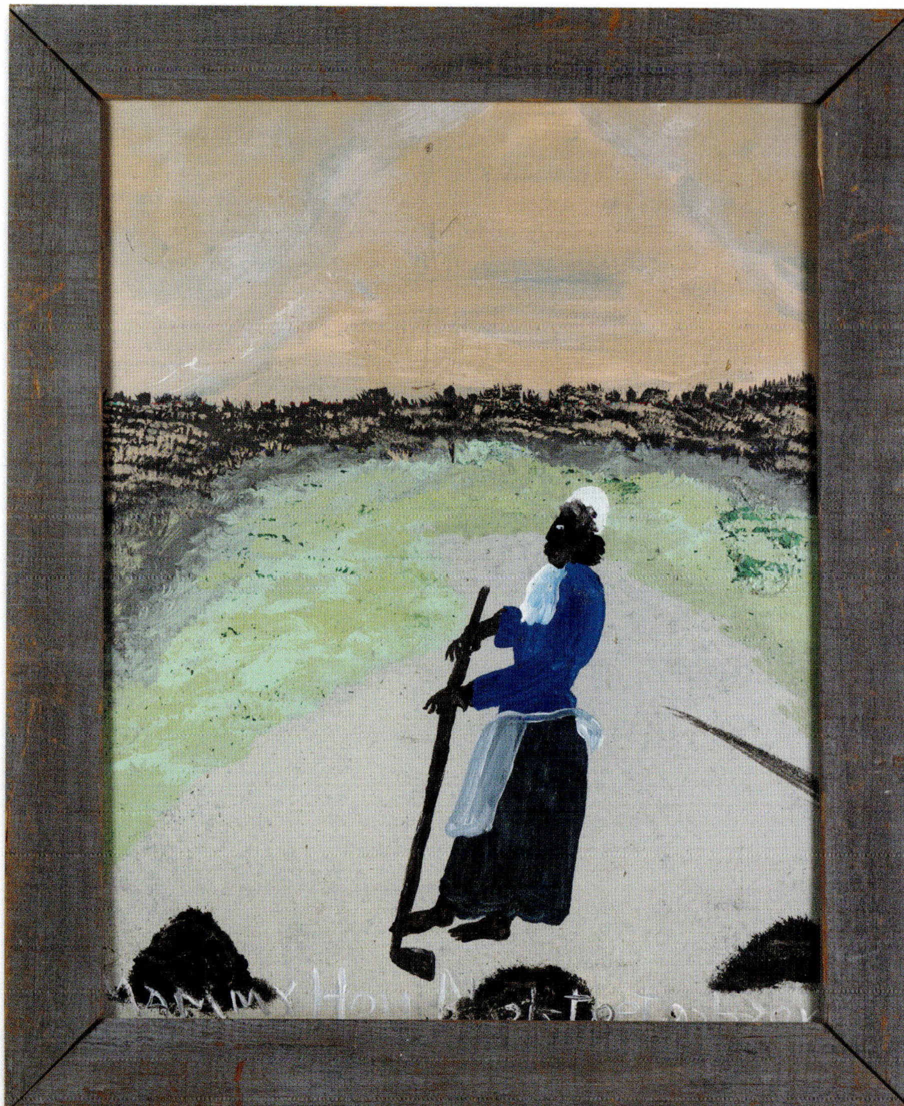

Plate 72. Black Joe Jackson, *Mammy hon*. Paint on fiberboard. 23 × 18 inches.

Row Work

The regular work Shorty's family did was all row work, one row, then the next row, and the next and next, then on to another field. Repeat row by row. Plowing, planting, weeding, laying by, topping, suckering, worming, pulling. All the spring and summer seasons were mostly row work..

May weeds outgrew tobacco. Row work turned to hoeing. (Plate 72) Everyone, including women and children, hoed. Chop the weeds. Don't hit the tender tobacco plant, pull weeds into the middle of the row, cover roots with dirt. Finish one row, on to the next row. "Then we took those two white mules, one named Jim, other named Pet, and used the buzzard-wing sweep to pull dirt back up around each plant." (Larry Dixon)

Row work developed a particular kind of endurance. It felt like the job was endless because each row stretched to a vanishing point beyond your view and you knew there were more rows to do just like the one you were working. Repeating the same movement, say plowing or hoeing, day after day pained muscles to extreme and lulled your senses, but if you didn't pay attention, mule got spooked, you had to catch him and start the plowing over. (Plate 73)

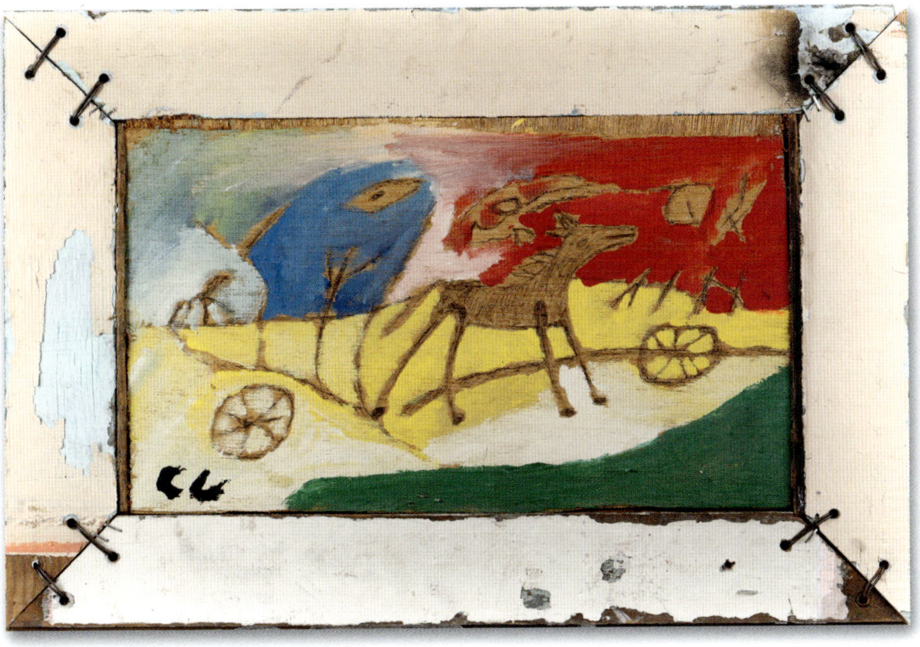

Plate 73. Charlie Lucas, *On the Farm*. Pen or pencil, paint on wood, staples, wire. 14 × 20½ inches.

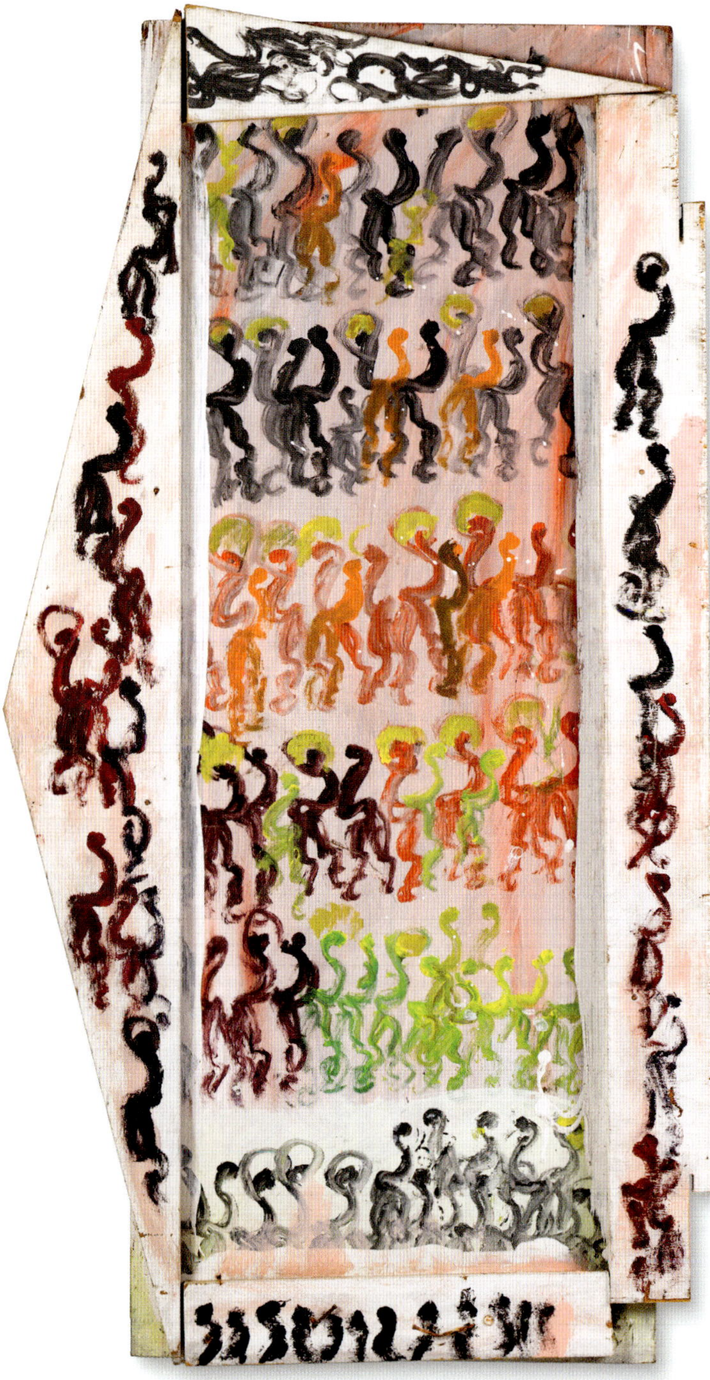

Plate 74. Purvis Young, *Untitled*. Paint on wood, painted wood cutouts for frame. 39 × 20 × 2 inches. Shorty Lawson Museum Collection. © 2024 The Larry Clemons Collection/Artists Rights Society (ARS), New York.

"We had to work, and we had also to pay attention. We had to learn surviving. We had to learn that everything you want to do, you got to struggle for it." (Thornton Dial) The stamina gained from row work paid dividends in stick-to-it-ness throughout life. Row work also taught you to keep your eye on the prize even when dealing with the most mundane detail. It shapes a person who can pursue a lofty vision and maintain focus at the same time.

From plowing and planting to hoeing and harvesting, every day was the same row work for several weeks or more for each task. The measure of life for six months from March to August, some years into September, was the distance along one familiar field line to another.

To grow 30 acres of tobacco required walking over 60 miles row by row for each task. Add in corn, hay, beans, milo, and other crops, you walked and worked 80 to 90 miles every week for six months, planting, hoeing, or harvesting, from dawn to dark. At sunrise rows offered a beautiful dew-laden fresh start. By sundown purple shadows were dulled by repetition and exhaustion.

Pulling bottom leaves of tobacco was the hardest, dirtiest, most humiliating row work. Suck the spirit out of many a man. Purvis Young painted this perfectly with endless rows of repeated action. (Plate 74) Bend over. Pull two tobacco leaves, one half-buried in the dirt, store the leaves under your left arm. Repeat, bent over fully at the waist, only standing upright when you can hold no more leaves under your arm. Put your tobacco leaves in a neat pile in the slide. Firmly tell the mule to "come up." Repeat the same action for five hours in the morning and five hours after dinner, for several weeks, every day covered from head to toe in sticky tobacco gum.

Pulling tobacco got easier as the season progressed because after bottom leaves you got to work up the stalk, pulling several more leaves each week. After pulling those leaves on the ground, you next pulled the lugs, then the cutters, then what was called leaf about midway up the stalk to the top. By August you could pull the last leaves standing up.

"I was never as fast or skilled as Shorty, but I learned to nearly match his endurance, just one gift he gave me. He taught me to work beyond exhaustion. Shorty pulled two rows of tobacco at once and finished those rows while I pulled only one row even when I was in high school. Without a disparaging word he always helped me or anyone lagging behind." (Randy Hester)

Annie and Shorty farmed with a handmade stringer called a "horse" and a pair of mules. Stringing tobacco required rhythmic hand-eye coordination, aggressive grace, and command of her "horse." Fieldwork required less finesse, more strength, and endurance. "Shorty was the hardest-working man I have ever known. One day I told him that. He smiled. Some weeks later he said to me, 'Mr. Randolph is the hardest-working White man I know.' I asked if he meant my daddy worked hard, or that most White men didn't. He smiled. Not a word spoken in response." (Randy Hester)

The Lawsons' reputation for hard work spread and lasts, decades later. "Everywhere I work, if people knew Mama and Daddy, they expect me to do more, fast, better than anybody else." (Carolyn Lawson) And she excelled in high-pressure manufacturing jobs.

Motorized farming upended the Lawsons' world: the "horse" stringer was replaced by a giant sewing machine, mules by tractors. A tractor was capable of hauling more, plowing faster, mixing speed with sleek, ironic machine "horsepower" whose horse power the machine replaced. Maybe more important, a farmer's status increased when a mule was replaced by a small Ferguson. Status expanded exponentially when the little Ferguson was replaced by a John Deere tractor, bigger and twice the power.

Less widespread but more captivating was the heavenly powered advance airplanes represented. Progress brought more status and unexpected curses. Some "progressive" farmers hired pilots with bi-wing planes to spray their crops to kill insect pests from the air. One of these crop duster planes hit a power line, crashed at Hesters Store, and killed the pilot.

Both the power and danger of flying fascinated Shorty. The farm was in a north-south flight path. There weren't many flights in those days, so every commercial or military plane merited a pause in fieldwork. He studied each one. "Once he asked if I believed people could fly. I responded that they certainly could, starting with the Wright brothers and all those passengers in the plane overhead. All those people are flying. He shook his head, said nah, that he meant could folks be flying like hawks or owls or buzzards. I told him I didn't think so. He was quiet for a few rows of work, then responded that even if he could, he was staying put. I forgot about Shorty's question and conclusion for decades." (Randy Hester)

Years later a student at Berkeley doing her master's thesis on Gullah culture told Randy about slaves in the Sea Islands who, when the beatings by the cruelest masters became unbearable, would have an elder say magic words, and they would fly away, fly right out of the field. (Plate 75)

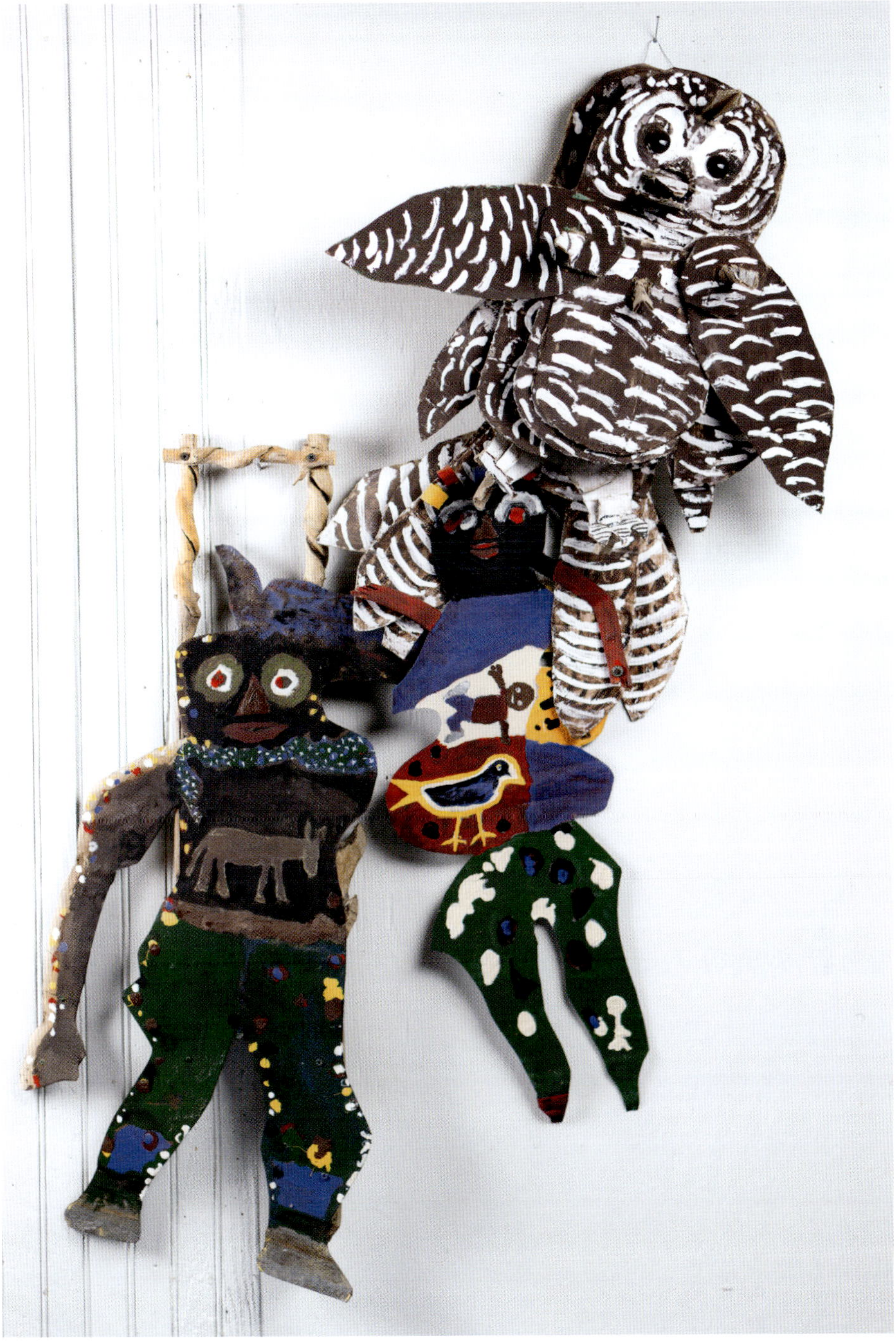

Plate 75. Brent Brown, *Owl with Randy Hester, Ancestors Flying to Africa.* Painted cardboard owl, cutouts assembled three-dimensionally, taxidermy eyes; enamel and acrylic paint on roofing tin, pastel, twigs, whorled wood, pierced earring, male and female figures. 49 × 31 × 8 inches combined.

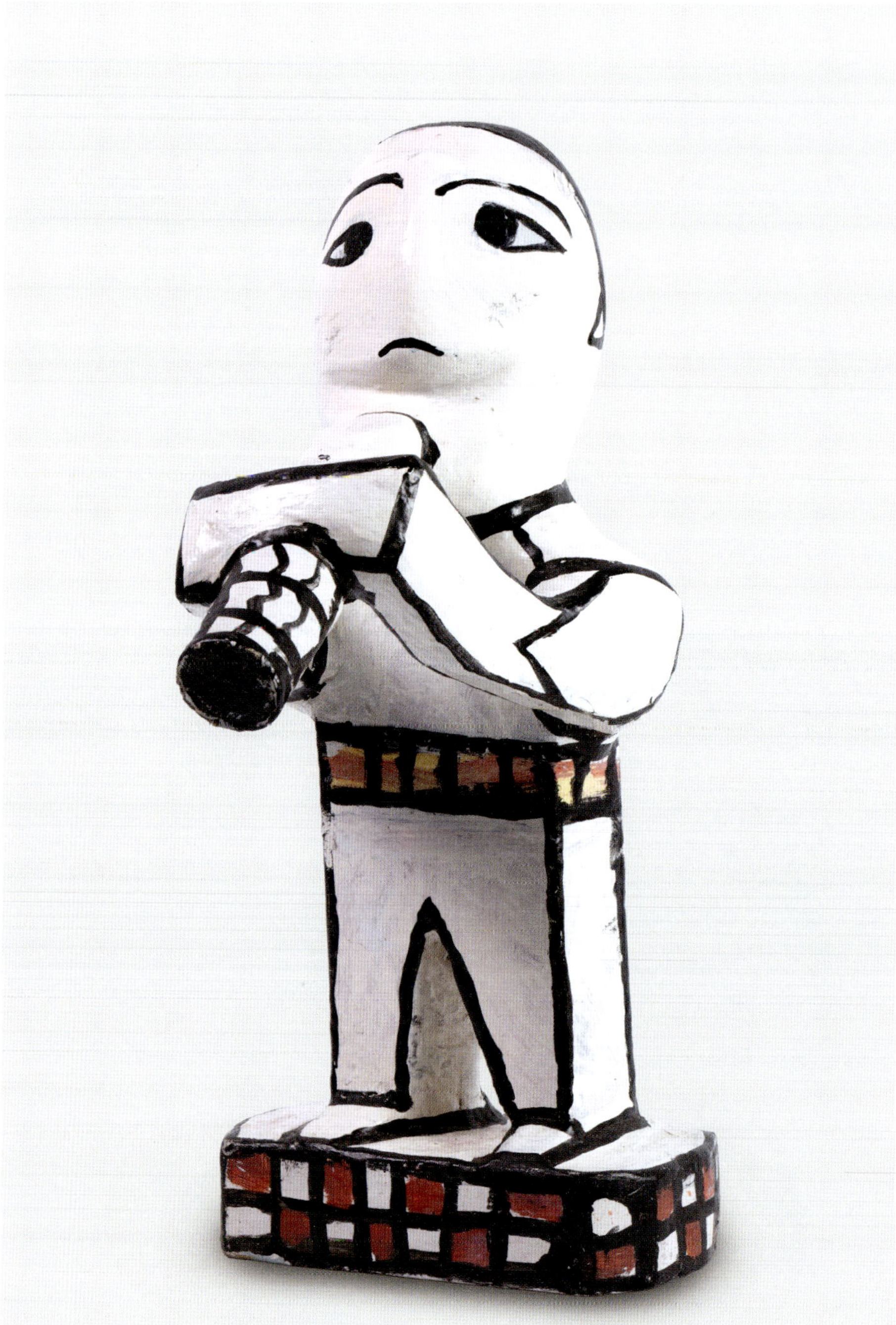

Plate 76. Hubert Walters, *Flute Player*. Wood, bondo, paint. 14½ × 6¼ × 9 inches.

An owl or hawk picked them up, and off they flew to Africa, free of the tortures of slavery. One story claimed that the slaves changed from human shape into vultures, called "buzzards" around here. Sometimes dozens of slaves flew off together either because the magic words worked or they rediscovered the wings each had been blessed with but had lost.

At the time Randy didn't know enough to ask Shorty if he had heard those stories. Had his grandparents told him about Flying Africans? Did his ancestors believe that those who flew off made it to the homeland or did they crash and drown in the ocean? Maybe they looked over Jordan. Maybe they just made it to heaven with what wings they had. They all had wings, once, you know. Remember the song "All God's Children Got Wings"? There is always truth in song and faith in ascension. Maybe the escape was created by Eshu, the flute-playing African god of uncertainty and conflict. (Plate 76) Speculation short-lived, the Lawsons were back to stringing tobacco. (Plate 77)

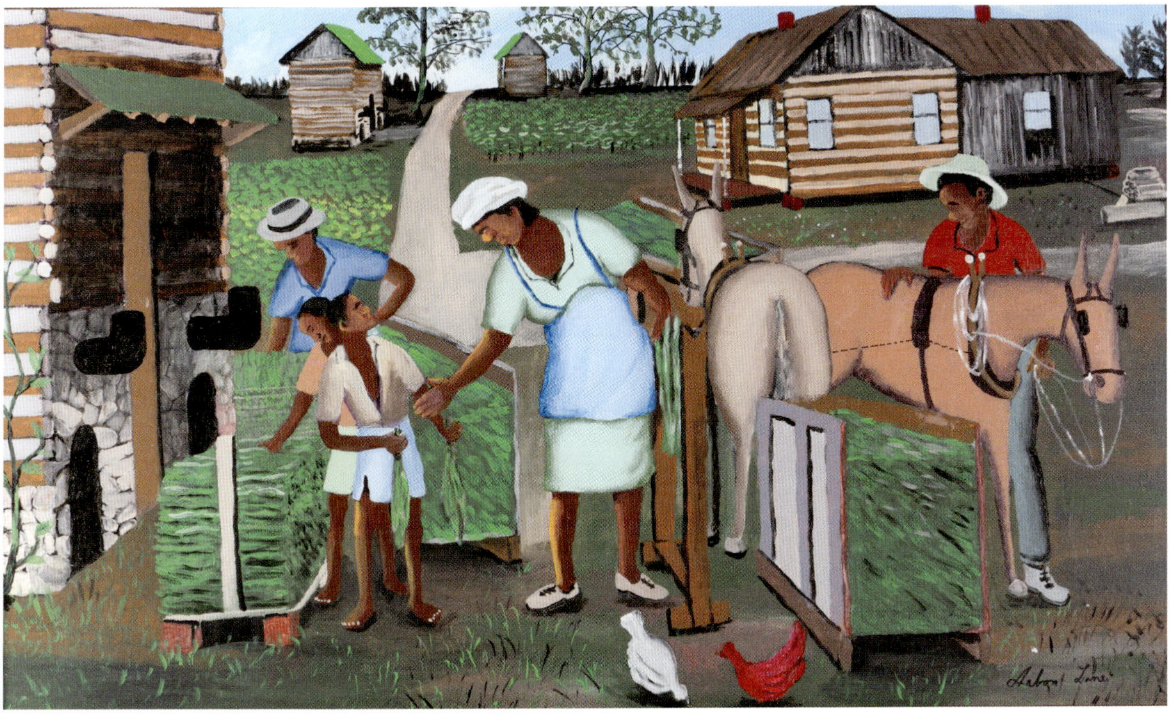

Plate 77. Arbon Lane, *Untitled*. Paint on thin plywood. 23¾ × 39 inches.

Philosopher-artist Joe Minter gifted the Shorty Lawson Museum his sculpture *African Queen*, a part of the African diaspora he has created in his Birmingham neighborhood. "Did his ancestors have Shorty's character, skills, and beliefs?" (Joe Minter) Minter questions such things. He asked how the Lawsons reconciled biblical damnation and eternal life with spiritualism and lingering African practices. Standing in the midst of his art world Minter speculated about what roles Shorty's and Annie's ancestors had in their African societies. Hearing stories about the Lawsons he concluded, "Shorty's forefathers had to be superior athletes, desirable to slave buyers, strong, agile, and fast. I wonder did his ancestors try escaping? Annie had to come from a royal African family who arrived in her new world wrapped in chains." (Plate 78) Thinking out loud he traced the centuries from slave ship to tenant farmer. Minter paused and wondered, "What did they do when Abraham Lincoln freed us?" (Joe Minter)

No one in the family has any details. They know that the Lawsons didn't leave Caswell County after Emancipation. By Shorty's time much history, even oral traditions, were unspoken. He may have remembered Flying African stories, but he didn't speak about Africa, slavery, the Underground Railroad, or breaking free.

Shorty's news was confined to local gossip. Current events seldom reached his ears, even something about a local man, T. T. Clayton, or his role in a new city two counties away where Blacks would provide labor and share the capital return. There, "We intend to work, and to work hard. But we do not intend merely to work. We intend to own." (Floyd McKissick)

Shorty's life was the present tense. He knew Sandy Richmond personally before Sandy left tobacco farming on the Woody Farm for New York. Sandy got a job driving a taxi. And he heard that a lot of Black folks went north, to Washington and New York, but he was as likely to fly back to Africa as to go north. He had a place, in fact, an important place, where he was.

Shorty knew he was the equal of any man at Hesters Store. In what mattered most to him and others he proved his superiority every day: respected as the hardest-working, most principled man inside and out.

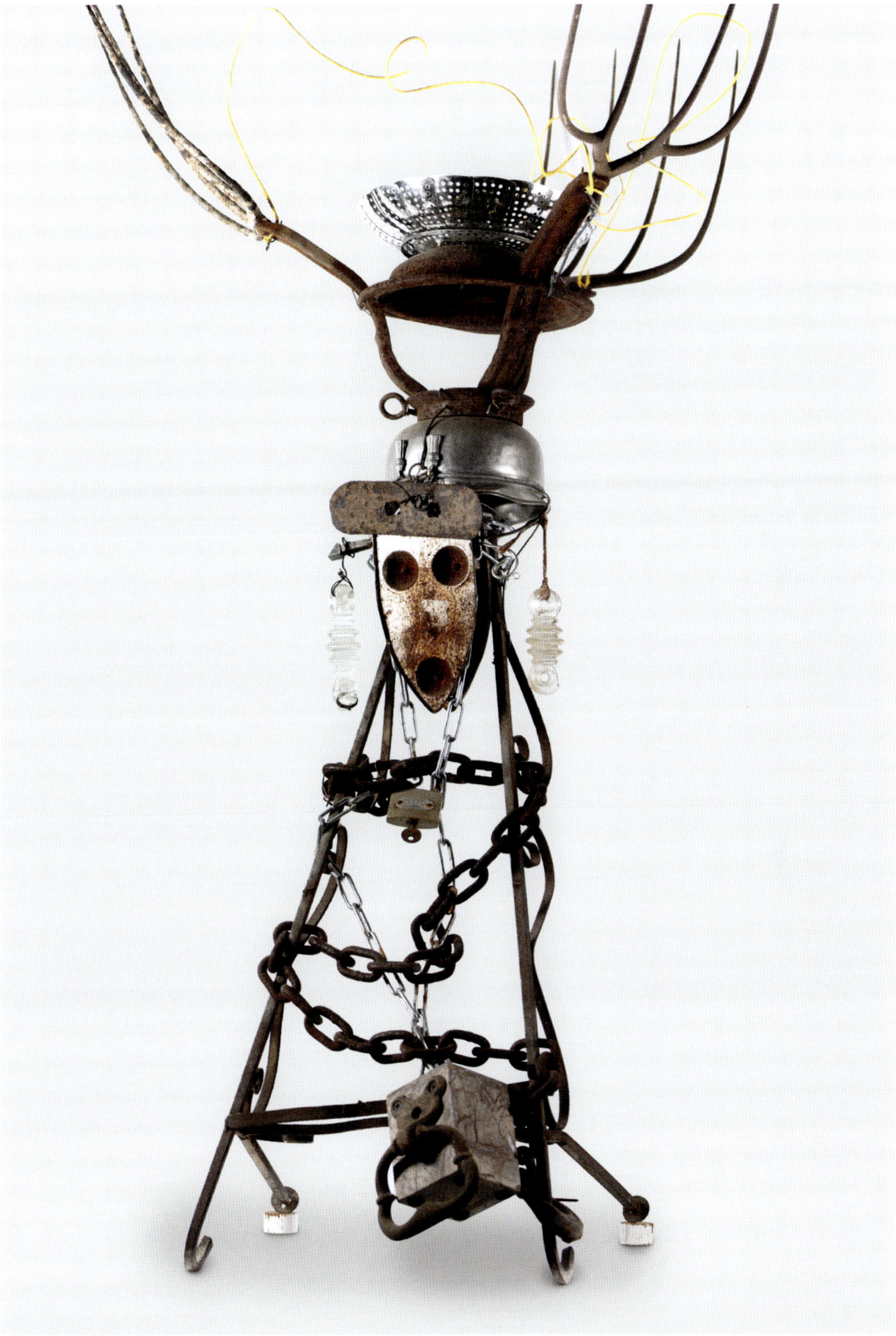

Plate 78. Joe Minter, *African Queen*. Found objects, metal frame, chains, lock, wire. 50 × 25 × 15 inches. Shorty Lawson Museum Collection.

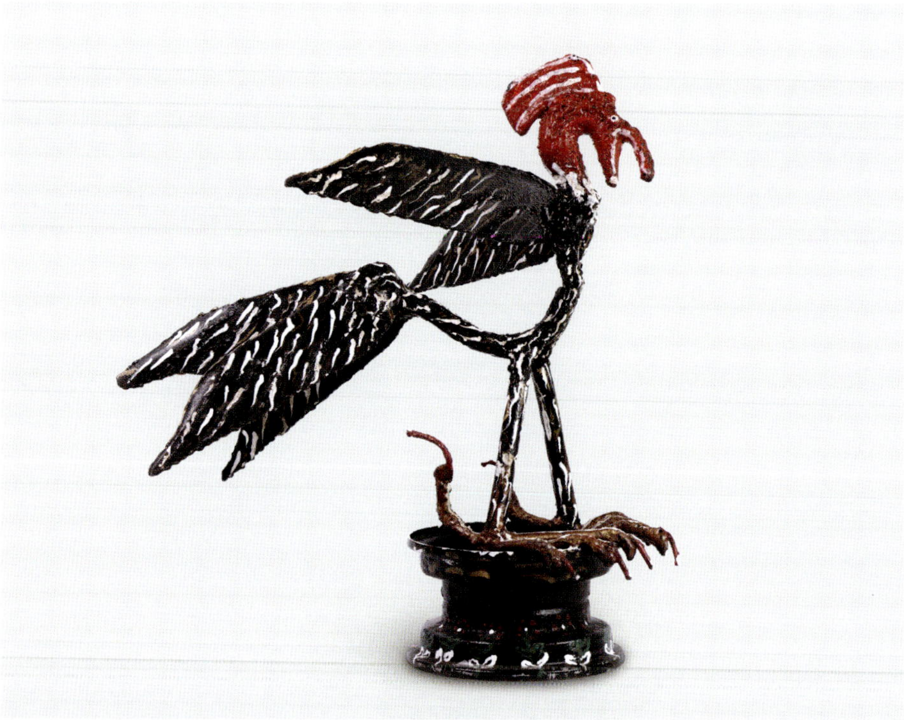

Plate 79. Willie Tarver, *Untitled*. Cut and welded metal, soldered and painted texture, wheel base painted with flowers. 19½ × 18½ × 11 inches.

Rooted, he intended to live right where he was and live within the law, raise boys to be men, and jockey only mules. He often raced the mules from the field at dinner and sometimes talked about the fastest mules he ever rode.

"It never occurred to me then that stories about the legendary Black North Carolina horse man, Austin Curtis, likely had been passed down for generations, certainly for the 147,000 pounds of tobacco he won in the race of the ages during slavery times." (Randy Hester) Shorty and Curtis were much alike. They shared unmatched sensitivity for and uncanny knowledge of their steeds. And both were respected for their character in their communities.

Shorty and I shared racing stories often. But "We talked about race only when it confronted us in the moment. He shared his Negro spirituals, yet Larry says his favorite was Johnny Cash. One day Jerry Clark rubbed stinging nettle on my arm. I jumped him. He was much bigger, outwrestling me until I got him in a scissors, squeezed the breath out

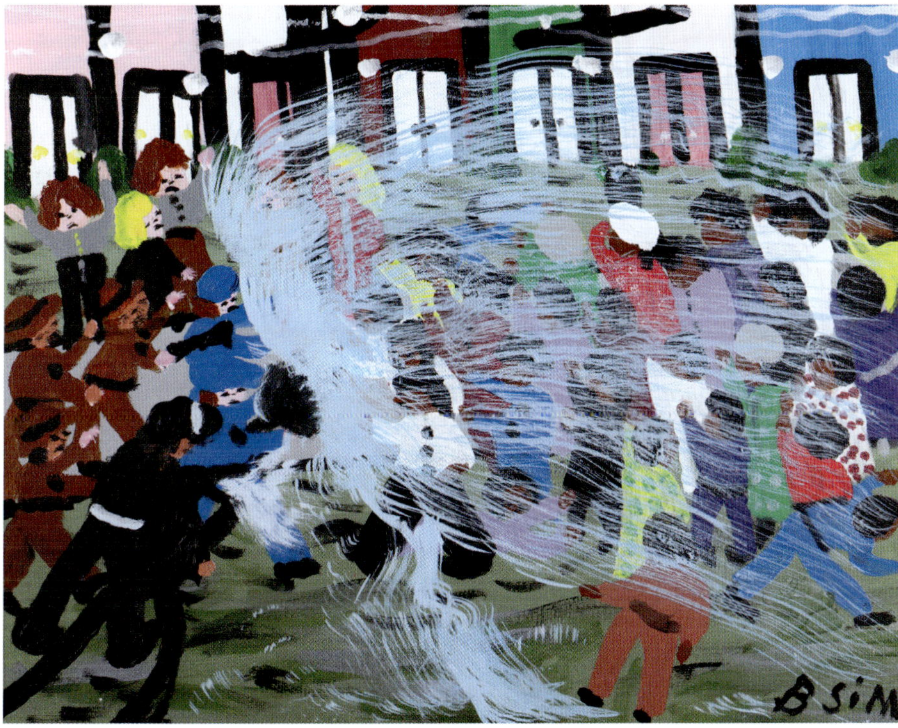

Plate 80. Bernice Sims, *Unleashing Police Dogs and Fire Hoses, Birmingham, May, 1963*. Paint on canvas. 16 × 20 inches.

of him. He gasped, 'I give,' I looked up at Shorty, his whole face a smile. Later he recounted the fight with considerable pride, summing up, 'You whipped that White bully's ass for both of us. You're the top rooster now.' (Plate 79) If Shorty himself had beat up Jerry, he knew he would have been in trouble, probably have faced jail time." (Randy Hester)

When something like that happened, Shorty and Randy might acknowledge inequities, but racial events beyond the farm were incomprehensible to them. Dr. King issued a call to action in Greensboro, less than an hour away. In 1960 the A&T Four initiated lunch counter sit-ins, a world alien to both Shorty and Randy, neither of whom had ever been to Greensboro nor eaten at a lunch counter.

In May 1963, when Bull Conner unleashed police dogs and fire hoses on children in Birmingham, Shorty and Randy were plowing. (Plate 80) The Lawsons had a television by then, but nobody remembers watching that news. Events roiled the nation with little immediate impact on their daily lives.

In time Civil Rights impacted most lives and forced challenging decisions about liberty and responsibility. "'But freedom, true freedom, is a master too, you see—one more dogged, more constant, than any ragged slave-driver,' she said. 'What you must now accept is that all of us are bound to something. Some will bind themselves to property in man and all that comes forthwith. And others shall bind themselves to justice. All must name a master to serve. All must choose.'" (Ta-Nehisi Coates)

Summer of 1964 was difficult. For some the masters had shifted. Randy came home from college full of freshman ideas about activist roles to combat inequality. Witnessing a KKK cross burning in Durham, racial injustice became personal, peopled with ones who loved and mentored him. (Plate 81) Shorty tolerated Randy's talk, but it didn't make much sense. When the Civil Rights Act was signed by President Johnson before July 4, it was miserably hot, and tobacco needed to be pulled.

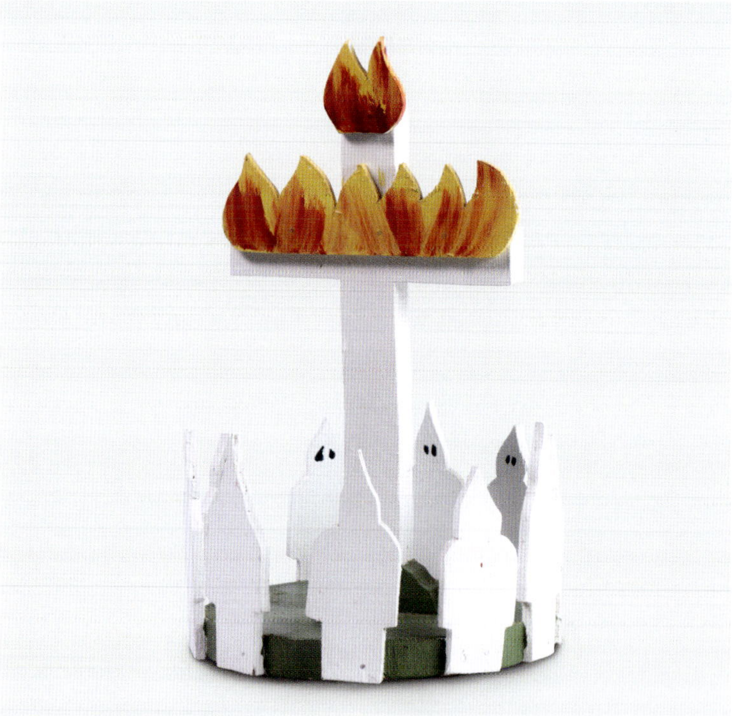

Plate 81. Unknown, *KKK Cross Burning.* Painted cut-out wood shapes. 12 × 7 × 7 inches. Shorty Lawson Museum Collection, gift of George and Sheila Borum.

Randy persisted. In 1965 he volunteered to lead an after-school program for the local Office of Economic Opportunity in Chavis Heights, the Black ghetto in Raleigh. Shorty was mystified. At the end of that tobacco season, months after confrontations at the Pettus Bridge in Selma dramatized barriers preventing Blacks from voting, Congress passed the Voting Rights Act. (Plate 82) Shorty only voted after Curtis Bradsher started picking him and Annie up and driving them to the polls. That was when Mr. Bradsher first ran for county commissioner.

Shorty was never confronted with a "Whites Only" sign at Hesters Store. The front door of the store served all men, and segregated territories were understood by all. White men conversed in a circle inside the store. Blacks gathered under the big oak tree outside. Women, Black or White, seldom entered the store. In Roxboro many places served only White people. "Toufie's Hot Dog Place behind the taxi stand only serve us from the back side." (Carolyn Lawson) To avoid swimming with Blacks the White community built a private swimming pool in Roxboro. Mixed-race swimming and seining in farm ponds persisted, where Randolph and Shorty were the ringleaders.

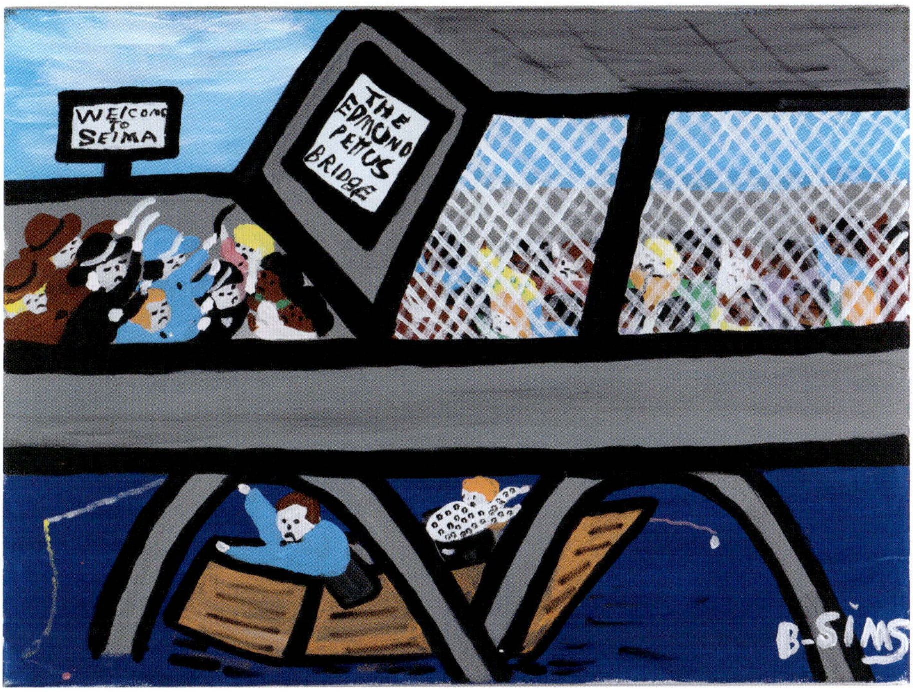

Plate 82. Bernice Sims, *Edmund Pettus Bridge*. Paint on canvas. 18 × 24 inches.

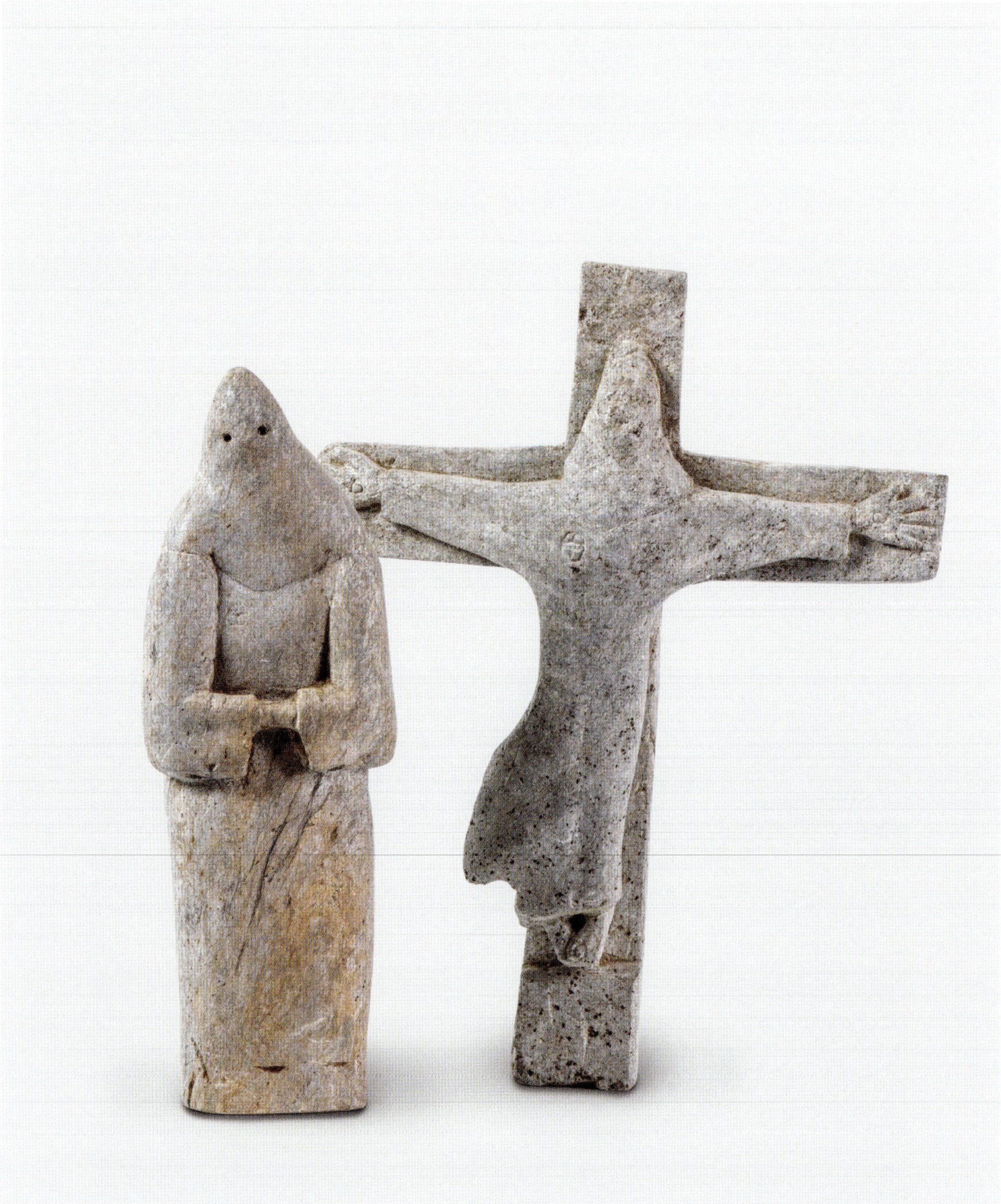

Plate 83. Charles Archer, *Klansman and Jesus Crucified in Klan Robe*. Two carved stones. Klansman 10 × 2½ × 2¼ inches, Jesus 11½ × 9 × 1¾ inches.

Intimidation continued close to home, and sometimes came to the secluded farm on Tom Bowes Road. "Larry was off at work, boys at school. I'll never forget. I was at home alone, hanging out clothes. White guy drove slow past the house. He yelled, 'Nigger, what are you doing?' at me. I called back, 'Excuse me, I know I'm a Nigger, but you don't have to call me outta my name. Still, you are not going to run me away from my home.'" (Stella Dixon) "The inability of one race to exterminate another gives rise to mutual understanding, reciprocity, and liberty." (Anna Julia Cooper)

The Klan in the 1960s was usually depicted in art by unaccomplished clumsiness, playing to fear of change, White Supremacy challenged. It is creepy, disgusting, but not truly fear evoking. It is difficult to imagine anyone buying that art or displaying it in home or business, which may explain why much is still stored in outbuildings. More recent sculpture by Charles Archer, however, is terrifying viscerally and intellectually. A Klansman, beautifully sculpted in a single gesture of hooded regalia, claims superiority of race and artistry. His eyes pierce the viewer's heart. He is accompanied by Jesus crucified, also a hooded Klansman with KKK insignia, claiming not only superiority of race and artistry but also religion. (Plate 83)

Larry said he was kinda scared but not Shorty, because they were prepared for the Klan. Still, they didn't go far from home until the Klan calmed down. Locally Jim Crow outmaneuvered the federal laws that sought to guarantee equal rights for all people. (Plate 84) In time there were occasional Civil Rights and personal victories, but that is not Shorty's story. Those victories simply occupied the same time but in a far different space. Shorty seemed bound to some master known only to himself.

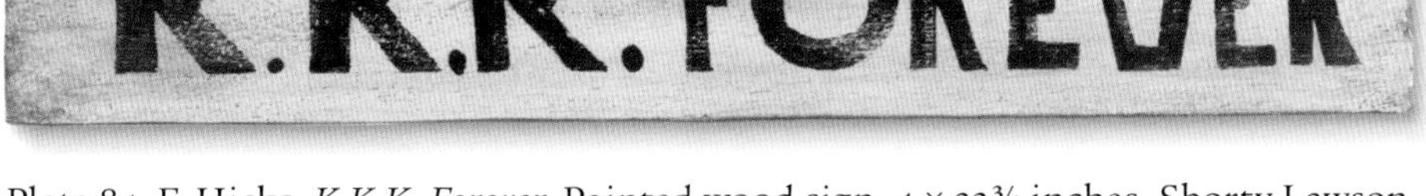

Plate 84. F. Hicks, *K.K.K. Forever.* Painted wood sign. 4 × 23¾ inches. Shorty Lawson Museum Collection, gift of George and Sheila Borum.

Black, White, Landed, and Tenant

At Hesters Store most men farmed during Shorty's lifetime. Black, White, landowners, and tenants interacted daily, often working side by side, but social distinctions between Black, White, landed, and laborer were clear and impenetrable. These differences determined income and net worth; dress; personal privilege; access to power; car, home, and appliance ownership; church and school attendance; and the women a man controlled or was controlled by.

Shorty knew the danger of cross-racial relationships. His mother likely told him about the lynching of Edward Roach in 1920 for attempted rape. He could not avoid the fear in his community after Henry Marrow was murdered in Oxford in 1970. The Teel boys claimed that Marrow had made an ugly remark to Larry Teel's wife so they brutalized and killed him. A White jury: not guilty.

Shorty knew that he and Annie were strong survivors in spite of the seemingly powerless places of Black men and women. In some ways Annie was both more powerful and more powerless than he was. Often, she stared down the tiger. Annie was true to their bed. She nurtured the family. She worked side by side with him in the fields. She embodied pleasure and struggle. (Plate 85) "The struggles we all have did, those struggles can teach us how to make improvement for the future." (Thornton Dial) Some battled publicly. The Lawsons' struggles were in daily life. Both battles counted.

Shorty understood the public struggle largely by hearsay. He was pleased that C. T. Vivian compared Randy to H. Rap Brown, but only after he was told who both Vivian and Brown were. Then he said to Randy, "You got room to be a troublemaker." At that moment Shorty acknowledged the roles, defined by gender, race, and class, that each person could play. He finally accepted his own outsized influence far beyond the farm when Randy moved into Chavis Heights and stopped the North-South Freeway and urban renewal clearance that threatened to destroy the homes of thousands of Black people. He didn't usually bother too much with distant racial conflict.

Shorty considered race in terms of what he knew: tobacco and kinship. His response: he touched Randy's hairy arm covered with sticky tobacco gum, comparing it to his hairless, gumless arm, and said, "There are 'vantages to being Black." Several washings with pine-tar soap didn't remove all the gum on Randy's arms and hands, sticky brown weeks after tobacco season.

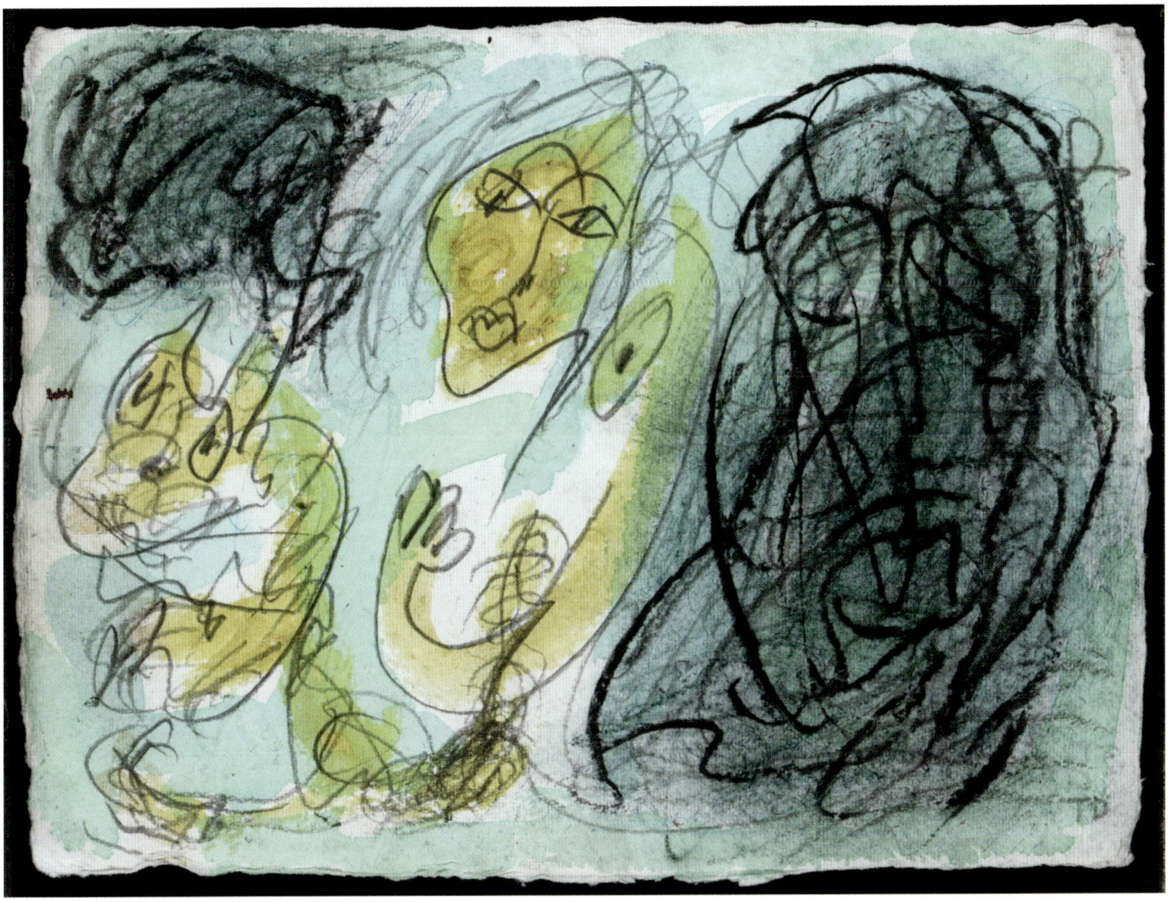

Plate 85. Thornton Dial, *Green Lady Facing the Tiger.* Watercolor, charcoal, pencil on paper. 10 × 12¾ inches.

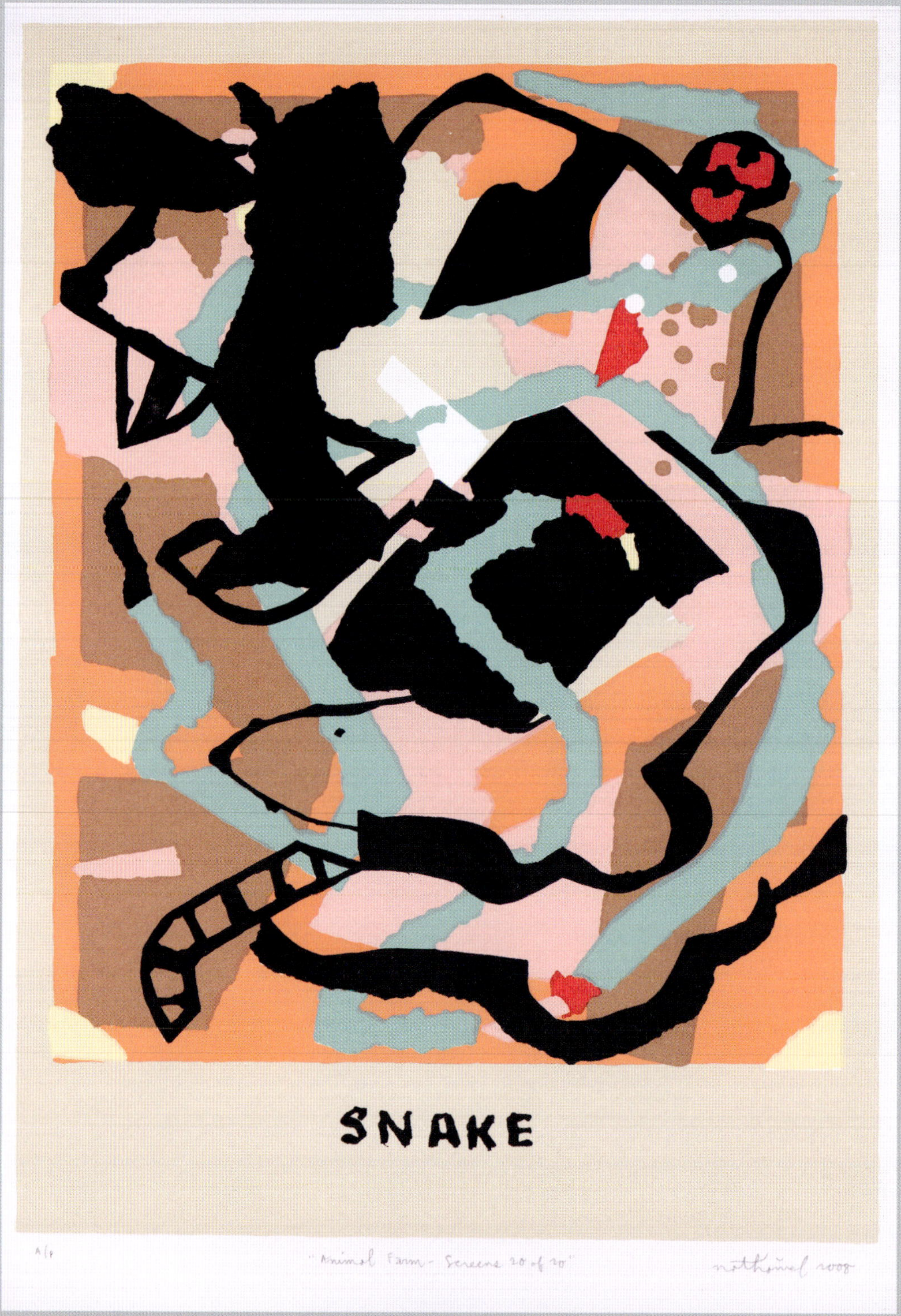
SNAKE
A/P
"Animal Farm - Screens 20 of 20"
nathaniel 2008

BOYS' ROOM

Failings, Fear, and God

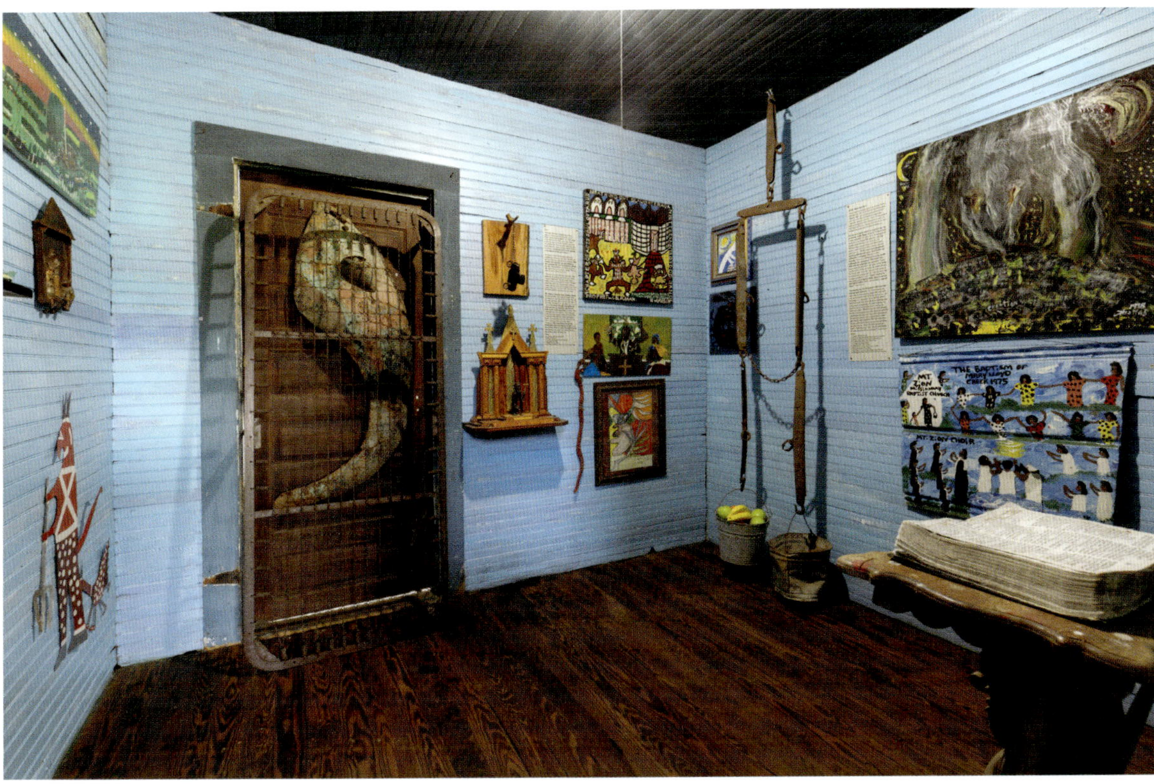

Plate 86 (facing). Nate Hester, *Snake*. Screen print from *Animal Farm*, screen 20 of 20. 17½ × 12 inches. Shorty Lawson Museum, gift of Nate Hester.

Hang the Car

The boys' bedroom measured 8 feet 4 inches by 9 feet 9 inches and had no window. Two bunk beds and a single slept five. Cramped quarters, but plenty of room for aspirations. Growing up, Larry drew the objects of most boys' desires: cars, cars, and more cars, still on the wall when the museum was created. Enduring craving. Likely to appease those who raised moral objections to the automobile, the license plate on his convertible proclaims, "I love God."

Wiley Bradsher, the preacher over at the Church of the City of God in the Wilderness, considered cars the ruination of the Black man. The car made it easy to run off, spend hard-earned money on gas, waste more money selling your soul for booze, gambling, and somebody else's woman. (Plate 87) Shorty had a streak of anger and was plagued by weekend drunkenness, characteristics he shared with the farm owner. Selling the escape of corn liquor, the Devil preyed on their addictions. Liquor "enslaved the souls of men." (Ta-Nehisi Coates) But Shorty drank only on

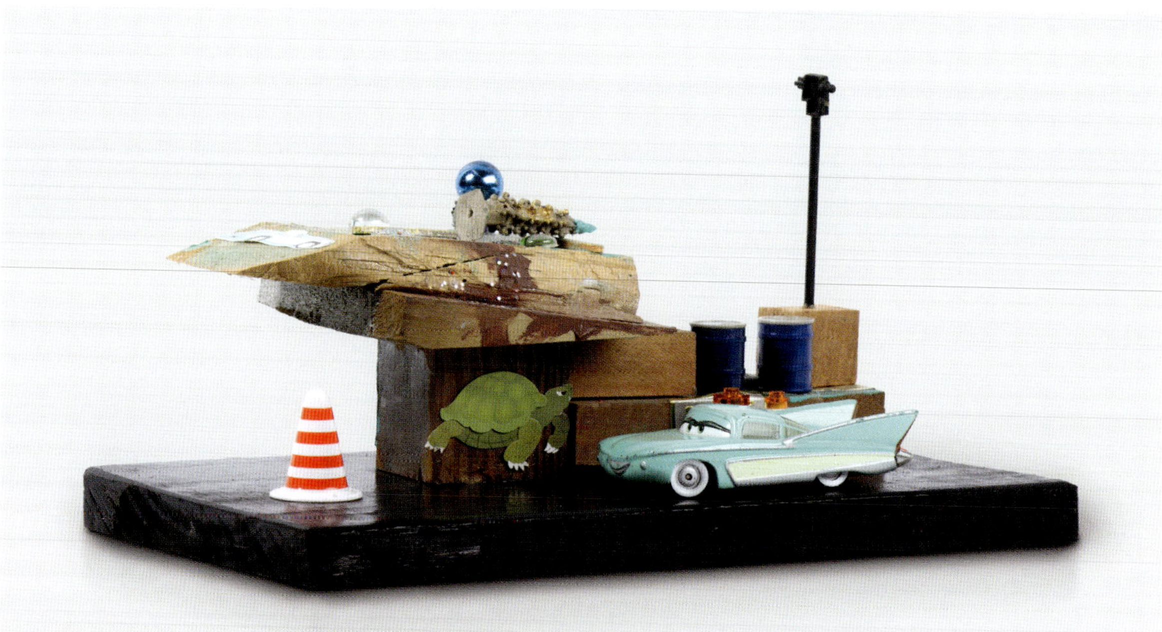

Plate 87. Randy Hester with Atticus Hester, *Fill 'er Up, High Octane*. Painted cut-out wood, Lego parts, buttons, stone, model Japanese pagoda, stickers, plastic barrels and eyeball, warning cone, metal *Car Story* car, Christmas decorations. 6¼ × 10¼ × 5½ inches. Shorty Lawson Museum Collection, gift of Randy Hester.

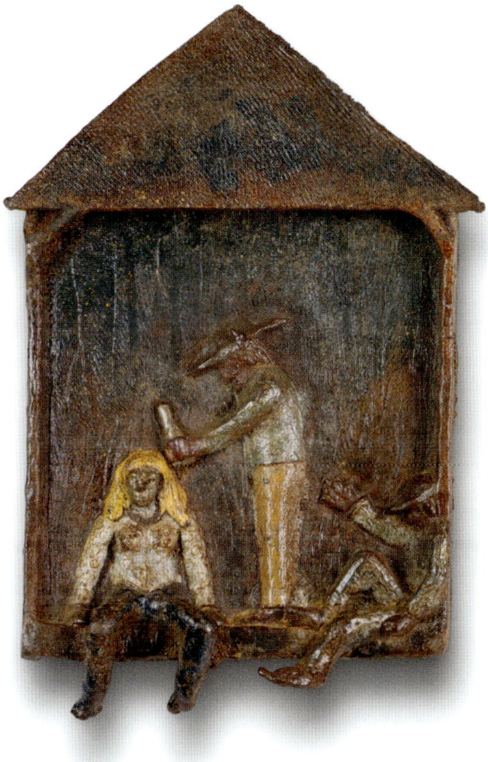

Plate 88. Unknown, *Untitled*. Cast, welded, and painted metal. 13 × 8½ × 1 inch. Shorty Lawson Museum Collection.

weekends away from home, usually at a juke joint or some house that sold white lightning. (Plate 88) Drinking and dancing, leaping from the floor onto a table to the beat of the huckabuck. There were plenty of ways to fail the God that Preach knew, but the Lawson home harbored few.

The evils of the car made sin easy and Black men indebted consumers; Wiley Bradsher preached buying land instead. Land was power and long-term security. Well-regarded tenant farmers like the Lawsons, who sharecropped, pocketed half the profits each year, enough to make a substantial downpayment on a small farm or buy a good used car. Preach Bradsher encouraged them not to waste all their earnings on a car loan that invited the Devil and distracted them from landownership.

With dramatic effect, Preach lynched a car from an oak tree at the church, touching nerves, past and present. No exaggeration. In spite of Preach Bradsher's warning all the boys wanted cars. But he was the moral authority in the Lawson household. Annie's family attended his church, believed on him, bowed at his altar. After they married, Shorty pushed his car down in the gully, never owned another one. Parts of the car were dug up a few years ago, a poetic reminder of Preach Bradsher's power. (Plate 89) Shorty never bought land.

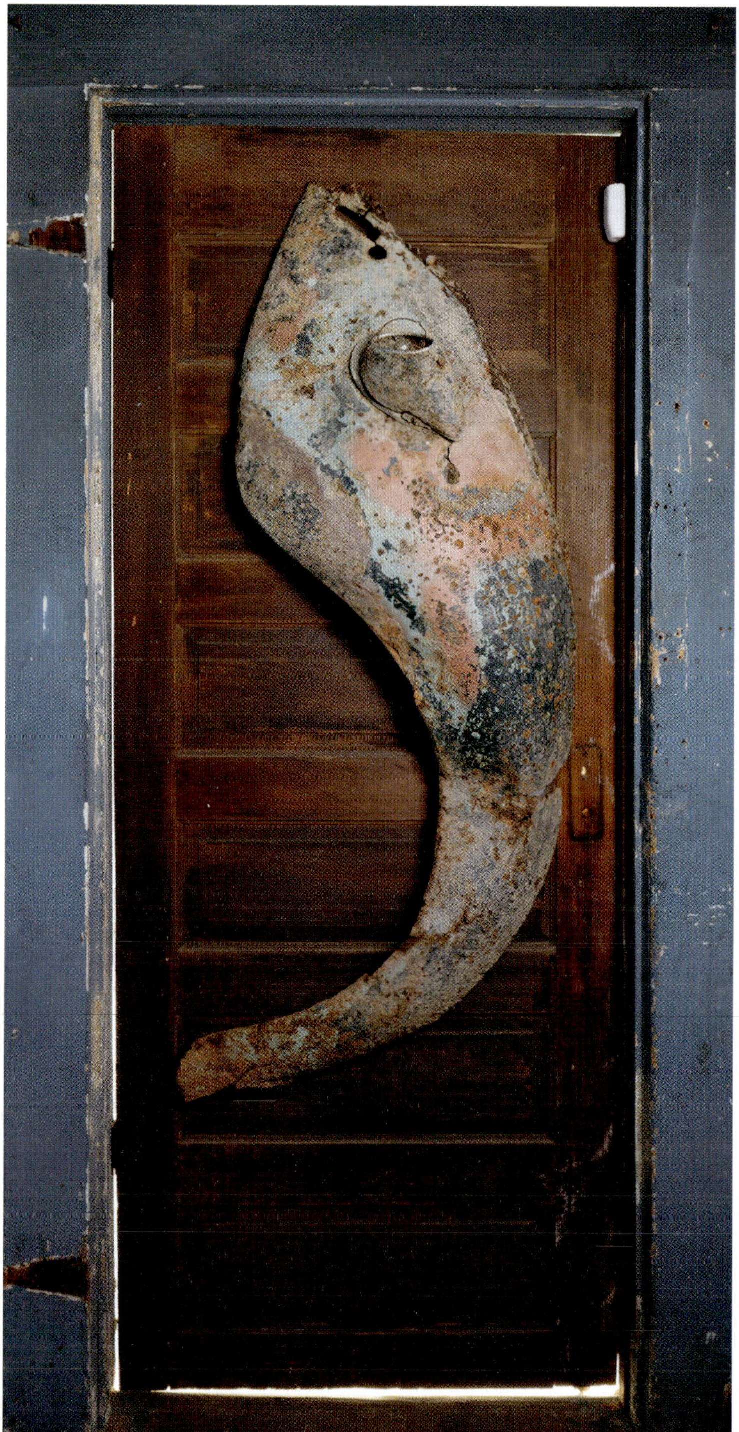

Plate 89. Unknown, *Untitled*. Fender of Shorty Lawson's car abandoned in gully behind house. 57 × 24 × 10 inches.

Snakes and the Man

Although there were dangers everywhere in daily summer life, Shorty's family most feared snakes. (Plate 90) It didn't matter whether snakes were God's curse or the work of the Devil, a copperhead sent you to the hospital, and a water moccasin's bite could kill you.

Snakes remained a fear without remedy. So too the Man. The Lawsons respected the landowner for working as hard as they did, side by side with them. But he wasn't consistent. "I loved Mr. Randolph. He was good to us." (Brenda Lawson) "He always brought us a big box of fruit and stuff at Christmas, but he never built us the well he promised." (Stella Dixon)

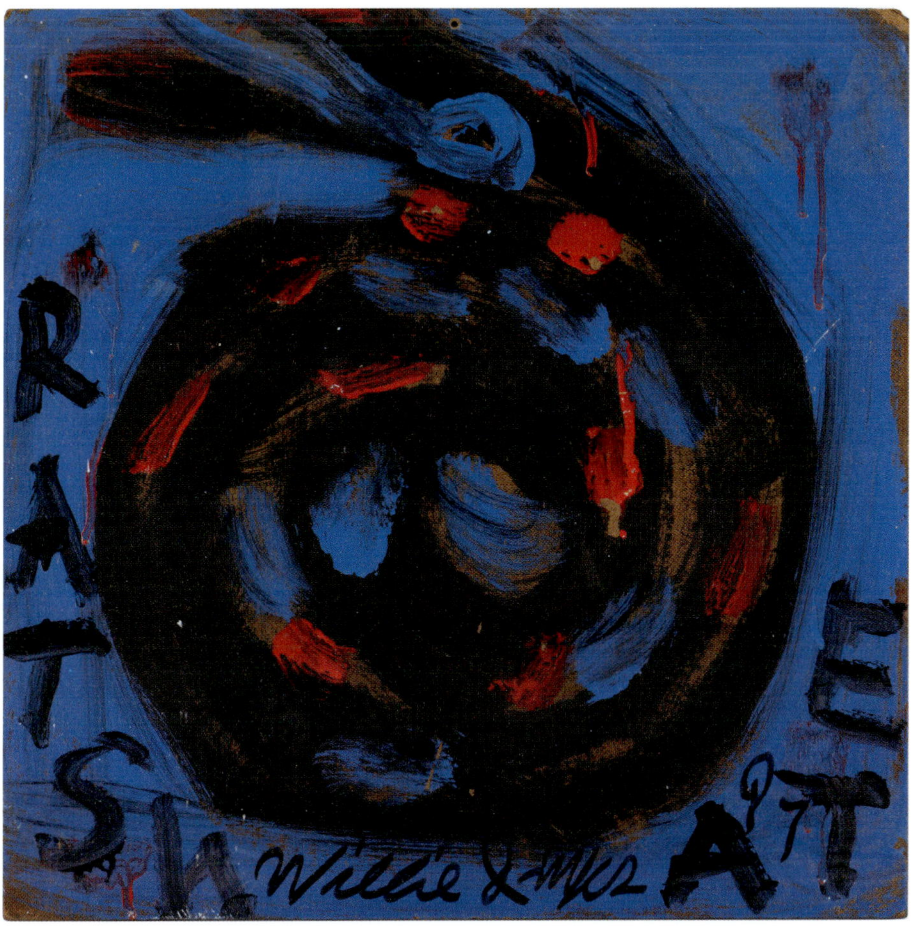

Plate 90. Willie Jinks, *Rat Snake*. Paint on Masonite board. 15¼ × 15 inches.

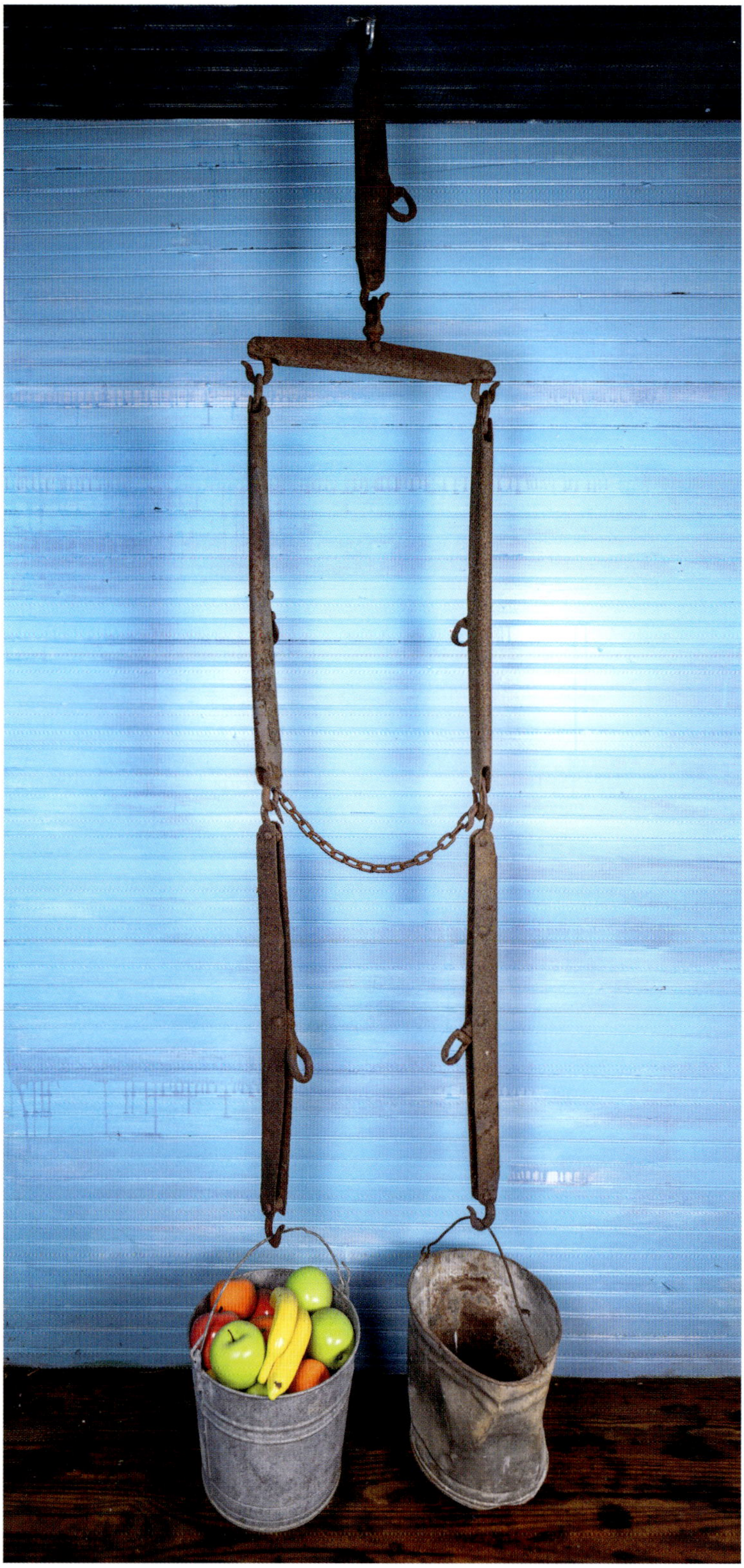

Plate 91. Randy Hester, *Randolph, Stubborn as a Mule, Fruit, No Well.* Metal single trees, chain, buckets, plastic fruit. 96 × 24 × 12½ inches.

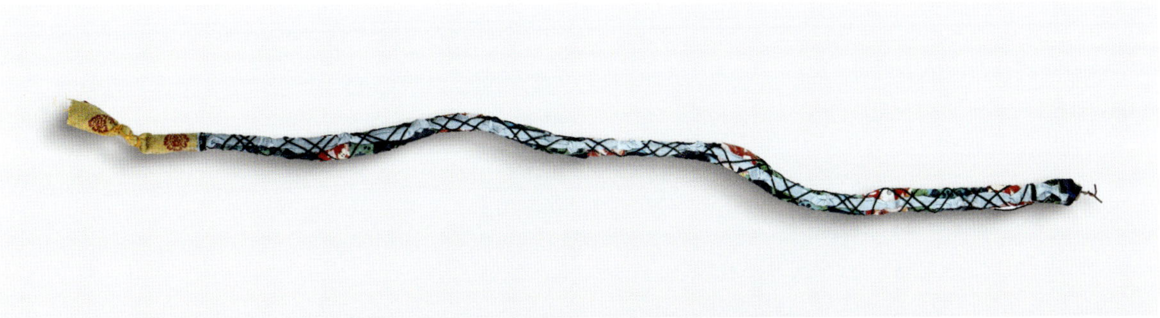

Plate 92. Marcia McNally, *Cotton Snake*. Woven fabric and thread over wood, wire, sequins. 38 × 1 × 1 inch. Shorty Lawson Museum Collection, gift of Marcia McNally.

Yet he defended them from racism. "This White guy called my boys niggers. Randolph warned him to shut up every day for a week, but the guy kept it up, 'Nigger this, Nigger that.' End of the week Randolph busted his face with one fist." (Larry Dixon)

That same fury scared everyone. "My grandfather was afraid Randolph would turn his gun on him." (Debra Davies) Shorty knew a complex Randolph who could be unusually big-hearted with presents at Christmas, but who could just as readily disregard the Lawsons' desire for a new well. (Plate 91) Shorty accepted Randolph for what he was. Strong and stubborn as a mule. Love and generosity mixed with anger and pride. And they saw eye-to-eye on most matters—big things like the value of hard work and toughness, and little ones like cuckoos and snakes. They believed cuckoos predicted rain. They respected but weren't terrified of snakes as most folks were. (Plate 92)

Preach Bradsher played on the visceral fear of snakes. To be certain the Sunday collection resulted in a big heap of money, he kept a black snake in the church, threatening to turn him loose if there were inadequate offerings in the collection plate. Sambo the snake encouraged the congregation to tithe generously. Preach was unusually wise and honest. A White man sold him the first land he owned. "But when Grandfather set a price, Preacher decided it was a bit low. So he paid Grandfather $100 more for the property than Grandfather had asked." (James Earl Hester) That was around 1888.

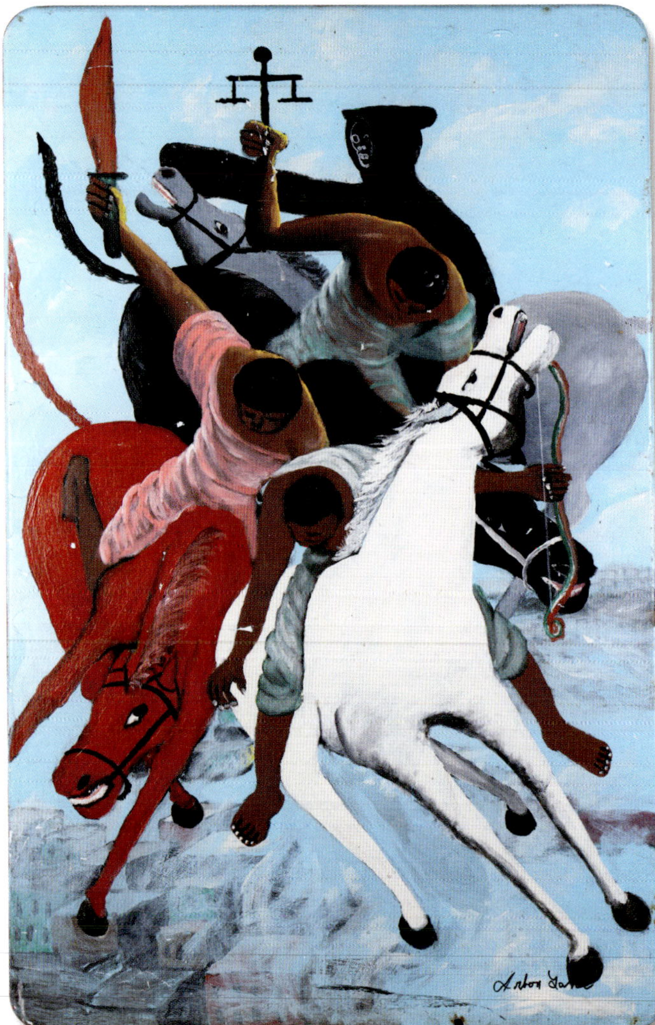

Plate 93. Arbon Lane, *Untitled*. Painting of *Revelations* on metal table top. 40 × 25 × ¾ inches.

Preach also had a store across the road from the church with basic supplies but no checkout clerk. A "customer" was on the honor system to pay for whatever he or she "purchased." He left coins in a box, tempting and testing his faith and the congregation's honesty. "Nor did any of us ever bother stealing anything, even though times were hard." (James Earl Hester)

Experience taught Shorty plenty about the complexity of God and the Devil. He saw both good and bad in everyone and everything. Most

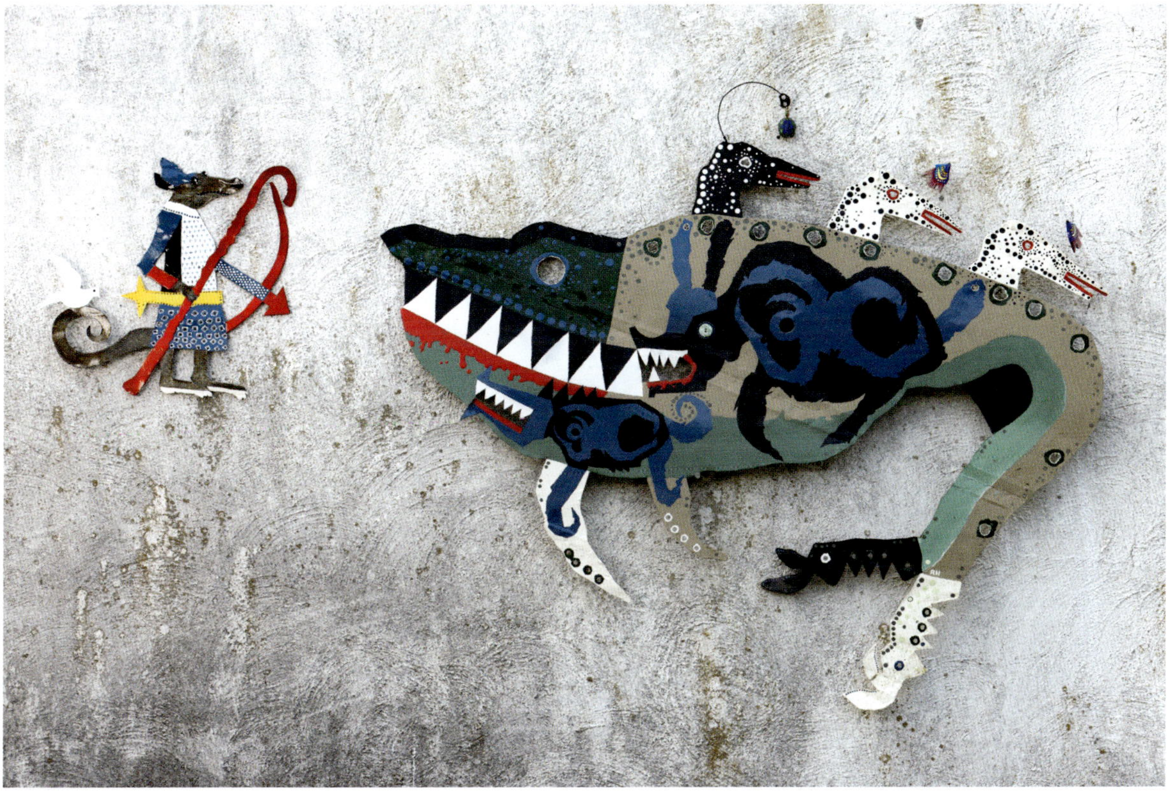

Plate 94. Randy Hester, *Ratty Goodfellow Versus the Sea Monster of Revelations.* Two painted roofing tin figures, tin, button, wire, toy fish and turtle, in style of David Butler. Ratty Goodfellow 13½ × 14 inches, Sea Monster 33 × 40 inches.

snakes were harmless, several poisonous, and a blessed few were downright beneficial; yet they all scared you. Shorty explained why Jerry Clark was mean as a snake, "He just gets the Devil in him, that's all."

It wasn't clear if Shorty was afraid of the Devil, or if it was just an expression, but he practiced ways to mediate fear. To keep ghosts out your house, paint walls electric "haint blue." There was a lot of "haint blue" in the Lawsons' home. Keep a rabbit's foot in your pocket to avoid ill fortune and bring good luck. To gain some measure against servitude look over Jordan for angels coming to take you home. Forestall death by returning the owl's hoot. Shorty didn't speak of an apocalypse, but he didn't speak of the Bible at all, and his evangelist sister-in-law Stella's Bible only marks a few verses in Revelations. (Plate 93) But the imagery sure inspires fear and a lot of yard art. (Plate 94)

Annie and her family grew up in and always attended the Church of the City of God in the Wilderness, founded by Wiley Bradsher and his wife. It is now called Union Grove Baptist Church. Annie made sure that all the children went to church with her. The Lawsons went to church in Caswell County, but "Shorty didn't go to church except as a kid." (Larry Dixon)

Preach Bradsher was the pastor for forty years, including the most formative time of Annie's life, so he shaped the Lawsons' religion through Annie. Her family was certain that an omnipotent God formed the world. At first man and woman lived in paradise, but they fell prey to the Devil's serpent, ate the apple, sinned, and ruined it all. Pestilence and suffering followed, and continues to follow today if one does not abide by Jesus' teachings.

In Annie's home there was no doubt that God's Son performed miracles and died for humankind. His crucifixion was for us. (Plate 95) The disciples of Jesus created the church in his name. Sins were washed away through baptism. Belief in Him comforted the oppressed, promised a better life, guaranteed the believers eternal life, and condemned the nonbelievers. "Gods always behave like the people who make them." (Zora Neale Hurston) And that is the all-powerful, sacrificing, new-life-granting God that Preach Bradsher and his people found comfort in and gave action to.

It is hard to know which was greater for Annie Lawson: faith, hope, or love. Without faith, it was impossible to know God. Unfailing faith made the near impossible possible, yielding mostly good fortune if not miracles. Without hope, tough times—and there were plenty—could not be endured. Hope allowed optimism. "If the Lord is my shepherd, surely goodness and mercy shall follow me all my life. A brighter future. My favorite." (Stella Dixon) Without love the world collapsed into meanness. And there was plenty of meanness all around, but little on Annie's watch in her home.

"We loved God first and our neighbors as ourselves." (Stella Dixon) Stella marked those passages in her Bible and others about avoiding the wrath of God by living right. Xs in the margins call attention to virgins and whores and the rewards for using God-given talents wisely. "Didn't matter if they had a lot of skill or little, those Lawsons used their abilities fully, never hid or wasted them." (Donald Hester)

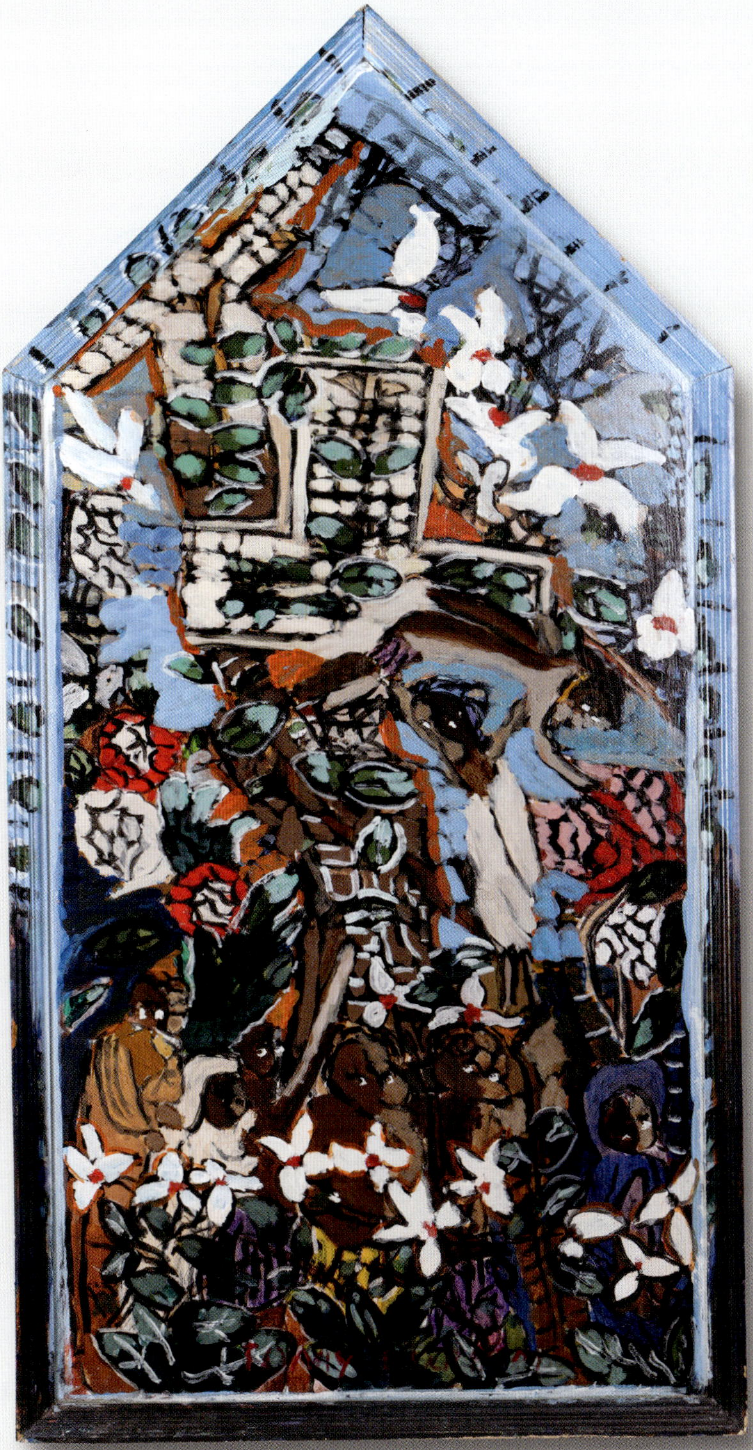

Plate 95. Tommy Durham, *Crucifixion*. Paint on wood. 48 × 24 × 3 inches.

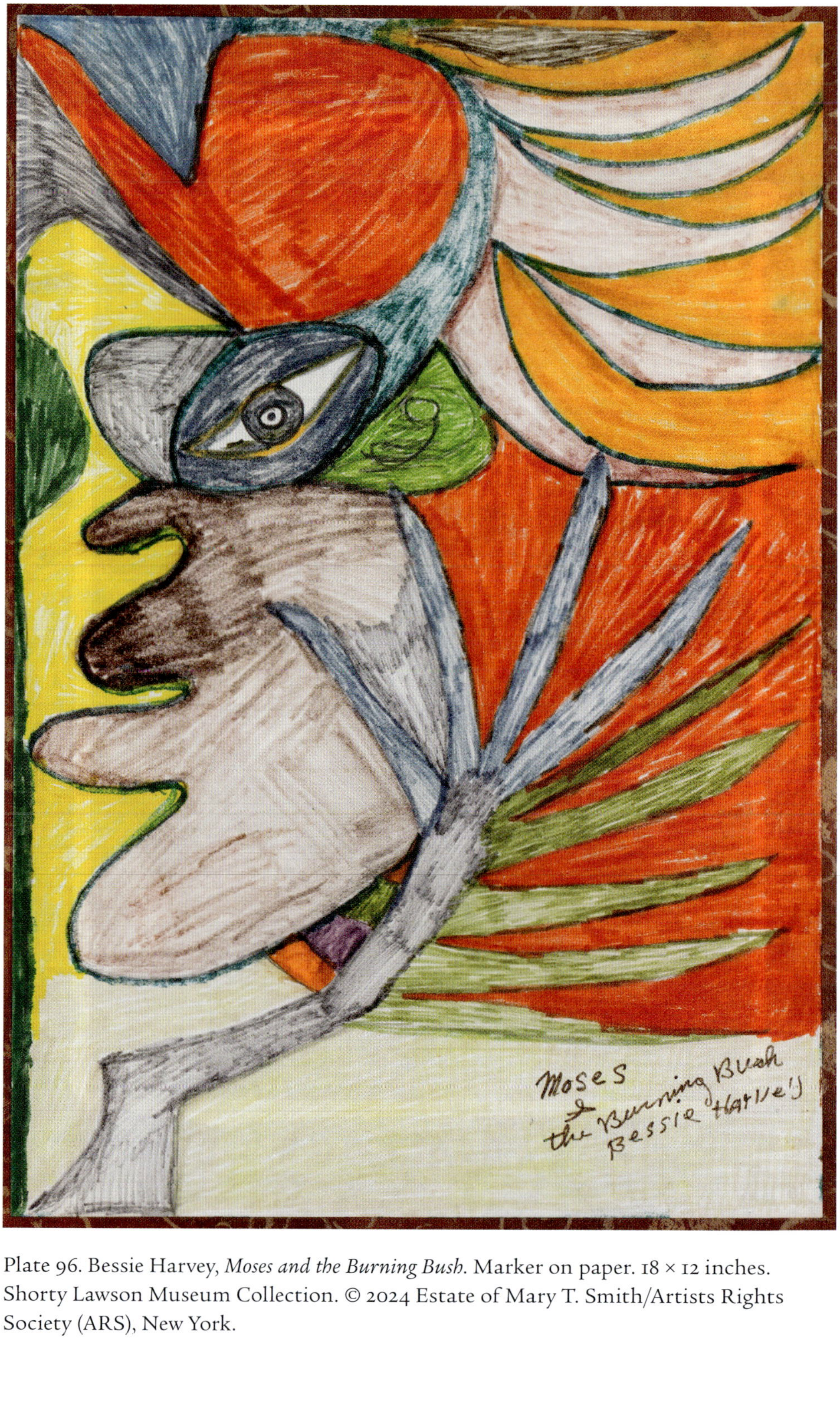

Plate 96. Bessie Harvey, *Moses and the Burning Bush*. Marker on paper. 18 × 12 inches. Shorty Lawson Museum Collection. © 2024 Estate of Mary T. Smith/Artists Rights Society (ARS), New York.

Nonetheless the Devil lurked to distract you from proper behavior. "It's Sunday. I woke up blessed so I don't have time for the Devil's mess." (Stella Dixon) Preach knew each person had a choice between the Anger Bar and Grill and the Salvation Café with Millions Served. He preferred the rewards of good living to the damnation of evil. He had Psalm 1:1 inscribed on an obelisk where the Lord saved him from death by lightning. If we avoid wickedness, sin, and mocking, we shall be like a tree beside water; our leaves shall not wither. Whatever we do shall prosper.

Shorty lived by practical rules based on what he observed to be right and wrong. He followed the 10 Commandments and the Golden Rule. (Plate 96) He used his talents, was of good spirit, cared after his family and neighbors. (Plate 97) He didn't seem to worry much about the Devil, but he worried when Shotgun Howerton drove by real fast, kicking up a dust storm, "Hope the kids get out the road. Shotgun gonna run over somebody." "Practical, God-respecting. Maybe Shorty got all the spiritual counsel he needed from the land, creeks, and woods, I don't know, but Shorty lived as decent a life as anybody I know." (Randy Hester)

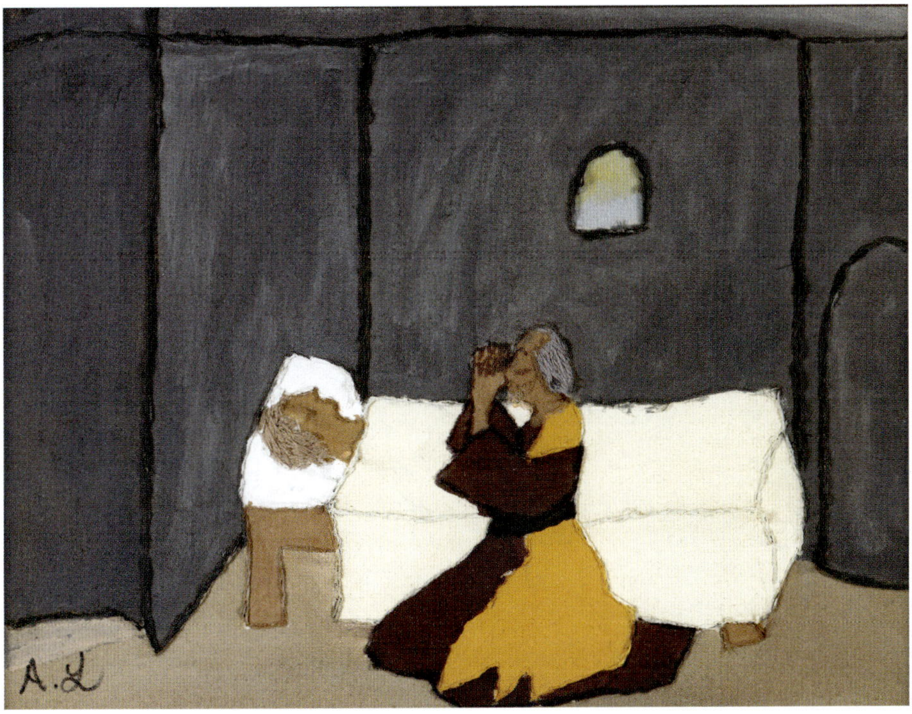

Plate 97. Annie Lucas, *Elijah and the Widow's Son*. Acrylic paint, needlework on canvas stretched onto wood. 11 × 15 inches.

What Does Shorty's Shared Crop Say to Tomorrow?

From Shorty to Us

As a sharecropper Shorty rose to be what he could be. He worked halves, getting 50 percent of the profits from each crop of tobacco, many years enough to make significant improvements in his family's life. He literally shared the crop, an appropriate basic interpretation of the meaning of this book. He never achieved the mandate Wiley Bradsher preached to own land. Would he have, had he lived a longer life? That would have made a sweet ending. The children achieved ownership in the next generation, but he didn't live to see it. Ending otherwise does not diminish Shorty Lawson's lessons for living.

The most important vision of tomorrow is embedded in the man himself. Shorty was undoubtedly a man motivated by his own internal drummer, with no apologies and unmeasured satisfaction, all this at considerable risk for a Black man at a time when deference was expected. It is worth repeating Shorty's essence. In "Poem 27" Arbon Lane asserts, "I am a man in the shadow of another man, and that is where I will always be, for I am a man in the shadow of another man, and that other man is me." (Arbon Lane) In this era most tenant farmers lived in the shadow of the owner; Shorty's shadow was his own. He possessed a keen sense of who he was, with clear intention and pleasure.

Teach by Example

Shorty Lawson shared his crop of wisdom by example. He and Annie raised their children with purpose, teaching them skills that prepared them to make their ways in a changing world. "Us children had chores back then. We knew we were important to our family, no room for slacking off." (Carolyn Lawson) The parents challenged each child to live in no other shadow except one's own. They inspired the children to be true to self and become who each is capable of becoming. In the Lawson world everyone had to work hard to survive. But to thrive one had to work hard

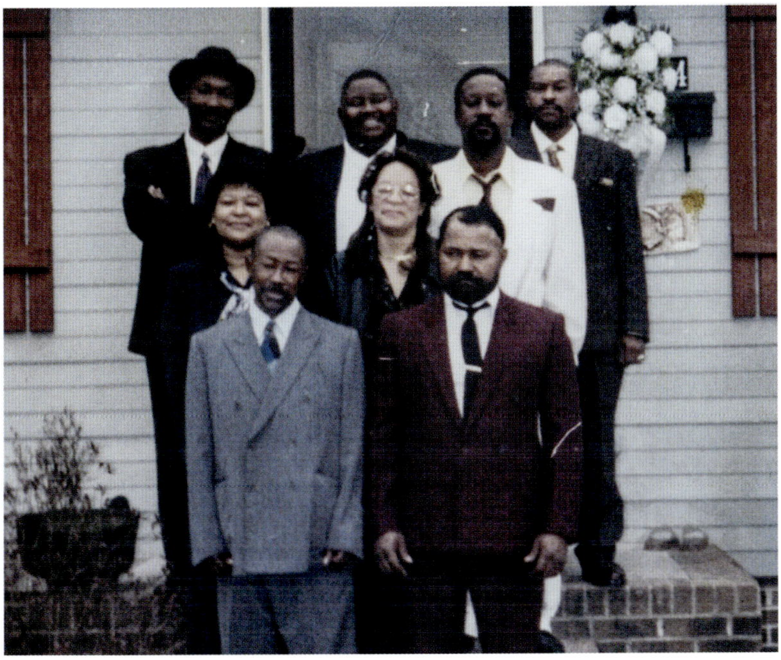

Annie Lawson's children at her funeral.

and enjoy it. Each one had to contribute what each was capable of by age and gender, to pitch in across gender expectations when required, to gain new skills, to master a multitude of specialized tasks yet be nimble enough to improvise under pressure, to accept criticism without sulking, and to never whine. They learned teamwork. For his family and for me that shared crop of shared responsibility was a priceless gift. These wisdoms, broadly reseeded throughout society, might strengthen a sense of shared purpose, mutual regard, and national reconciliation.

Teamwork

Consider the teamwork required in stringing a shared crop of tobacco depicted by Arbon Lane (Plate 98) on the following pages. The focus is Annie stringing the leaves as two children hand them to her. One lags behind, not getting the leaves to her quickly enough, breaking Annie's efficient rhythm. He gets a sharp glance of disapproval. Annie likely calls out "Leaves," so he is publicly chastised. Reminded that his job is essential, he won't let that happen again. When Annie completes stringing each stick, the man in the blue shirt, likely Jasper, takes the full stick of tobacco and carefully stacks it to be housed at the end of the day. If one of the children

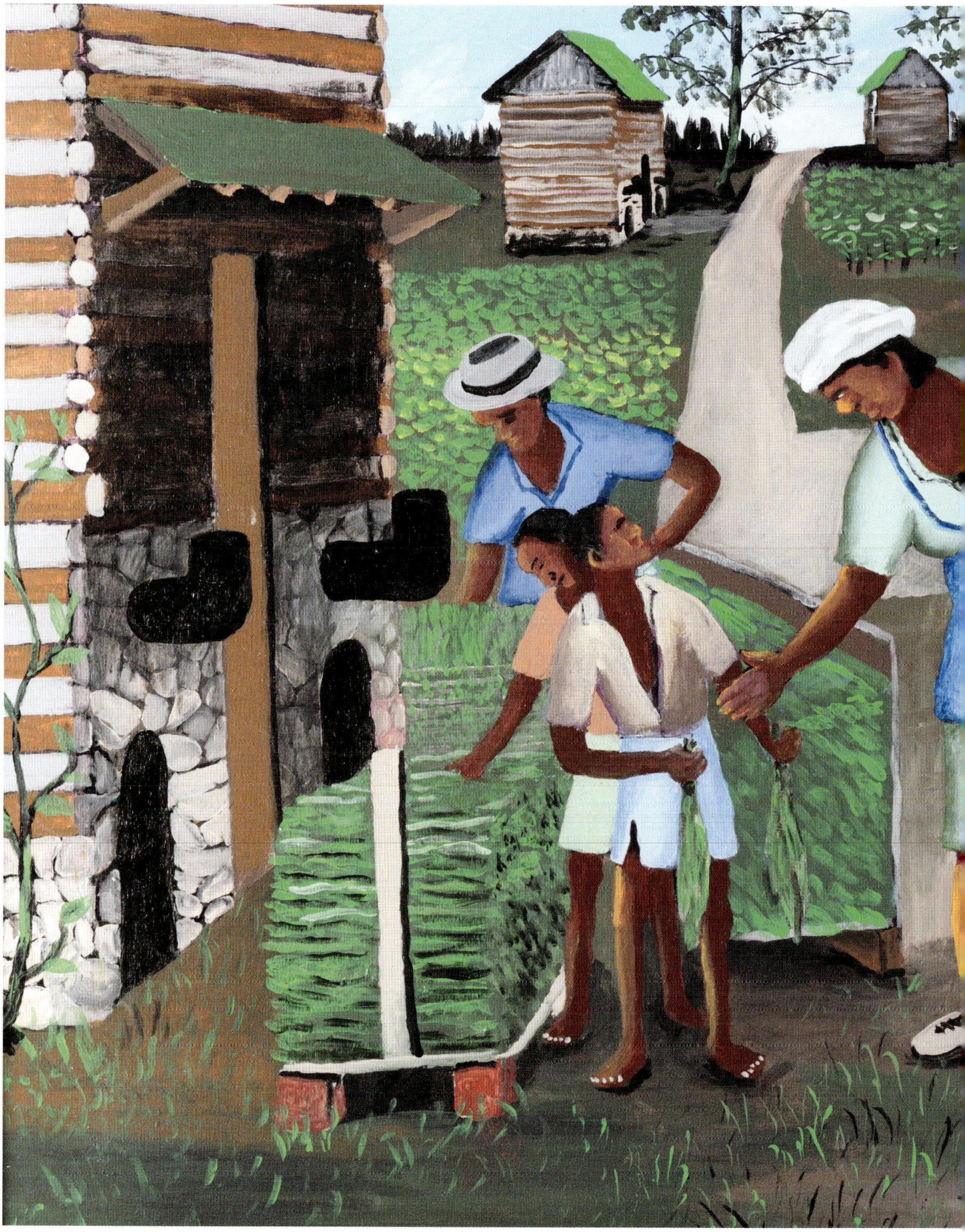

Plate 98. Arbon Lane, *Untitled*. Paint on thin plywood. 23¾ × 39 inches.

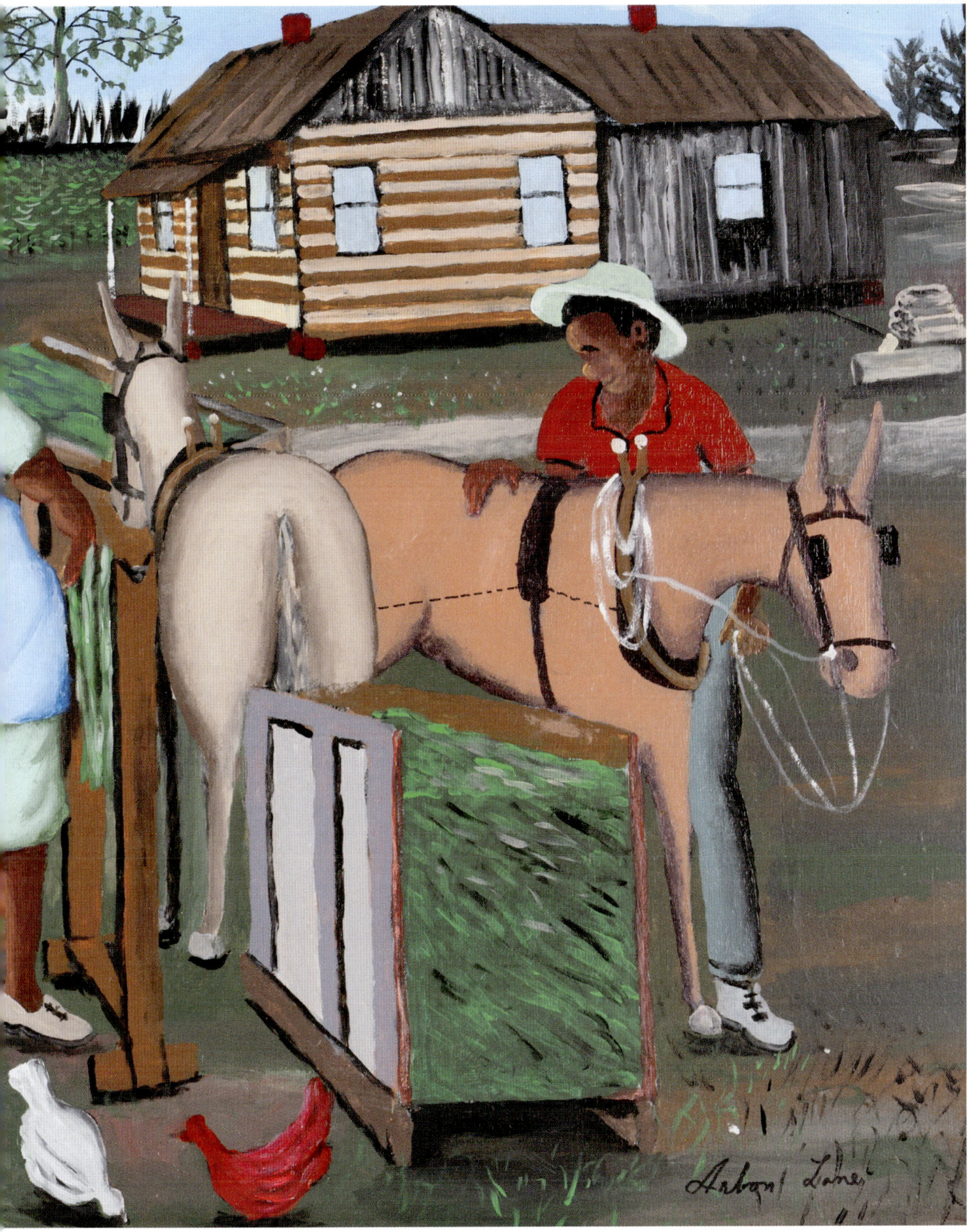
Arbont Lanes

hasn't already given her a new stick, Annie calls out for one. The man in the red shirt is running slides of just-pulled tobacco from field to barn. He is challenged by rough topography to keep slides on schedule and upright; hitting a rock easily upends the slide, ruining a mess of tobacco and delaying delivery. He unloads one slide, hitches a mule to an empty slide, and returns to the field for another load. Implied in the picture are other tasks. Chickens, mules, and cow were fed before daybreak. Cow milked. Breakfast and dinner were made before fieldwork. Someone will have to gather eggs and milk again later. Tobacco will be housed at dusk and fires tended all night. Outside the picture Shorty, Randy, and maybe Kenny are pulling tobacco. Shorty keeps up with how much needs to be pulled to fill the target of one barn each day. It is a shared crop requiring each member of the team to perform well. Pretty strenuous training for life's challenges.

A shared crop required each person to do one's personal chores well (Plate 99) and to help out doing whatever else was needed. (Plate 100) In spite of his work ethic Shorty made plenty of room for everyday joys. He integrated simple pleasures like a muleback ride into daily life and fishing and swimming into time off. Nature itself provided enough free entertainment to sustain him and his family. Little need to consume artificial thrills when you had nature as a playmate. This too is a crop worth sharing and spreading in the future.

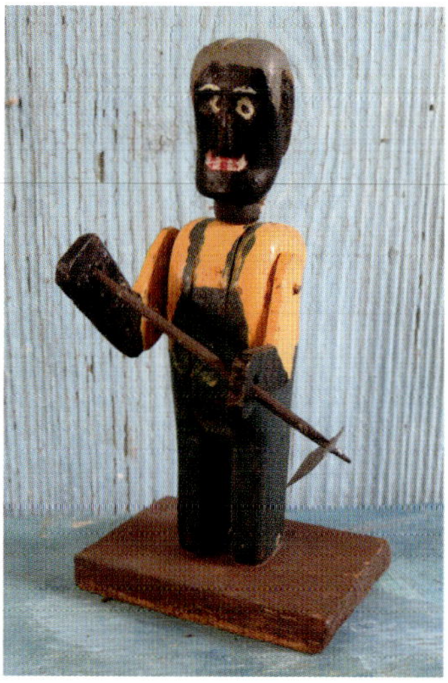

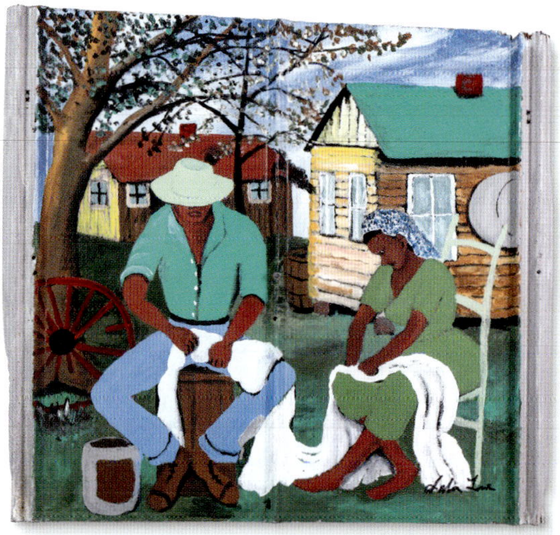

Plate 99. Unknown, *Untitled*. Carved and painted wood in man shape with moving arms working a metal hoe. 4¼ × 2¼ × 1½ inches.

Plate 100. Arbon Lane, *Untitled*. Paint on roofing tin. 25 × 26 inches.

Unforget the Past. Greet the Future as Uncharted Territory.

At a time of unprecedented discussion about these matters their story helps us unforget the past and greet the future as uncharted territory. As simmering responses to the "other" have taken central stage in national politics, the Lawsons offer a way to shape a path forward from unlistening to common ground. The values Shorty and Annie Lawson embodied reflect larger than race or class, larger than Black or White (Plate 101), larger than tenant or owner, larger than rural versus urban, larger than one religion or political persuasion over another, larger than my gain at your expense. They reflect honesty and decency. They reflect doing one's part and more as needed. They reflect life as a crop shared with others.

If the Lawson story inspires others, the legacy will live many lifetimes and add to humanity's search for meaning. The Cornell "Shorty" Lawson family has a lot to say not only about the past but also about the future.

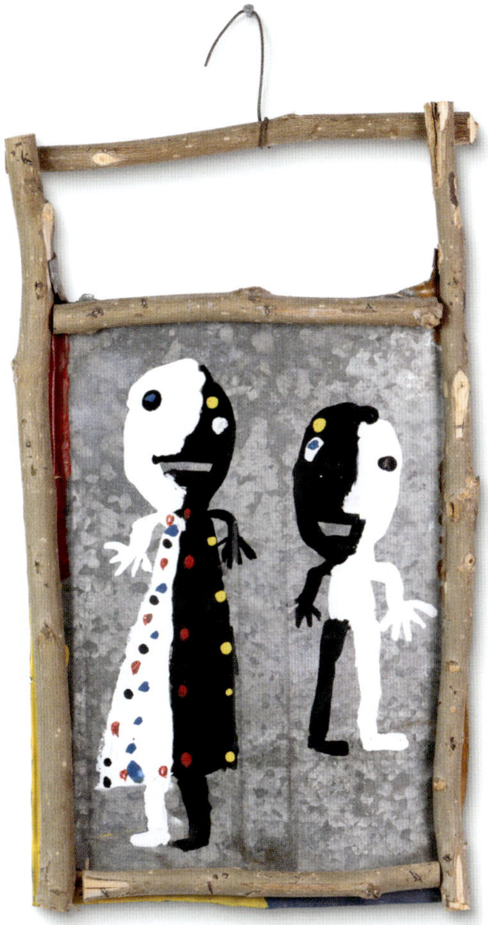

Plate 101. James Buddy Snipes, *Halloween People*. Paint on tin, sticks, wire. 16½ × 9¼ × 1 inch.

Making the Museum

Stabilizing Shorty's House

When I retired in 2009, I returned to live at the Bowes Farm where I had worked as a youngster, in high school, and college summers. I started to tend to the decade of deferred maintenance and neglect after my father died. One of the projects I undertook in 2015 was to stabilize a near-collapsed tenant house. The south wall, having suffered one hundred years of sun exposure, had fallen out into the yard. Foundation rocks lay scattered about. The oak foundation sill had rotted. Leaks had declared victory over interior walls and floors. I wasn't sure where to start. I just started.

One day a neighbor stopped by and asked me why I was wasting all my time fixing up that rundown tenant house, and without thinking, I blurted out, "I'm making a museum for Shorty Lawson." His expression dropped derision. He nodded approvingly. He had known Shorty well.

Until that instant all I wanted was for Shorty's house not to fall down, but at that moment we started making a museum. I had never made a museum.

Jamie Hughes helped me raise the house inches enough to replace the rotten sill and make other two-person repairs, then I did the remainder of the restoration myself, reusing materials found on the farm: discarded beadboard, roofing tin, and nails, paint, and scrap metal left in the shop. There were piles of oak, pine, and poplar that my father Randolph, Shorty, and I had timbered and stacked years before. Once I began, I did know what to do. I realized that making do with what is available must be like riding a bike. If you learn early in life, you never forget. I had not forgotten how to improvise with what was at hand. That was the only way my family and Shorty's made ends meet and got a little ahead in the 1950s.

My cousin Donald stopped by most days to check on the progress. A decade younger than me, Donald had worked with the Lawson children for years and knew them in ways I didn't. He was generous with his memories and encouragement, but left me to the labor. Another cousin who

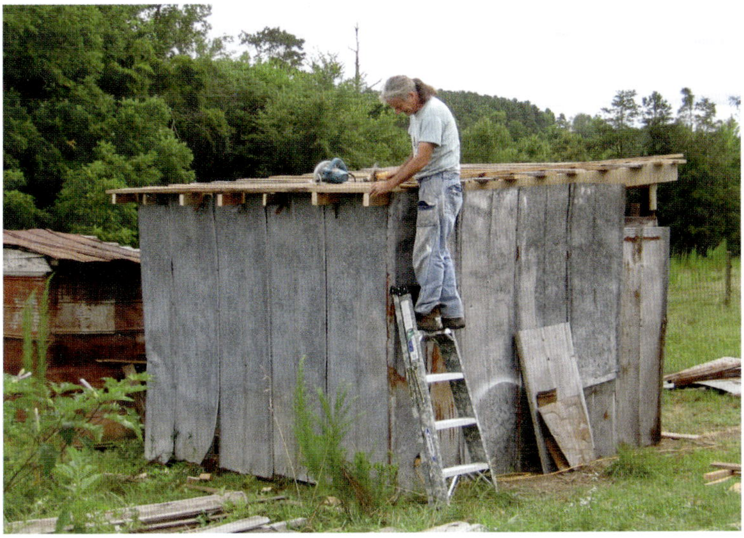

Reconstruction of wood shed in 2018.

is an interior designer, Leigh Blow, advised on paint colors that retained the history.

Once the house was stabilized, I worked room by room, deep cleaning ceiling, walls, and floor, replacing beadboard surfaces, and patching rotten floors. I did all that work myself, alone, surrounded by traces of lived lives and sometimes Shorty's voice, retelling me stories long forgotten. Each room wanted to tell its history and offer instruction. Each night at dinner (supper in the 1950s) I'd recount to Marcia, my wife and business partner, what I had accomplished, and she would help plan what needed to be done next. She brought order to every step in making the museum. From these notes it will be clear that this is a DIY museum, for better and worse.

Never Made a Museum Before

Although we had no experience in making such a museum, decades of professional design practice helped guide us. Marcia and I had often found inspiration in cultural history and myth as part of helping communities to evolve in ways true to themselves, not trying to be something they were not. We used overlooked resources endemic to the place to create unimagined futures. We called that finding fish heads, for example, turning an auto repair shop into an exhibit hall in Castle Rock, Washington, and a pipe graveyard into Parque Natural in South Central Los Angeles. Our design approach was unconventional, outside the mainstream of elite architecture. We worked transactively with communities, mapped power, environmental injustices, and daily life patterns. In those we discovered a sacred structure of communities, a most empowering aspect of city design. We often worked with marginalized groups, minorities, Native Hawaiians, new immigrants, gangs, and homeless, making designs that confronted dominant values and power, and frequently winning. Had Shorty inspired that in me many decades earlier? Creating the story of Shorty Lawson with his family was not a totally foreign action for us.

Carolyn Lawson Got the Best Stories

Intimidated by the thought of making a museum for Shorty Lawson, we set out on a participatory strategy that we knew well from our design projects: listen to the people. Marcia and I had kept in touch with the Lawsons when we visited my family. Shorty's brother Sam and his wife Brenda lived on the farm and worked with my father until his death. We hosted lunches at the Bowes house where Sam and Brenda had lived and we now live. We would all eat and share stories about their family. Carolyn Lawson insisted she had the best stories, and indeed she recalled, in detail, bushels of pointed memories that shaped the way their story is told. But other family members overflowed the lunch table with their distinct perspectives, sometimes contradictory, each experienced with different young or older eyes, at the barn or in the field, doing men's or women's work, house or garden chores. The memories of Brenda Lawson and Stella and Larry Dixon filled the house. Marcia asked questions, I took notes. It was clear that the collective memories, richer than the soil out of which they grew, should be preserved. Ben Premeaux, a noted filmmaker, agreed to film the family members as each told his or her stories. He also wanted to film my cousin Donald to place the Lawsons in the larger frame of the community of Hesters Store. I asked Angie Brown and Ray Jeffers to provide the broader county and state political context. Mrs. Brown participated in early sit-ins as a student at North Carolina A&T and is revered for her local activism. Ray Jeffers is our house representative in the North Carolina General Assembly. All of these oral histories are on the museum website, and are a most important contribution to tobacco farming history, in and of themselves.

About this time, we realized that making the museum was much like raising a profitable crop. Everyone pitched in what they had to offer, from construction and organizational skills to best stories and filmmaking. We were a shared crop.

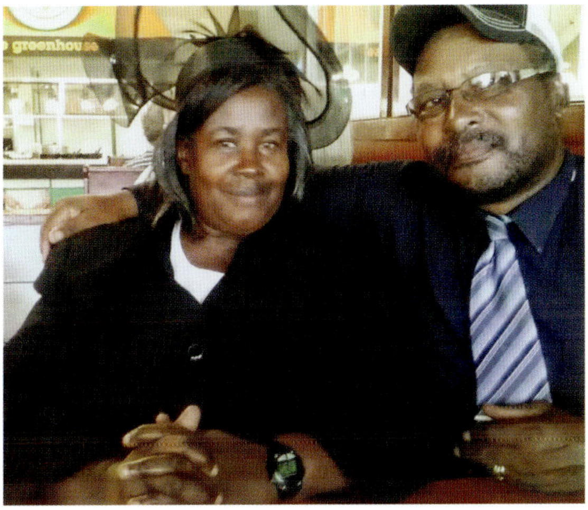

Larry Dixon, Shorty's half-brother, who grew up as one of Shorty and Annie's children, married Stella, raising his own family in the Lawson home.

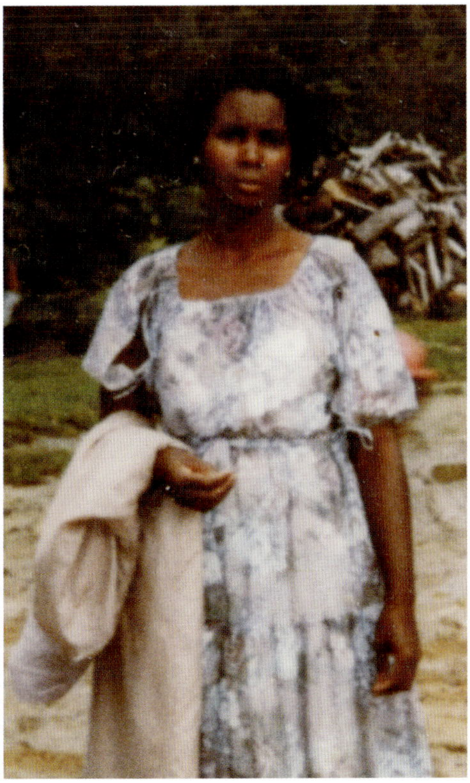

Brenda Lawson, bull whisperer and wife of Shorty's brother Sam, when she lived in the big house.

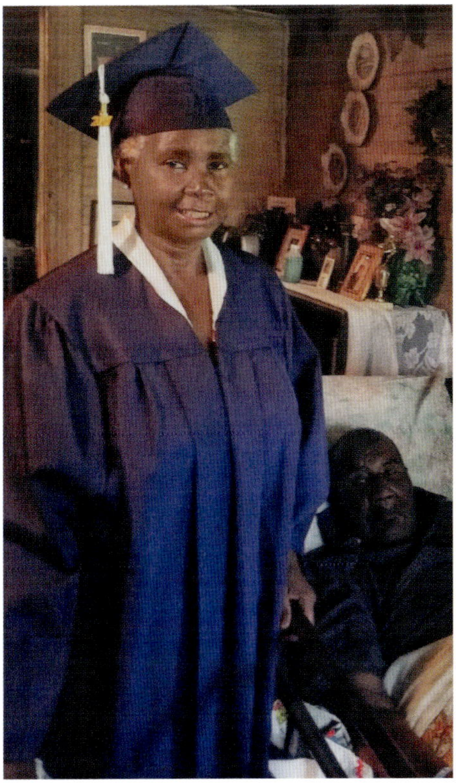

Brenda Lawson in high school graduation regalia as a senior citizen.

How Can We Shine a Light on the Stories?

We had many bushels of stories and little clarity about what to do next. Someone said that we had to show the stories, not just tell them. The time-tested approach called for furnishing the house in period furniture, but that would have told an incomplete story of tenant farming in the barns, fields, and woods. And furnished rooms often paint a static lifeless picture.

What about pictures being worth a thousand words? How much would pictures and rich stories together be worth? It must have occurred to Marcia first that outsider art could be the equivalent of a thousand words, illuminating the oral histories. The Thornton Dial show in Indianapolis in 2011 lingered in her mind. *Lost Cows* foretold Carolyn's story of milking Jasper's cow before school.

We were soon tutored on outsider art that might give visual form to the everyday lives of the Lawson family. Patsy Bonafair, a local resident and collector of outsider art, offered a crash course introduction to outsider artists whose work paralleled the stories we had recorded. Soon after, Marcia and I set off on a Civil Rights tour, stopping at outsider art galleries along the way, and spending days with Joe Minter and Charlie Lucas.

We purchased pieces that illustrated topics from the oral histories. Jeanne Kronsnoble, Marcia Weber, Matt Ledbetter, the Jeffrey Lovetts, Gregg and Karen Mack, the George Borums, and Laura Baldree embraced our search for appropriate art. Other galleries, auctions, and the internet broadened the possibilities.

We preferred African American, outsider, and North Carolina artists, but we were not rigid about that; the art simply had to illuminate the Lawson stories.

I value outsider art because it addresses topics familiar to tenant farming. In addition, the label "outsider" appeals to me. I know for some it diminishes the standing of the artists, marginalizes them. Not for me. My profession of architecture, landscape architecture, and city design aspires to the high arts, catering to wealth and power, excluding others, and ignoring the everyday places of most people. I am continually at odds with, often in battle with, the controlling elites for the soul of my field. I choose to serve those without a voice, stopping freeways that would destroy minority neighborhoods, providing parks where there are none, and developing local bottom-up economies. The status-seeking dominant culture of conspicuous consumption is a danger to an ecological

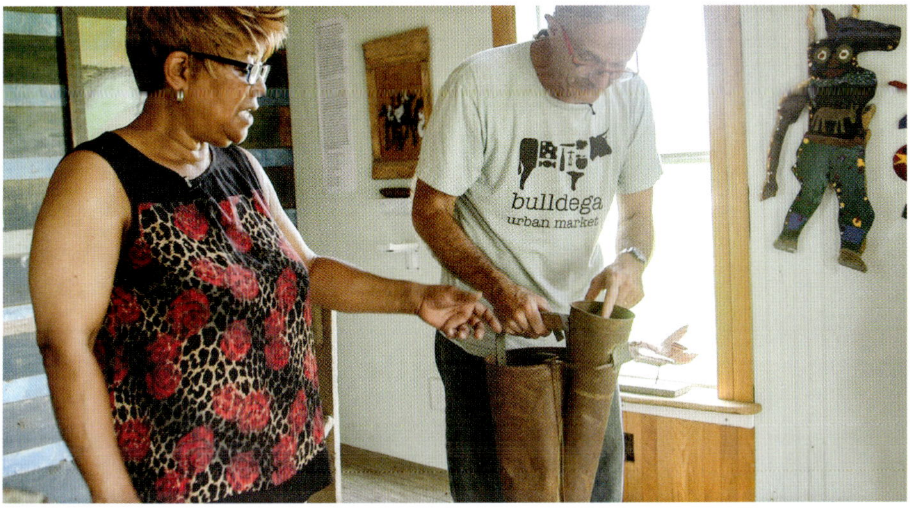

Carolyn Lawson, elder daughter of Shorty and Annie, telling Randy one of her best stories about the tobacco planter.

democracy and a more perfect union. Reformation always requires outsiders. There is no place I want to stand, except as outsider. And it is likely that Shorty shaped me thusly.

Museum as Graphic Novel

By 2017 we had a trove of oral histories and art encapsulating the daily lives of the Lawson family, but it was not organized. Rebecca Hoffberger gave us ideas when she showed us how she ordered the American Visionary Art Museum. Carolyn Lawson envisioned the framework for her family museum. One day as she and I roamed the house, in each room a single memory came to her mind and crowded out all others. Those memories organized the mass of stories into categories. In the room she shared with her sister her dominant recall was how the seasons controlled their lives. So the "Girls' Room" became summer, fall, winter, and spring. The kitchen was unquestionably her mother's domain, where women's rules oversaw everything from cooking and eating to bathing and studying. The room Shorty added off the kitchen Carolyn described as sort of a halfway house, halfway in, halfway out, between outdoor work and indoor work, churning the milk and washing clothes. Her parents' room evoked lessons and pleasures learned from them. The big room reminded her that their collective hard work provided luxuries like a TV and news

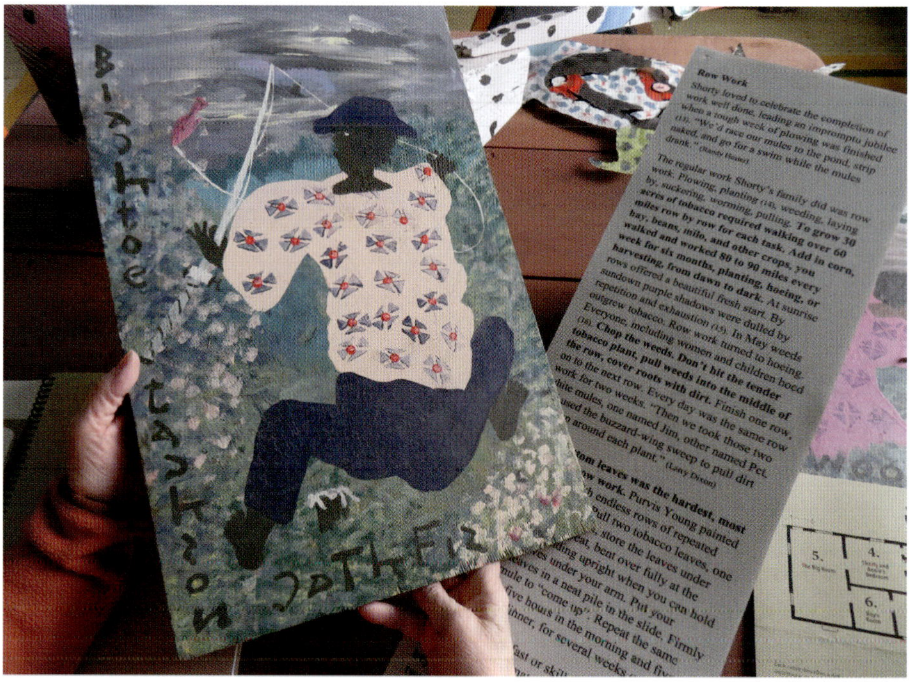

Marcia McNally matching text of an oral history with art illustrating the story.

of the world. Carolyn remembered the "Boys' Room" as overcrowded, full of dreams and devilment.

Based on her dominant memories we sorted the stories into rooms where they best fit. As I hung art in the assigned room, Marcia said that the stories should be hung next to each artwork. I took on the task of tying the stories together and creating panels of text matched with the art. That is when we realized that the museum was akin to a rough draft of a graphic novel, except it was graphic nonfiction. That distinguishes the museum.

Phil Freelon raised another challenge and offered a solution. He thought the farm itself told the story. The house might be the focus, but barns, outbuildings, fences, fields, woods, and springs each had lead roles in the narrative. To Phil the relationship of Shorty's house overlooking the land reflected Shorty's shared control of the territory. Isolated topography distinguished the Lawsons from other tenant farmers. Phil wanted to make visible these aspects hidden in the landscape. In response we mapped the places sacred to the Lawsons, from the feed barn where Shorty calmed and harnessed the mules to the creeks where the kids caught knotty heads. The distance to White neighbors marked autonomy. The well was a place of unresolved contention for the Lawsons, much like the Woolworth lunch counter was for the A&T Four. As a result of Phil's thinking the museum spilled out of the house onto the farmland. We looked for art of plowing with mules. I rebuilt a barn and basketball goal. We are still working on these moments in the landscape.

Read, Reflect, Enrich, Test, Repeat

I had grown up in the fields laboring under Shorty's guidance and later worked in the Civil Rights Movement, both of which offered advantages of lived experience during Jim Crow. I admired the uncompromising Fred Shuttlesworth and the thoughtful C. T. Vivian, but I was unread in the classic literature. I started with Anna Julia Cooper, Richard Wright, Zora Neale Hurston, and Paule Marshall, then found my way to the present with James McBride and Ta-Nehisi Coates. Each demanded space to speak of the Lawsons. Henry Louis Gates Jr. and Maria Tatar's *Annotated African American Folktales* answered questions Shorty raised as we worked tobacco fifty years ago. The text was reconsidered. Juxtaposed with the oral histories, quotes from African American writers elucidate key moments in Shorty's life.

I reread John Beardsley, whose theory of aesthetics helped me believe in the beauty created by everyday people. I found Bernie Herman, who unsettles revered foundations of art built on quicksand. I immersed myself in the Arnetts, who saw great art before anyone else and saved stories from the mouths of artists that now inform us.

Matt Ledbetter shared books by the North Carolina artist Arbon Lane, who not only, better than anyone else, painted the everyday lives of tobacco tenant farmers but also described those lives in poetry. In "Poem 16" he details never-ending tasks, "After working a hard day of work, grubbing plowing planting making some mollases, cutting down some treese, and cutting up some wood, milking the old cow, giving the old mule some corn, and slooping the old sow, with all her little pigs, now we get our stuff together." (Plate 102) After all the work Lane describes a night of big-time hunting "under the light of the shining moon" and bringing home "a prise like coon." (Arbon Lane) That echoed Shorty's embrace of hard work and equal play.

Each encounter helps explain the story of Shorty Lawson and forces updates to text, finding art that is truer to the story. And the family keeps adding stories. The museum is a memory palace for the family. When one

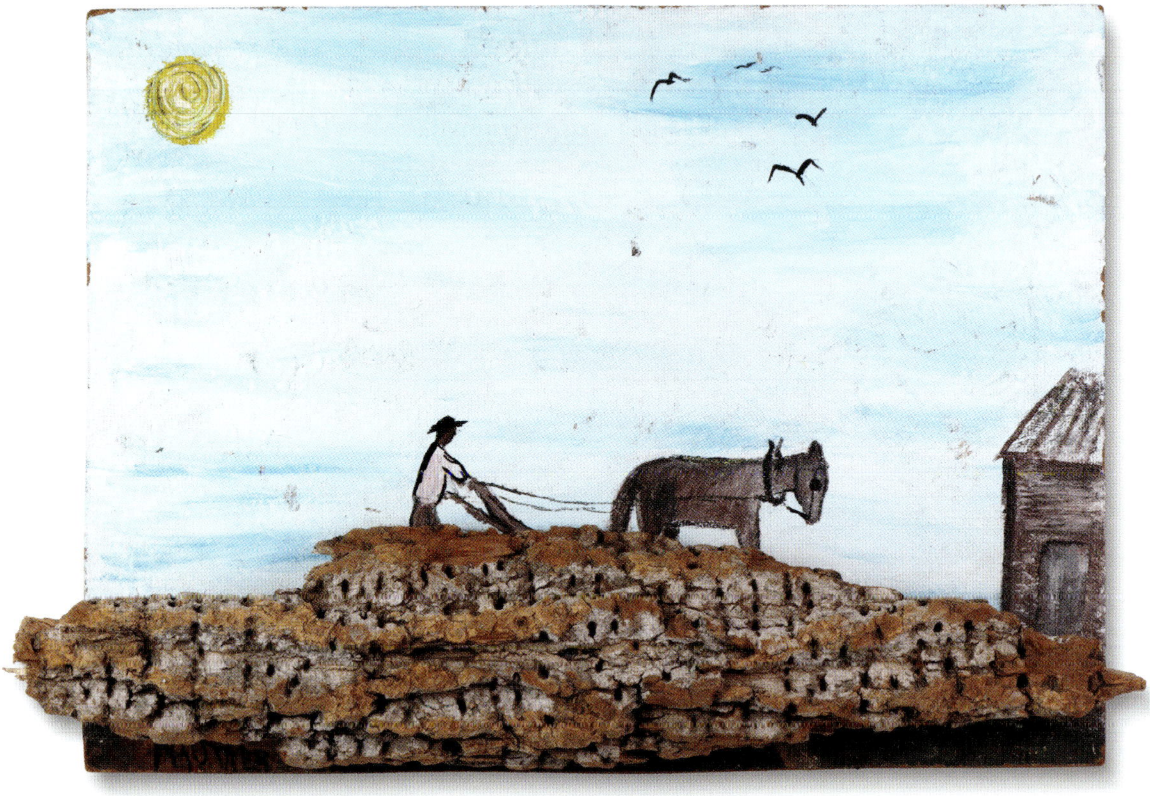

Plate 102. Mother, *Plowing Hilly Furrows*. Paint on Masonite, bark of tree. 18 × 26 × 5 inches.

of Shorty's grandsons visited for the first time, he stopped at the photograph of his grandfather. In silence he studied it, an image so true to his genes to be a mirror reflecting himself. After long minutes he turned to me and said, "I never see my grandfather before." He wanted more, but there are no other pictures, all lost in fires.

What of other visitors? They too prompt change. Whether family, neighbor, college class, book club, or church group, each shares personal stories, notes favorite art, and makes suggestions: "You need a roadmap of each room" or "Show me where Shorty hid to be sure the children kept a lifeguard as others went swimming." Evaluations ensure revisions. I understand the burden of every museum director. It is never done. Do other directors have to sweep the floors?

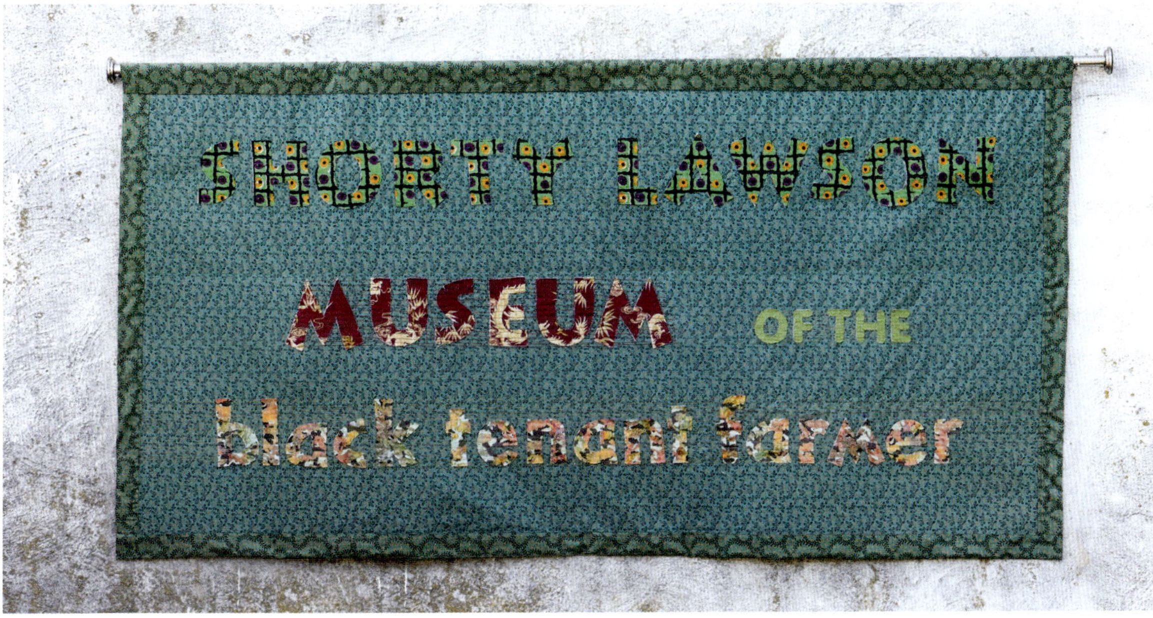

Homemade quilted museum sign by Marcia McNally.

Marcia's Inventory and Catalog

Marcia keeps good household records. She insisted on the same for the museum, starting with expenses to restore the house. As we acquired art, she filed who, what, when, where, the price and provenance of each purchase as best she could determine. She kept an inventory that now, years later, is the only way to recall important information.

Neighbors Bob and Elizabeth Babcock expanded her effort. Bob shared catalogs that he had curated at Yale: "You need to make a similar book, and you must write why you bought each artwork." Marcia then had two files, an inventory and a catalog. The catalog includes size, medium, and, as Bob instructed, the reason for purchase. It is organized by room with numbers that relate art to text. Visitors rely on the catalog for details about the art, and we use it to verify locations, make text revisions, track changes, and, most recently, seek permissions.

Marcia also sews homemade things for the museum. Her cloth snakes demand attention, but aren't dangerous. Her fabric banners announce the museum. Most important, she created the settings for discussions about the nuanced impacts on the Lawsons' daily lives when Jim Crow challenged federal authority. Those talks shaped the way a complex story is told. (Plate 103)

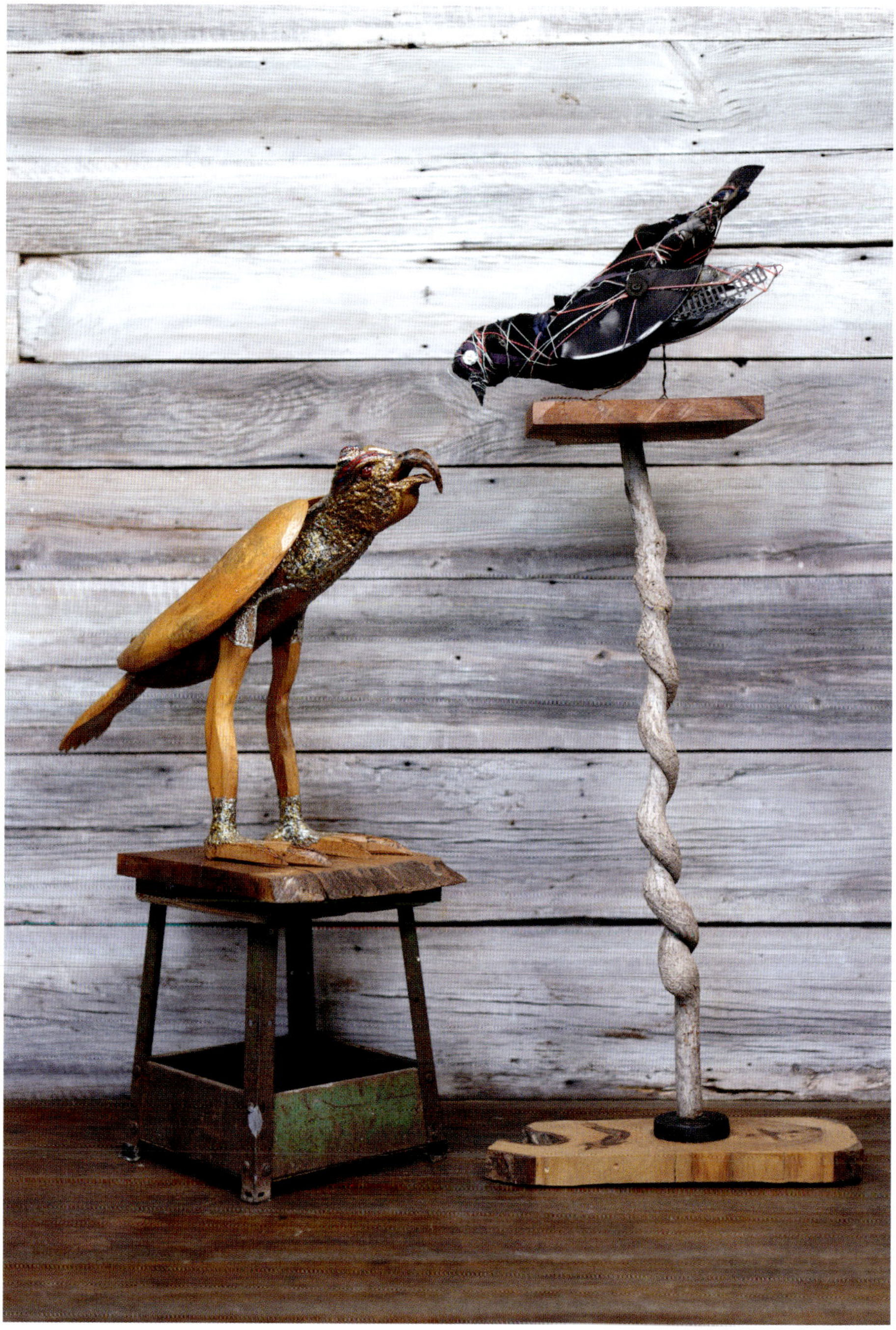

Plate 103. O. L. Samuels, *Eagle*. Carved wood, glitter paint, found objects. 20 × 22 × 12 inches. Bryant Holsenbeck, *Crow*. Recycled materials, fabric, records, ribbon, thread, colored twine, buttons, clear plastic, sequins, wire. 11 × 17 × 10 inches.

Aspirations

We now know that a museum like the one that tells the Lawson family story is never finished, but the completion of the book *Shared Crop* puts the effort in perspective, allows a pause for reflection, and impels discussion about what is next. Asking visitors after a tour to recall a favorite story or artwork has unexpected outcomes, often stimulating reflection about long-lost impulses to make art themselves. I sometimes hear someone telling a friend that the art of Shorty's half-brother, Larry Dixon, inspires them to try it themselves. I remember early on hoping that the stories, paintings, and Larry's art would have this effect.

After we started work on the museum, we began to understand its importance to the collective memory of the Lawson family, the community, and the histories of tenant farming and the tobacco industry. Although well documented, the history of tenant farming often overlooks the nuances of daily life. The Lawsons' stories fill in missing detail and challenge the depiction of Black tenant farmers as a generalized one-size-fits-all category.

Shorty exercised unusual authority over the farm, embraced decision making, thrived on hard work, and provided pleasures and conveniences for his family. All this informs history.

In another realm the Lawson's story stirs reflection about class, race, landed, and tenant, then and now, in a more informed manner. In the museum four chairs are tightly arranged in a square, facing each other: a somewhat worn, comfortable armchair of the landed faces a sharecropper's straight back. Another straight back painted white with padded seat faces a rickety straight back painted black with a metal crow occupying much of the hard sitting area. Whenever a visitor is invited to sit, he or she invariably chooses the landed chair, stirring a spirited discussion. If self-awareness breeds empathy, this is a valuable prompt. Indeed, the Lawson story is about race, yet far more complex. It is about multiple legacies of slavery, Shorty's era of Jim Crow and Civil Rights, affirmative action, and backlash resentment.

These contrasting narratives require more attentive listening and honest face-to-face sit-downs than most folks are brave enough to entertain. The museum offers a safe setting for civil discussions about some of today's most contentious issues. Our hope is that this setting will continue to inspire understanding, empathy, and a way forward for our community and others.

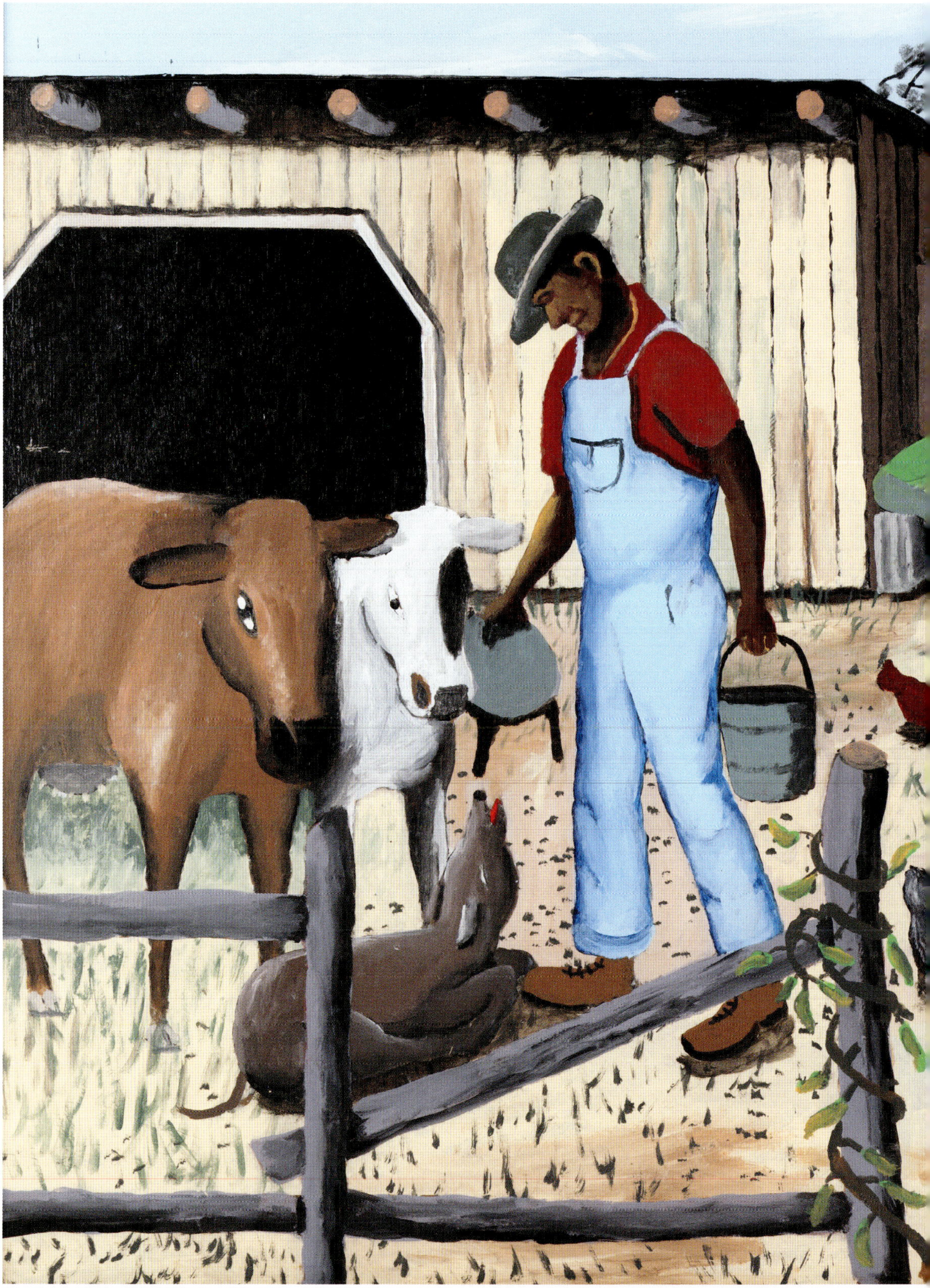

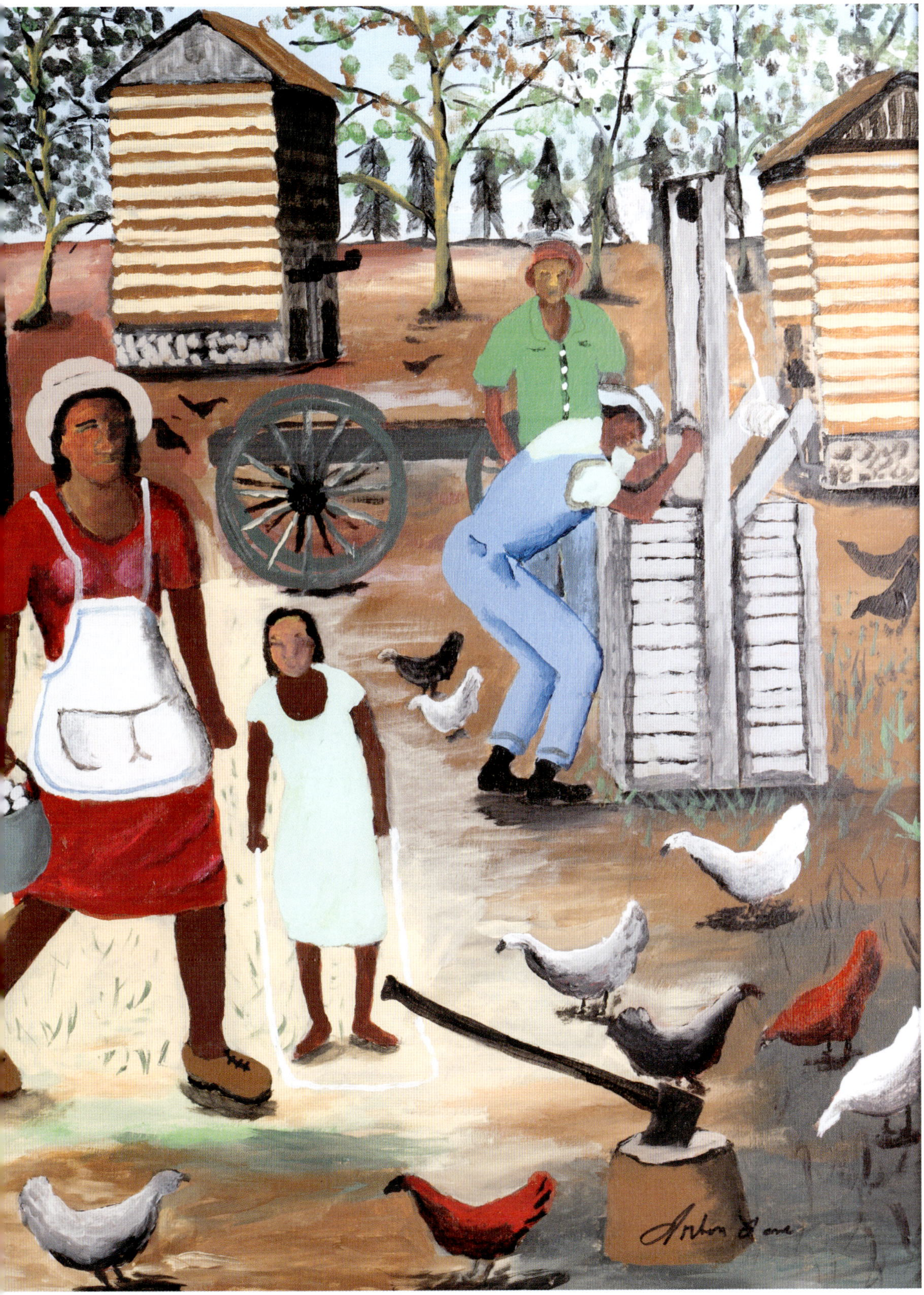

Source Notes

Introduction

page 3: Arbon Lane, *One Finger at a Time, Poems by Arbon Lane,* Book 3 (Roanoke, VA: Bill Jones Gallery, n.d.), 18.

page 7: Creola Bennett Pettway, in Valerie Cassel Oliver, *Cosmologies from the Tree of Life* (Richmond: Virginia Museum of Fine Arts, 2019), 76.

page 7: Anna Julia Cooper, *A Voice from the South* (1892; reprint Oxford: Oxford University Press, 1988), 173.

page 9: Thornton Dial, "Mr. Dial is a Man Looking for Something," in Timothy Anglin Burgard, ed., *Revelations* (Munich: DelMonico Books, n.d.), 30.

page 9: Donlyn Lyndon and Charles W. Moore, *Chambers for a Memory Palace* (Cambridge, MA: MIT Press, 1994).

page 9: Maya Angelou, *I Know Why the Caged Birds Sings* (New York: Ballantine Books, 2009), 1.

page 9: Lane, *One Finger at a Time*, Book 3, 9.

Girls' Room

page 17: Ta-Nehisi Coates, *The Water Dancer* (New York: One World, 2020), 307.

page 25: Marvin Finn, February 28, 2025, marvinfinn.weebly.com.

page 27: Coates, *The Water Dancer*, 308.

Kitchen

page 33: Zora Neale Hurston, *Their Eyes Were Watching God* (New York: Amistad, 2013), 40.

page 37: Cooper, *A Voice from the South*, 27.

page 37: Cooper, *A Voice from the South*, 60.

page 39: Cooper, *A Voice from the South*, 90.

page 39: Richard Roebuck, February 23, 2025, Possum County Folk Art, sheila@possumcounty.net.

Room Off the Kitchen

page 48: Coates, *The Water Dancer*, 347, 348.

Shorty and Annie's Bedroom

page 58: Dial, "Mr. Dial is a Man Looking for Something," 56.

page 59: Cooper, *A Voice from the South*, 78.

page 59: Martin Luther King Jr., *Martin Luther King, Jr. Companion* (New York: St. Martin's Press, 1993), 21.

page 61: Zora Neale Hurston, *Mules and Men* (New York: Harper Modern Classics, 2008), 270.

page 65: James McBride, *The Color of Water* (New York: Riverhead Books, 2006), 262.

page 65: Zora Neale Hurston, *You Don't Know Us Negroes and Other Essays* (New York: HarperCollins, 2022), 115, 234.

page 67: Hurston, *Mules and Men*, 269.

Big Room

page 81: Edward P. Jones, *The Known World* (New York: Amistad, 2003), 320, 321.

page 83: Cooper, *A Voice from the South*, 30.

page 87: Dial, "Mr. Dial is a Man Looking for Something," 27.

page 92: Floyd McKissick, in Divya Subramanian, "The Lost Plan for a Black Utopian Town," *New Republic*, March 17, 2021, article 161745, newrepublic.com.

page 96: Coates, *The Water Dancer*, 155.

page 99: Cooper, *A Voice from the South*, 160.

page 100: Dial, "Mr. Dial is a Man Looking for Something," 31.

Boys' Room

page 104: Coates, *The Water Dancer*, 252.

page 109: James Earl Hester, *More Wisdom Than I Possess* (Roxboro, NC: Person County Museum of History, 2014), 174.

page 110: Hester, *More Wisdom Than I Possess*, 172.

page 112: Zora Neale Hurston, *Tell My Horse* (New York: Amistad, 2009), 219.

What Does Shorty's Shared Crop Say to Tomorrow?

page 116: Lane, *One Finger at a Time,* Book 3, 18.

Making the Museum

page 129: Lane, *One Finger at a Time,* Book 3, 10.

The author gratefully acknowledges:
The Lawson and Dixon families who tell the stories
The artists who illustrate the stories
The writers and poets who speak in ways the author cannot
Marcia McNally, who shaped the book from concept to conclusion
Ben Premeaux, whose photography gives life to the stories
Julie Allred, BW&A Books, Inc., whose design and production sing in harmony with the Lawsons
Greg Gundlach, whose work on the photographs elevates the book's design
Alan Berolzheimer, whose editing lets the Lawsons tell their stories their way
Jacqueline Simon, Artists Rights Society, who led me by the hand
Carrie Currie, Person County Museum of History, who wants everyone's story told
John McLeod, UNC Press, who brought the book to others

Unless otherwise noted, photographs are by Ben Premeaux, courtesy of the Shorty Lawson Museum Collection.

pages ii–iii: James Buddy Snipes, *Untitled.* Painted tin, wood, glass bottles, pipe tobacco tins, leather harness, cow horns, marbles. 32½ × 63 × 8½ inches.

pages 134–35: Arbon Lane, *Untitled.* Paint on plywood. 27½ × 39 inches.

The Shorty Lawson Museum of the Black Tenant Farmer can be found at www.shortylawsonmuseum.org

Artist information can be found on site in the Shorty Lawson Museum of the Black Tenant Farmer Catalog written by Marcia McNally.

Library of Congress Control Number: 2025914986
ISBN: 978-0-9914797-2-6 (paperback)
ISBN: 978-0-9914797-3-3 (cloth)

Printed in the United States of America by Versa Press
First edition, first printing, October 2025